DYNASTY'S END

1969 World Champions (standing left to right): trainer Joe DeLauri, Emmette Bryant, Don Chaney, Tom Sanders, Rich Johnson, Jim Barnes, Bailey Howell, Mal Graham. (seated left to right): Don Nelson, Sam Jones, player-coach Bill Russell, president Jack Waldron, general manager Red Auerbach, captain John Havlicek, team physician Dr. Thomas Silva, Larry Siegfried

DYNASTY'S END

BILL RUSSELL
and the 1968–69
World Champion
BOSTON CELTICS

Thomas J. Whalen

NORTHEASTERN UNIVERSITY PRESS
Boston

Northeastern University Press

Library of Congress Cataloging-in-Publication Data
Whalen, Thomas J.
    Dynasty's end : Bill Russell and the 1968–69 world champion Boston Celtics / by Thomas J. Whalen.
        p. cm. — (The Sportstown series)
    Includes bibliographical references and index.
    ISBN 1-55553-579-8 (cloth : alk. paper)
        1. Boston Celtics (Basketball team)—History. 2. Russell, Bill, 1934– 3. Basketball players—United States—Biography. I.Title. II. Series.
    GV885.52.B67W53 2004
    796.323'64'0974461—dc21

                                                                                    2003012176

Designed by Books By Design, Inc.

Composed in Adobe Garamond by Books By Design, Inc.
Printed and bound by Thomson-Shore, Inc., in Dexter, Michigan. The paper is Dexter Offset, an acid-free sheet.

MANUFACTURED IN THE UNITED STATES OF AMERICA
08 07 06 05 04   5 4 3 2 1

For my stepfather, Joe

Sportstown Series Preface

It's been said that you can judge a city by its newspapers, bars, ballparks, and bookstores. By this reasonable standard Boston is world-class. Boston is to sports and literature what Paris is to painting and romance, London to drama and royalty, and Rome to ruins and traffic.

Sporting traditions dictate both the landscape and the social calendar of Bostonians. They literally plan their lives around the Marathon, the Beanpot, The Country Club, the Green Monster, and the Game. Not only has Boston produced and embraced the talents of such athletes as John L. Sullivan, Bobby Orr, Sam Langford, Joan Benoit, Bill Russell, and Ted Williams, but it is also the city that boasts of writers such as Phillis Wheatley, Nathaniel Hawthorne, William Dean Howells, Henry James, John Updike, and Edwin O'Connor, to name but a few.

It is no surprise that sportswriting talent developed in Boston and that the talented writers documenting the local sports scene have nearly matched the accomplishments of both their writing and athletic counterparts. For generations the sports pages of Boston's many newspapers have been among the best in America. Likewise, books depicting Boston's colorful and unparalleled array of athletes, events, and teams are among the best of world sports literature.

For years many of these books have been out of print. The Sportstown Series from Northeastern University Press, selected and edited by Richard A. Johnson, an author and the curator of the Sports Museum in Boston, seeks to reprint selected works from among these classics and also to publish original titles that illuminate one of the world's great sports regions. Among the subjects under consideration are the Boston Braves, 1913 U.S. Open champion Francis Ouimet, Rocky Marciano, and other legends. This volume in the Sportstown Series focuses on Bill Russell and the Boston Celtics.

The 1968–69 Boston Celtics bore the burden of impossible excellence. The defending world champions included a core of talent whose sole mission was the annual defense of their title. However, their middling regular season performance gained them a fourth place finish and the final playoff spot in the Eastern Conference. More than a few writers predicted the imminent demise of the dynasty. Waiting in the wings was a Laker team that had fallen in the finals in each of their six attempts against Boston. Most predicted the Celtics would be lucky to even make it to the inevitable Laker victory party.

The Celtics, known by their distinctive black sneakers and precise fast breaks, were as much a feature of the sixties as the Beatles or cold war while capturing ten of the twelve National Basketball Association finals contested since 1957. Led by center Bill Russell, the Celtics dominated their sport like no other professional team over a similar period in North American professional sports history. By April 1969 the team finally descended to the role of underdog. Their stirring playoff run, capped by an unforgettable seven-game final against the Lakers, was their finest hour and a fitting conclusion to the first chapter of their dynasty.

Historian Thomas J. Whalen has told their story with insight, depth, and grace while examining the season as well as the saga of the towering figures of Bill Russell and Wilt Chamberlain. For those of us fortunate to have enjoyed the '69 Celtics and the improbable resurgence of their playoff run, this book will rekindle much of the drama and joy of that spring. This book is well researched and places the franchise in the historic context of America's best sportstown as well as detailing much of the social history of the city and nation at that volatile time.

Richard A. Johnson
Series Editor
THE SPORTSTOWN SERIES

Contents

Illustrations

Bill Bradley, then with the New York Knickerbockers

Foreword

The 1968–69 season was particularly memorable for me, as it was my first full season in the NBA. It also was the first full season for our coach Red Holzman. Also, joining us that autumn were fellow '67–'68 rookies Walt Frazier and Phil Jackson and in December Dave DeBusschere, via a trade with the Pistons. Our Knicks team was just starting to show signs of the championship form that would carry us through a magical run of two NBA championships in three finals appearances in the four seasons from 1970 to 1973.

Part of what helped make this season a vital experience for our young, talented team was the opportunity to battle with our division rivals, the NBA champion Boston Celtics. It was also a virtual graduate school seminar on the game itself. It wasn't just basketball, it was Celtic basketball. With an ever-changing cast of solid role players around the core of stars such as Bill Russell, Bob Cousy, Sam Jones, and John Havlicek, the Celtics collected titles.

For the record we aced the course, dominating our "teachers" while capturing six of seven regular season games. The final exam, in the form of the Eastern Conference playoff final, was a different story as the defending champions beat us in six games, including two one-point losses.

I couldn't help but admire them as their championship run continued against a heavily favored Laker team in the finals. Following their improbable triumph in the seventh game in Los Angeles, Bill Russell captured the essence of their achievement when he remarked, "We won because of comradeship, friendship, and teamwork."

Championship teams share a moment that few other people know. The overwhelming emotion derives from more than pride. Your devotion to your teammates, the depth of your sense of belonging, is something like a blood kinship, but without its complications. Rarely can words fully express it. In the nonverbal world of basketball, it's like grace, beauty, or ease in other areas of your life. It is the bond that selflessness forges.

In his book *Dynasty's End*, historian Thomas Whalen captures the selflessness and absolute commitment to winning that made the '68–'69 Celtics intriguing and inspiring. It is a story that evokes countless memories of games played in that gym that was the other "garden" in which I played. It was my privilege to play against such men and gain inspiration from a team that treated winning as their right. Because they won with style, intelligence, grit, and grace, it didn't hurt as much when we lost and meant more when we won. I trust you'll also be compelled by their story.

Bill Bradley

Preface

The news came like an unexpected thunderbolt. In an exclusive cover story for the August 4, 1969, edition of *Sports Illustrated,* Bill Russell announced he was quitting the game of basketball for good, despite having a year remaining on his lucrative contract. "Since 1943, when I first saw a basketball," he attempted to explain, "I've played approximately 3,000 games, organized and otherwise. I think that's enough." After denying categorically his decision had anything to do with money, the philosophical player-coach of the Boston Celtics continued at length on his rationale for leaving: "There are professionals and there are mercenaries in sports. The difference between them is that the professional is involved. I was never a mercenary. If I continued to play, I'd become a mercenary because I'm not involved anymore. . . . I played because I enjoyed it—but there's more to it than that. I played because I was dedicated to being the best. I was part of a team, and I dedicated myself to making that team the best. To me, one of the most beautiful things to see is a group of men coordinating their efforts toward a common goal—alternately subordinating and asserting themselves to achieve real teamwork in action. I tried to do that—we all tried to do that—on the Celtics. I think we succeeded. Often, in my mind's eye, I stood off and watched their effort. I found it beautiful to watch. It's just as beautiful to watch in things other than sports. . . . Being part of that effort on the Celtics was very important to me. It helped me develop and grow, and I think it has helped me prepare for something other than playing basketball. But so far as the game is concerned, I've lost my competitive urges. If I went out to play now, the other guys would know I didn't really care. That's no way to play—it's no way to do anything."[1]

In truth, Russell had been secretly contemplating retirement throughout most of the 1968–69 season, but it was an event that occurred during a March 15 contest against the Bullets in Baltimore that finally convinced him to walk away. In the closing moments of a tight ballgame, Russell found his adrenaline rising as he called a time-out to rally his troops on offense. "Now we've got 'em!" he shouted as he excitedly pounded his fist into his hand for emphasis. "Now we've got 'em by the gym shoes! Let's go out there and kill 'em!" Then, as his fired-up team eagerly awaited instructions, Russell began to laugh hysterically. "Hey, Coach, what's the matter?" a concerned teammate asked. "What are you laughing at? What play are we going to run?" It took a moment for Russell to respond as he had to collect his thoughts and wipe away the tears from his eyes. Finally, he said, "Hey, this is really something. Here I am a grown man, 35 years old, running around semi-nude in front of thousands of people in Baltimore, playing a game and yelling about killing people. How's that?"[2]

Since that was hardly the answer they expected to hear, the team stared back blankly at Russell, no doubt expecting further elaboration. None was forthcoming as the Celtics went on to kick the ball away and lose the contest by a point. "That game," Russell later wrote in his 1979 best-selling biography, *Second Wind: The Memoirs of an Opinionated Man,* "confirmed my decision to retire; if there had been any doubt, it was erased. In all my years of laughs in pro basketball, I had never mocked the game itself. You can't give out what a game requires if you start focusing on its ridiculous aspects."[3]

Yet no one could characterize what Russell and the Celtics accomplished that glorious 1968–69 season as being ridiculous. A consensus preseason pick not to go very far in the playoffs due to their advancing age as a team, the Celtics overcame poor health, indifferent fan support, disruptive personnel changes, internal morale problems, and a disappointing fourth place finish on the regular schedule to capture the NBA championship, the franchise's eleventh in 13 years. "We felt we were good, we just didn't know how long we could keep it going," team captain John Havlicek later said. "We were just looking for one last gasp."[4]

Indeed, the 1969 championship marked the end of the greatest sports dynasty in history. No team in any sport at any time could match the

Celtics in terms of overall accomplishment. Not even the lordly New York Yankees of 1949–53, widely considered the best ensemble of baseball talent in the modern era, could match this string of success. After all, they could *only* manage to win five championships in a row, while the Celtics of the late 1950s and 1960s performed the feat an unprecedented eight straight times. "Ballplayers expect to win, but we more than expected to win," revealed defensive forward Tom "Satch" Sanders, an important contributor on six of those championship teams. "It was automatic. The key is having the same team together all the time. Roles were very clearly defined, and as long as you stuck with your roles, everything worked."[5]

Even fierce opponents like Jerry West of the Los Angeles Lakers admitted to having a grudging admiration for these Russell-led squads. "When you have people of that quality, those people can play at a higher level, period, and they do play at a higher level," said West, whose teams lost an unprecedented six NBA finals to the Celtics during this period. "When you have days of rest, and the ability to think and use your experience, the playoff atmosphere completely changes. Athletes are human. They know when somebody is really good, and when they're really good, you can't play at that level even when you're younger."[6]

Still, it looked as if the string had finally run out for the Celtics by the 1968–69 season. Russell was 35 and playing in considerable pain, due to a serious knee injury he had incurred in the middle of the year. He would average just 9.9 points for the season, the fewest in his illustrious career. Teammates Sam Jones, Larry Siegfried, Bailey Howell, and Tom Sanders also experienced their share of debilitating injuries and other problems that limited their overall effectiveness. Yet somehow the team managed to survive and thrive amid all the pressure to repeat as champions. As John Havlicek related, "When you're the underdog and can rally like the Celtics have, it makes it a little more satisfying, it builds on unity and closeness and character—the things that are required to win."[7] And win is exactly what the Celtics did in 1969.

Like any tale of heroic achievement, however, it is best to start at the very beginning.

Acknowledgments

I have found in writing this book, I am indebted to several people. For starters, I want to thank my mom, Mary Anne Whalen-Spinale, and my stepfather, Joseph Spinale, for providing me with constant encouragement and support. They are the best.

The latter can also be said of Dan Hammond and Chris Callely, who aside from being my best friends are also excellent writers in their own right. They were invaluable in offering suggestions on how to improve the book. I couldn't have done it without them.

John Weingartner and Robert Gormley, my editors at Northeastern University Press, did a terrific job in guiding this project through to completion. Their patience and good taste are much appreciated. Thanks also to Nancy Benjamin, Carol Keller, and Janis Owens at Books By Design for their work on this book.

A special debt of gratitude is owed Richard A. Johnson, curator of the Sports Museum of New England. He took time off from his busy schedule to review an early draft of the manuscript and was helpful at every stage.

Linda S. Wells, my dean at the College of General Studies at Boston University, was very supportive, as was my department chair, Jay P. Corrin. They have my deepest gratitude.

Fellow Bates grad and hoop fanatic Chris Fahy gets a big assist for his guidance and insights. Ditto for Joe King and Mike Feloney, whose humor and friendship I greatly appreciate. Sally Bryant patiently fielded many a late-night call on the West Coast to keep my spirits from flagging. She has my highest regard.

Special kudos to the staffs of the Naismith Memorial Basketball Hall of Fame, the Sports Museum of New England, the Boston Globe Library, and the Boston Herald Library for providing a highly professional and friendly environment in which to do my research.

Also deserving of strong praise are John Cronin, Leigh Montville, Bailey Howell, Emmette Bryant, Larry Siegfried, Don Nelson, Tom Heinsohn, George Plimpton, Bob Sales, Meghan Fay, Fred Hammond, Mary Alston-Hammond, Thomas H. O'Connor, Andrew Bunie, Betty Anderson, Barbara Storella, Scott Ferrara, and James Dutton.

Finally, I would like to thank all my students over the past three and a half years who have displayed enthusiasm and support of this project. They are my strength.

A Divided City
with a
Winning Tradition

Boston did not love its Celtics. Despite winning championship after championship in the 1950s and 1960s, the local entry in the National Basketball Association had never been able to capture a loyal following or the sporting imagination of the city. Beantown fans would flock to Fenway Park and the Boston Garden to see the Red Sox and Bruins play baseball and hockey respectively, but when it came to witnessing some of the world's greatest athletes perform acts of unsurpassed physical artistry around a basketball hoop, the interest level declined precipitously. Attendance figures tell the sad story. Between 1959 and 1966, the prime years of the Celtics dynasty, eight consecutive world championship banners were raised to the dusty Garden rafters, but only an average of 6,783 fans per game bothered to make the trek down Causeway Street. Since the Garden had a seating capacity of 14,000, this meant that the Celtics regularly played in a building that was less than half full. "There were always tickets," remembered *Boston Globe* sports reporter John Powers in *The Short Season,* a book detailing his experiences as a lifelong Celtics fan covering the team.[1] Fellow journalist and team chronicler Jeff Greenfield also detected a lack of broad interest in the club. "Building the world's greatest basketball team in the city of Boston had about it the quality of a Twilight Zone episode in which a man walks down a busy thoroughfare, desperately asking people to notice him, but going unseen and unheard," he wrote.[2]

Theories abound as to why this was the case, the most prevalent being that the city lacked the hoop tradition of a New York or a Chicago to appreciate the magnitude of the Celtics' accomplishments. The Boston public school system, after all, had eliminated the sport from its curriculum back in 1925, meaning that "thousands" had grown up "with no basketball in their sporting diet."[3] In addition, Bostonians seemed more temperamentally inclined to lace up a pair of skates and play hockey than go to basketball games in the dead of winter. All told, these factors made the city "an unlikely place to spawn a basketball legend," according to Bob Ryan, a longtime Boston sports columnist who penned several books on the Celtics.[4] Yet the great Holy Cross College basketball teams of the late 1940s had no problems selling out the Garden, especially when players like Bob Cousy, George Kaftan, and Dermie O'Connell electrified crowds with their up-tempo ball movement offense, the same kind of game the Celtics employed during their dynasty years. Indeed, when Cousy was a freshman member of the 1947 NCAA champion squad, more popularly known as the "Fancy Pants A.C.," the tiny Worcester school was the toast of the town. Holy Cross fever gripped the Hub in the same manner a Red Sox pennant race did in the hot summer months of July and August. "As we knocked off one opponent after another, the fans of Boston and New England went crazy," Cousy said. "They poured in the Garden to see us pile up our string of victories."[5]

So how was it then, when the Celtics began stockpiling championships of their own during the prosperous Eisenhower and Kennedy years, that Bostonians weren't eagerly caught up in the same kind of excitement and clicking through the turnstiles in record numbers? The brutal truth of the matter is that the city's majority white inhabitants felt uncomfortable paying money to see athletically gifted African-Americans run up and down a basketball floor, even when they were wearing Celtic green. Cheering on Holy Cross had been acceptable because their teams were predominantly white. The Celtics, on the other hand, possessed several top-quality black players who either started or performed high-profile bench roles. "Bill Russell's Celtics were always a lousy draw at Boston Garden," maintained authors Harvey Araton and Filip Bondy in their controversial 1992 best-seller, *The Selling of the Green: The Financial Rise and Moral Decline of the Boston Celtics*. "People would say Boston was a hockey town, surrounded by New England hockey villages. They would say the local media didn't know how to cover the sport. They never said that Bostonians didn't want to watch black basketball superstars."[6] Only when the Celtics began developing white superstars like Dave Cowens and Larry Bird in the 1970s and 1980s did fans begin to flock to the Garden. The composition of these crowds, needless to say, was mostly white, owing to the fact that African-Americans didn't feel particularly welcome in the cozy confines of the Garden. Indeed, blacks on the team were routinely subjected to racial taunts and other extreme forms of verbal abuse from the crowd. "People would walk past the bench and say, 'Cowens, Havlicek, you're great, the rest of you guys ain't worth a damn,'" one amazed opponent remembered.[7] A popular joke of the day went that when the Celtics won, a white player's picture would appear prominently in the next day's Boston sports pages, but when the team lost, that honor would fall thanklessly to a black player. "When I went there . . . I felt they had a code of conduct—first for athletes and another for black athletes," Bill Russell said.[8]

This kind of racially motivated fan behavior was directly linked to the city's own turbulent history of black-white relations. Up until the twentieth century, African-Americans had represented a small but vibrant portion of Boston's population. Settled along the northwestern slope of Beacon Hill, this community had played an active role in the struggle for emancipation in the years leading up to the Civil War. During the war, many local blacks deepened their commitment to the cause by volunteering to join the 54th Massachusetts Volunteer Infantry, the first African-American regiment raised by any northern state for the Union army. When several hundred members of the regiment were killed during a heroic assault on Fort Wagner, at the gates of Charleston, South Carolina, in July of 1863, their "common martyrdom," the late historian J. Anthony Lukas concluded, "helped cast a glow of brotherhood over the city's race relations."[9]

Alas, this "golden era" of racial harmony did not last very long. Black Bostonians continued to be subjected to the same traditional forms of racial discrimination that had existed before the war in terms of housing, schools, jobs, and public accommodations. By the turn of the century, little had changed in a real socioeconomic sense, apart from the fact that blacks now lived predominantly in the lower South End and Roxbury sections of the city. As scholar Stephan Thernstrom observed in his seminal book *The Other Bostonians*, "There was virtually no improvement in the occupational position of Black men in Boston between the late nineteenth century and the beginning of World War II. In 1890, 56 percent of the Black males employed in the city were unskilled day laborers, servants, waiters, janitors, or porters; three decades later the fraction was 54 percent, and, in 1940, it was 53 percent. As of 1890, a mere 8 percent of Boston's Blacks held white collar jobs; half a century later, the figure was only 11 percent."[10]

With the outbreak of the Second World War, however, came dramatic change. The city's black population nearly doubled from 23,000 in 1940 to over 40,000 by the end of the decade. The increase was part of a larger national trend that saw millions of blacks migrate from the Deep South to urban centers in the North and Midwest due to the wartime economic boom conditions that existed there. Boston was no exception as many blacks found good paying jobs in war-related industries. But along with this influx of newcomers came new problems. "Because no new construction had taken place in the Roxbury area since 1920," Boston historian Thomas H. O'Connor writes, "the overcrowded black population was literally bulging at the seams. By the late 1960s, African-Americans were starting to move beyond the confines of their traditional Roxbury boundaries, settling along the fringes of such formerly all-white neighborhoods as Dorchester, Mattapan, Jamaica Plain, Roslindale, and Hyde Park."[11]

This development in turn caused panic among ethnic whites, such as the Irish in South Boston and Charlestown, the Italians in East Boston and the North End, and the Jews of Mattapan, who felt their "turf" was in danger of being permanently overrun. As O'Connor notes, "Racial tensions quickly mounted as whites raised fears of blacks taking over their jobs, lowering the standards of their all-white schools, bringing down property values, and adding to the danger of crime in the streets. . . . At the same time, it stiffened the resolve of African-American residents to get their fair share of the American way of life before it was too late."[12]

Indeed, inspired by the success of the civil rights movement in the South in the 1950s and early 1960s, Boston blacks increasingly let it be known they were no longer going to sit back and passively accept the inferior social and political status the city had accorded them in the past. "We began to see ourselves differently," maintained local activist Mel King in his 1981 book, *Chain of Change: Struggle for Black Community Development.* "In this organizing stage, we understood that not only are we deserving of services in our own right as members of this society, but we are also capable of serving ourselves on our own terms. . . . Our collective voice began to be heard more clearly than our timid individual pleas for entry, and the political implications of working together began to be obvious."[13]

Decades of bottled-up racial tension and frustration would finally burst forth in a torrent of rage and violence during the summer of 1967. The precipitating incident involved a sit-in staged by a group of concerned African-American mothers at the Grove Hall office of the Welfare Department on Blue Hill Avenue. Outraged by the demeaning treatment they claimed to have received from "suspicious and insulting" social workers, these Mothers for Adequate Welfare (MAW) demonstrated for greater empowerment and the end of what they considered the "threatening presence" of police at local welfare centers.

Unimpressed by the group's demands and unwilling to negotiate, outgoing mayor John B. Collins ordered police to clear the city-owned building where a sizable crowd of mostly African-Americans had gathered outside. Violence soon erupted between bystanders and police as the crowd objected to the strong-arm tactics being employed. "When the police arrived they joked with the people at first and then all hell broke loose," remarked one witness.[14] Indeed, a full-blown riot occurred that engulfed the surrounding black neighborhood in a spontaneous orgy of looting, rock throwing, and arson. "It's just like a war," said another observer. "If the cops would go home there wouldn't be any trouble."[15] But trouble would continue over the next two nights as a series of violent outbreaks swept the area. As one newspaper account reported, "Bricks and bottles were hurled from rooftops and doorways the length of Blue Hill av. through the tense district. Several fires were set, one in a lumberyard. Cars were overturned or their windows smashed. A number of stores were looted by roving bands of youths." It was the worst rioting the city had experienced since the 1919 Boston police strike, and the event would go far in exacerbating the already volatile state of relations that existed between blacks and whites. As one disaffected teenager informed a reporter, "I'm going to throw bricks until winter. And when winter comes, I'm going to throw snowballs."[16]

Race also took center stage during the 1967 Boston mayoral contest that pitted Democrat Kevin White against former city school committee member Louise Day Hicks. A native of Charlestown and a graduate of Williams College, White was a "liberal-minded progressive" whose integrationist views and articulate manner made him "acceptable" to blacks and upper-middle-class groups. Hicks, in contrast, was a reactionary political firebrand from South Boston who positioned herself as an "outspoken champion of local autonomy and neighborhood schools."[17] Over the years she and her fellow colleagues on the all-white school committee had arrogantly dismissed charges that "de facto segregation" existed in Boston schools, despite all evidence to the contrary. This stance won her the enthusiastic acclaim of working-class whites throughout the city. "Boston for Bostonians" became her campaign rallying cry, and it did not require a major stretch of the imagination to determine who she meant by "Bostonians."

Thus, as election day approached, the two candidates presented voters with a compelling study of contrasts. White held out the promise for a broad inclusionist future, while Hicks offered a decidedly narrower vision predicated on her opposition to desegregation. Indeed, the entire election seemed to hinge on the question of race, which prompted the *Boston Globe,* a paper boasting a liberal readership, to break an 86-year tradition of withholding endorsements to political candidates. "There is a principle at stake in this election," the *Globe* editorialized. "In a city which once led the nation in public education and in calling for the end of slavery, it is now the principle of equal treatment for all people. And because principle rather than politics dictates its decision, the *Globe* today departs from its tradition and endorses Kevin White for mayor and hopes that Boston voters will support him."[18] Perhaps owing to the *Globe's* considerable political clout and influence, White was able to edge Hicks by a margin of 12,000 votes.

Yet White's troubles were just beginning. Just three months after White took office, the Reverend Martin Luther King Jr. was struck down by a white assassin's bullet in Memphis, Tennessee. Outraged by the slain civil rights leader's death, black ghettos across the country exploded into violence. Widespread looting, arson, and rioting resulted in the deaths of 46 people nationwide, all but five of whom were black, and property damage estimated to be over $100 million. In Chicago, 20 downtown city blocks were set ablaze, while large sections of Washington, D.C., were similarly torched before federal troops were called in to quell the disorder. Though Boston managed to avoid such wide-scale destruction, significant outbreaks of violence did occur in black neighborhoods throughout the city. In the Orchard Park section of Roxbury, for instance, one light-skinned African-American male was pulled from his motorcycle by a gang of angry rioters. "They thought he was white," reported Roxbury YMCA director Bill Wimberly, who fortuitously arrived on the scene to prevent further tragedy. "They were beating him when I got there and I recognized him and told the others that he was a Negro. I guess some of them then realized how senseless violence is. But the whole thing was ready to explode."[19]

White did his part to diffuse the situation by consulting with black community leaders around the clock and holding back overly zealous white police officers who were chomping at the bit to use armed force. The culmination of his efforts to ease racial tensions was his decision to address a mostly black audience before the start of a locally televised James Brown concert in Boston Garden. "Twenty-four hours ago," White said, "Dr. King died for all of us, black and white, that we may live together in harmony. Now I'm here tonight to ask you to make Dr. King's dream a reality in Boston. This is our city and its future is in our hands. So all I ask you tonight is this: Let us look at each other, here in the Garden and back at home, and pledge that no matter what any community might do, we in Boston will honor Dr. King in peace. Thank you."[20]

While these soothing words did much to calm the city in the immediate aftermath of the King assassination, they could not erase the racial enmity that had long existed in Boston. This ill feeling would flare into far greater violence in the decade to follow over the issue of federal court-ordered busing and school desegregation. By then, however, the word had already gotten out about the city. Far from being a "cradle of liberty," Boston revealed itself to be a seething cauldron of hate and intolerance, where the simple act of transporting black children across town to attend previously all-white public schools was tantamount to starting a race riot. Whites were furious because they felt federal desegregation laws denied them a voice in who could attend their neighborhood schools. They expressed their anger by hurling rocks and racial invective at the offending newcomers. As authors Emmett H. Buell Jr. and Richard A. Brisbin Jr. noted in their book on the subject, Boston replaced Little Rock, Arkansas, the site of the famous 1957 school desegregation battle, as the symbol of "white resistance." "Boston school desegregation was the most difficult in American history," they concluded.[21]

That such persistent racial strife would negatively impact fan attendance at Celtics games was perhaps inevitable. For not even the opportunity of seeing the greatest dynasty in the history of professional sports, one that would win ten NBA championships between 1957 and 1968, could convince local white sports fans to support the team in any appreciable numbers. The Celtics simply had too many "Negroes" playing for their collective tastes, and, if that wasn't bad enough, there was no longer the reassuring presence of a traditional white authority figure patrolling the sidelines. Starting with the 1966–67 season, the coaching reins fell to Bill Russell, a proud and defiant black man who wore a seething hatred of all things racist on his sleeve. He would, through his own steady leadership and stellar athletic deeds on the court, prove to whites in Boston and elsewhere that blacks were just as capable as they were in positions of power.

The times they were a changin', sang folk music legend Bob Dylan during these years of social and political upheaval. It was true of the country and also true of the local sports scene by the end of the 1960s.

Regarding athletic institutions, however, no team better exemplified Boston's historic racial divide than the Red Sox. Behind the unenlightened ownership of multimillionaire Tom Yawkey, the team had compiled an abysmal record when it came to hiring players of color within organized baseball. Indeed, the Sox waited until 1959 to have an African-American on its team roster, thus earning the dubious distinction of being the last ballclub in the majors to do so. Ironically, the team could have been the first to break baseball's color line in 1945 when future Hall of Famer Jackie Robinson and two other Negro League stars, Sam Jethroe of the Cleveland Buckeyes and Marvin Williams of the Philadelphia Stars, were given a "tryout" at Fenway Park. Despite performing impressively in a workout supervised by then Sox coach Hugh Duffy, Robinson and his comrades were never given a second look by the club. "We were fairly certain they wouldn't call us, and we had no intention of calling them," Robinson later revealed in his controversial autobiography, *I Never Had It Made*.[22] The reason the ballplayers felt this way had to do with the "insincere" nature of the tryout. The Sox had agreed to stage one only after receiving pressure from a Boston city councilman about the team's lily-white employment practices. The councilman, Isadore Muchneck, "threatened" to initiate legislation that would ban Sunday baseball games if the Sox persisted in excluding blacks from job consideration. "I still remember how I hit the ball that day, good to all fields," Robinson said. "What happened? Nothing!"[23]

By failing to sign Robinson and other talented black players, the team missed a golden opportunity at making history and securing a potential baseball dynasty. Regarding the latter, the Sox of the immediate postwar period always seemed to be a quality player or two short of winning it all. Having a couple of players the caliber of a Jackie Robinson then might have made a crucial difference in putting them over the top. As it was, Robinson would go on to play for the Brooklyn Dodgers in 1947 and lead the team to six pennants and one World Series championship over the next eleven seasons. "Had the Red Sox done it, had they had a two-year jump on the Dodgers and every other team in baseball in terms of signing African-American players," baseball historian Glen Stout remarked, "can you imagine the addition of a handful of any of two dozen guys who were available in 1945, what that would have meant to those powerhouse [Sox] teams in the late '40s and early '50s?"[24]

Four years after letting Robinson slip through their fingers, the team passed on an opportunity to sign an even greater black talent in Willie Mays. A Hall of Fame center fielder who would hit 660 home runs over a dazzling 22-year career, Mays was then a promising young star with the Black Barons, a Negro League team that had an agreement with a white Boston farm club operating in Birmingham, Alabama. In return for allowing the Negro Leaguers use of their home ballpark, the Sox farm team received "first refusal on any Black Baron players." Given Mays's exceptional abilities on the baseball diamond, it seemed a given the Sox would sign him to a contract. But the Boston front office determined that Mays was "not the Red Sox type" and instead opted to sign an aging Negro League veteran named Lorenzo "Piper" Davis to a minor league contract. Davis would not last a full season in the organization, despite leading his Class A Scranton, Pennsylvania, team in hitting and stolen bases. He was unceremoniously informed by club officials that his release was due to "economic conditions."[25] Not until infielder Pumpsie Green was brought on board in the late 1950s did the Sox even attempt to acquire another black ballplayer of comparable major league ability.

As to why the team dragged its feet so long regarding integration, the burden of responsibility lies squarely on the shoulders of Tom Yawkey. A resident of South Carolina and a graduate of Yale University, Yawkey possessed views on race that were all too common of that era, namely that blacks were inferior and that they should be segregated from white society. To this end, he saw nothing wrong with employing managers like Mike "Pinky" Higgins, who vowed there would be "no niggers on this ball club as long as I have anything to say about it."[26] Yawkey himself is suspected of being the unidentified heckler who shouted, "Get those niggers off the field," when Robinson, Jethroe, and Williams were trying out at Fenway Park in 1945.[27] More significantly, he supported the findings of the "highly classified" Major League Steering Committee report of August 27, 1946, that condemned efforts to sign black ballplayers. "Certain groups in this country including political and social-minded drum-beaters, are conducting pressure campaigns in an attempt to force major league clubs to sign Negro players," the report warned. "Members of these groups are not primarily interested in Professional Baseball. . . . They know little about baseball—and nothing about the business end of its operation. They single out Professional Baseball for attack because it offers a good publicity medium."[28] That same year, fellow owner Larry MacPhail complained to Yawkey during a night of "talk and drink" at New York's famed Toot Shor's restaurant that integration was going to "ruin" their business.[29] Yawkey could only nod in agreement. "The buck stopped at the top," Stout maintained. "Yawkey was someone who almost had no life outside of being owner of the Red Sox. This was not a man who was going to take dramatic action. He was someone that allowed a temperament to proceed after it had disappeared elsewhere or was beginning to disappear elsewhere."[30]

The bad racial vibes would continue in the Red Sox organization even after the team bowed to the inevitable and began signing African-American ballplayers in large numbers in the 1960s. Pitcher Earl Wilson, the team's second black player, who went on to become a 20-game winner with the Detroit Tigers, later told author and Red Sox historian Dan Shaughnessy about the unease he felt playing for a racist owner like Yawkey. He "had his farmers on his farm," Wilson said. "They were black. What other people call great is bad for other people. Some people probably thought Hitler was a great person. And they truly thought he was, but they wasn't Jewish and didn't have to deal with it. But once you're in that little guy's empire—everybody's got their cronies and junk. I don't know. I might have been a public pressure. You never know."[31] It was only in the late 1990s, more than two decades after Tom Yawkey's death, that the organization would shed the image of being a hostile place for minorities to play.

Unlike the Red Sox, the Celtics were in the forefront of efforts to integrate their sport. In 1950 the team made history by selecting All-American forward Charles "Chuck" Cooper of Duquesne as its number two pick in that year's NBA draft. The choice effectively smashed a long-standing bar against African-American athletes that had unofficially been in place since the league's founding in 1946. In short order, the rest of the NBA fell in line and began integrating team rosters, albeit at varying rates of progress. "I am convinced," Cooper later said, "that no team [w]ould have made the move on blacks then if the Celtics had not drafted me early."[32] New ground on the integration front was also broken during the 1963–64 season when the Celtics became the first professional basketball team to play five blacks on the court at the same time. Indeed, of the five starters on that year's Celtics squad, only one, power forward Tommy Heinsohn, was white. "It was no big deal," longtime Celtics coach and general manager Arnold "Red" Auerbach insisted. "I didn't even think about it. I just did it."[33] The team continued to make waves in 1966 when it named Bill Russell player-coach, the first African-American to helm a major league sports team.

Providing the impetus for these far-reaching changes were two individuals unhindered by the popular prejudices of their day. Walter Brown and Red Auerbach could hardly be considered social revolutionaries, but, unlike many of their contemporaries in the NBA and elsewhere in American society in the 1950s and 1960s, they instinctively embraced a philosophy of color blindness. If someone possessed the God-given talent to play in the NBA, they reasoned, then that person should be granted the opportunity to perform up to his fullest capabilities, regardless of racial heritage or ethnicity. "I don't give a damn if he's striped or polka dot or plaid," thundered Brown when informed by a fellow owner that his team was drafting a "colored boy" in 1950. "Boston takes Charles Cooper of Duquesne."[34]

"Walter Brown was 100 percent for it," Auerbach later claimed. "Without his decision, it never could have happened. I couldn't have done it without him. If he could play, he was going to take him, no matter what color he was, what religion he practiced. If he could play, Walter didn't care."[35] Cooper concurred with his former coach and mentor on this important point. "I had nothing but respect and admiration for [Brown]," Cooper said. "He was a gentleman with backbone. Give all the credit to that man who wasn't afraid to stick his neck out all the way. He made it all possible when nobody else would."[36]

A graduate of Phillips Exeter Academy, Brown began his nearly five-decade career in sports under the supervision of his father, George V.

Walter Brown
Courtesy of the Boston Public Library

Brown, the general manager of the Boston Garden and founder of the
Boston Marathon. Learning the business literally from the ground up,
young Walter rose steadily through the ranks by performing such diverse
tasks as collecting tickets, editing programs, and promoting local amateur sporting events. In 1934 he was tapped to be assistant manager of
the Garden, and, when his father passed away five years later, Brown succeeded him as general manager at the relatively young age of 33. As a tes-
tament to his skill and professionalism as an administrator, Brown was
promoted to Garden president in 1941, a position he would hold until a
heart attack claimed his life in 1964. Under his innovative leadership,
the Garden became a preeminent sporting venue, the site of several first-
rate prizefights, professional ice hockey battles, and college basketball
showdowns. In addition to these accomplishments, Brown cofounded a
professional ice skating show called the Ice Capades, served as president
of the Boston Bruins, and sponsored a popular annual collegiate hockey

tournament known as the Beanpot. Along the way, he picked up the title of "Boston's greatest sportsman," an honor venerable sports historian Richard A. Johnson argues Brown richly deserved. He "was simply a model of modesty, competence, and gentility in a profession filled with self-promotion, greed, and envy," Johnson wrote.[37]

Brown was also, according to many who knew him, kindhearted to a fault. He would give you his shirt, one friendly columnist wrote, and never bother to take out the cuff links.[38] This behavior, however, did not necessarily make him a good businessman. "You couldn't be as generous as he was and still be shrewd in business," former Celtics and St. Louis Hawks center Ed Macauley observed. "Very few people ever asked him for a salary figure they didn't get. Most people will ask for, say, 15 and you know they'll take 12. But if you asked Walter for 15, you got 15, or whatever the figure might have been. That's just the way he was. He cared for his players. And he was the most loyal man I ever knew. There were people who worked in the Garden back then who'd worked there when his father [George V. Brown] was president before him. If you'd ask them what function they performed, they'd have been hard pressed to come up with an answer, but as long as Walter was around they always had a place on the payroll."[39]

Brown was not without personal shortcomings. He possessed a volcanic temper that could erupt at a moment's notice. Yet his anger passed quickly, and he usually went out of his way to make amends with whoever was on the receiving end of his wrath. "In my rookie year," Bill Russell once recounted, "we lost our last game of the regular season to Syracuse, the team which had been murdering the Celtics in the playoffs up until then. Walter walked in and said: 'You bunch of chokers! I'll never come into this dressing room again.' The next day, while we were getting dressed for practice, he came in and stood there with his hand in his pocket kicking the floor. He said, 'I'm sorry. I'm just a fan, and I was so scared we were going to lose again that I got frustrated. I didn't mean what I said. I was upset. I apologize.'"[40]

What impressed Russell the most about the incident was the willingness of Brown to admit his error. "He owned the team," Russell said. "He didn't have to say that. But that's the way he was, a decent human being, and he'll always have the hearts of the guys who played for him."[41] Said Celtics Hall of Fame swingman Frank Ramsey, "There was a gentleness and fineness to this man which words cannot capture. His word was everything. He brought grace and dignity to the profession of sports and everything else he did."[42]

Brown earned his employees' trust and respect through his obvious integrity and tireless efforts to put the best possible entertainment product on the Garden floor every night. "Walter works hard, too hard," his wife, Marjorie Brown, said in a 1962 interview. "His days are endless. I really don't know how he stands it. He'll be up and out of the house at 9 a.m. and off to his office at the Garden. At 5:30 in the evening he'll be home, eating with an eye on the clock. He's gone an hour later. He just has to be back at the Garden when the doors open for an evening event or be there no later than one in the afternoon for a matinee, or else he feels he isn't doing his job. He loves his work. He'd work at what he has been doing now for 30 odd years for no money at all rather than make all the money in the world in some other field."[43]

Indeed, Brown was always cognizant of the fact that his chosen profession was unlike any other. "You can't treat this like a straight business," he liked to say. "It is too much of a business to be a sport and too much of a sport to be a business. It is sort of a hybrid affair." To this end he spent countless hours in his office trying to devise creative new ways to fill the Garden. He would book ice shows, three-ring circuses, rodeos, hockey tournaments, and wrestling matches—anything that had the potential of drawing a large audience. His operating philosophy was straightforward and unassuming. "It's not what I think that counts," he said. "What I think is immaterial. It's what the crowd wants."[44]

Sometimes the roaring masses got more than they bargained for, however. "One time we had a bring-'em-back-alive show," Brown recalled. "On closing night, someone forgot to lock the door to the monkey cage and 75–80 of those Rhesus monkeys got loose. Murder. We tried everything but couldn't get them down from the rafters. A couple of sports shows came and went but the monkeys stayed, thriving on the peanuts and hot-dog remnants and other morsels. It was strange, all those people watching a sports show and all those monkeys watching them, chirping and leaping and waiting for the fans to leave—feeding time. A real jungle backdrop. We tried everything to lure them, even some limburger wrappers contributed by the late Ernie Doody, one of our superintendents, who was a cheese lover. The monkeys got a sniff of the limburger-bait, actually reeled, and beat it back to the belfry again."[45] It was only through the intercession of a naturalist that the monkeys were finally induced into leaving their newly adopted Garden habitat.

Troublesome human beings were another matter. On one particularly memorable occasion, two inebriated sailors climbed down from the stands to participate in a bull-throwing contest that a visiting rodeo was holding. "They made straight for an ugly-looking Brahma as the cowboys stood aghast, their mouths open," Brown said. "The crowd bellowed, thinking this was a comedy act in the show. That bull caught one of those sailors and sent him cartwheeling, right into the first row of the box seats where he landed upright in a chair, unhurt. His mate was rescued. Had they been sober, both might have been killed."[46]

Through it all, Brown somehow managed to maintain his poise and sense of humor, qualities that came in handy when he launched the Celtics in 1946. He had earlier hit upon the idea of starting a new professional basketball league out of a desire to boost Garden attendance. Like other arena owners of his day, he grew alarmed at the thought of his building having "dark nights." He felt he needed a major new attraction to keep people coming to the Garden in the winter when his hockey Bruins were on the road. Basketball seemed like a logical choice. The sport was gaining in popularity around the country, as evidenced by the runaway success of annual collegiate basketball competitions like the National Invitational Tournament in New York. In addition, a pro circuit calling itself the National Basketball League had built up solid fan followings in upstate New York and in the Midwest in just under a decade. Indeed, if ever there seemed a more propitious time to start a new hoop league, it was during these early postwar years. The economy was booming, and returning GIs from the battlefields of Europe and the Pacific were looking for fresh avenues of entertainment to divert themselves. Thus seized with the idea, Brown successfully lobbied his colleagues in the arena business, respected figures like Al Sutphin of Cleveland and Ned Irish of New York, to join him in the enterprise. From their combined efforts emerged the Basketball Association of America, later to be renamed the National Basketball Association in 1950. The NBA turned out to be far from an overnight success story, but, thanks to the foresight and perseverance of these pioneering entrepreneurs, the league eventually grew to a point where it was able to take a place alongside baseball, football, and hockey as a major professional sport.

Yet all this was in the distant future for Brown in 1946. Having played a decisive role in giving birth to the league, his main concern now lay in getting a franchise up and running in Boston. As to what the team would be called, Brown had little difficulty in coming up with a name.

"Wait, I've got it—the Celtics," he excitedly told his publicist, Howie McHugh. "We'll call them the Boston Celtics! The name has a great tradition. And besides, Boston's full of Irishmen. We'll give them green uniforms and call them Celtics."[47] Unfortunately for Brown, finding an appropriate team moniker was about the only thing that went right that first season. A self-admitted basketball novice, Brown tried to make up for his lack of hoop knowledge by hiring an experienced head coach. However, his first choice, the highly regarded Frank Keaney of the University of Rhode Island, bowed out after having led Brown to believe he was going to take the job. Desperate to find a replacement, Brown settled on John "Honey" Russell, the former pilot at Seton Hall University who had led the Pirates to a 43-game winning streak between 1936 and 1941. But since he had been hired long after most teams had finalized their coaching selections, Russell was at a competitive disadvantage when it came to securing talent for the Celtics. Other coaches had already finished stocking their rosters with the "best and the brightest" the amateur and pro ranks had to offer, leaving Russell to scramble for whatever crumbs they left behind. He "missed out on players he might have garnered had he been able to start his recruiting earlier," Jack Russell, Russell's son, later said. "It was the kind of thing that put him and the Celtics management in a situation where the odds were against them."[48]

The odds grew steadily worse as the season progressed. Though the team possessed the league's third leading defense, the Celtics had difficulty putting points on the board. In fact, they could muster only 60 points a game, placing them dead last in offense. Only one player, center Connie Simmons, averaged double figures. In light of such pathetic scoring, the team won only 22 games for the season, finishing in a tie for last place with the Toronto Huskies in the Eastern Division. While the club lacked on-court success, it was not without its share of interesting characters and personalities. Topping the list here was eccentric pivotman Kevin "Chuck" Connors. Nicknamed "Li'l Abner" after the title hillbilly character of the popular Al Capp comic strip, Connors became an instant fan favorite with his offbeat brand of personal humor and irreverent showmanship. Indeed, his antics caused the team's first home opener of November 5, 1946, to be delayed by one hour. Showing off during warm-ups, the future star of *The Rifleman* television series shattered the glass backboard at the west end of the Boston Arena. (The Boston Garden was unavailable due to a rodeo booking.) Since no other backboards were on site, a shooting contest was staged on the east end side to keep fans entertained until a suitable replacement was brought over from the Garden. When play finally got under way, the Celtics dropped a heartbreaking 57–55 decision to the Chicago Stags before a less than spectacular turnout of 4,329 fans. Making partial amends for his earlier mishap, Connors became the team's third leading scorer on the evening with seven points. "Anyone who knows anything about the Boston Celtics knows that when they started they were the strongest team in the league—in the cellar holding everyone else up," he later joked.[49]

The Celtics avoided last place during the 1947–48 season and even made the playoffs before being summarily dispatched by Chicago in the first round, two games to one. Nevertheless, the team finished eight games below .500 during the regular season and showed few signs of real improvement. Brown did his best to try to rectify the situation by firing Russell and replacing him with Alvin "Doggie" Julian, who was coming fresh off an NCAA championship with Holy Cross. But the change in coaches made little difference. Over the next two years the team continued to falter and lose money, almost a half million dollars by one estimate. "Things were going so bad that even my wife wanted me to get out of the business," Brown said. "I remember her telling me: 'we've had a lot of teams that have lost—but they were trying to win.[']"[50] He thus found himself at a personal and professional crossroads as the 1940s drew to a close. He could either fold the team or risk his life savings in a desperate bid to keep the "rapidly sinking" franchise afloat. Against all common sense and the advice of family and friends, he opted for the latter course of action. He took out a second mortgage on his home and cashed in his stocks to stave off team bankruptcy. These drastic financial measures all might have been gone for naught, however, if he did not come to another fateful decision during the summer of 1950 that would forever alter the future of the Celtics and the NBA. On the advisement of good friend and team investor Lou Pieri of Providence, he hired Red Auerbach as his new coach.

In terms of competitive drive, intelligence, and sheer chutzpah, no one was better qualified for the task of reversing the team's moribund fortunes than Auerbach. "This is an opportunity that makes me very happy," he informed an assemblage of local media upon accepting the job. "I know the crying need for immediate success, and I fully intend to do everything within my power to give Boston the best basketball team that can possibly be put together."⁵¹ Losing had never been an acceptable option for Auerbach. He believed in success. Period. Nothing annoyed him more than players who did not share a similar sentiment. "Red knew how to judge talent and how to motivate it," former St. Louis Hawks forward Bob Petit said. "Plus he commanded respect. I don't care who it was, if one of his players stepped out of line, Red would descend on him with both feet. On my team I think we had 11 [coaches] in 11 years . . . and when some of them got up to yell and scream, the players would laugh at them. No one paid any attention to them. They sounded tough, but they weren't tough, not the way Auerbach was. Red was different. You had to respect him, even if you didn't like him."⁵²

No one was above the team in Auerbach's mind, and that included certain superstar centers. Early in his 1956–57 rookie season, Bill Russell displayed a distressing penchant for contracting minor injuries that cut back on his playing time. Auerbach thought he was excessively "moaning" about his ailments and using them as an excuse not to perform up to his usual high standards. When he saw Russell lying on a training table before a game against St. Louis complaining of a "tight hamstring," the Celtics' boss could no longer contain his displeasure. "Get off that table and get suited up and get out there and play," he roared. "We're paying you damn good money and we're expecting you to perform." Without a word, Russell got up and proceeded to play a "great game." When later asked by Celtics broadcaster Curt Gowdy if he had run the risk of permanently alienating the feelings of his prize rookie, Auerbach could only shake his head. "If other players know I let someone get away with something, they'll completely lose their respect for me," he said. "They may not like me, but I know one thing. They have respect for me."⁵³

Vituperative outbursts aside, Auerbach displayed an unflinching loyalty toward his players. A case in point involves the harsh treatment Chuck Cooper received when he broke in with the Celtics in the early 1950s. The first black to break the color barrier in the NBA, Cooper endured a mountain of abuse from opposing players and fans alike. In one noteworthy 1952 contest against the Tri-Cities Blackhawks in Moline, Illinois, Cooper was called a "black bastard" by an opponent. "I asked him what he said and he repeated it," Cooper told an interviewer in 1977. "So I pushed him in the face as hard as I could. I wanted to fight him, but I wanted him to throw the first punch. He wouldn't fight—but everyone else did." Among those rushing to Cooper's defense was Auerbach, who took the opportunity to vent his displeasure at the way his young forward was being treated by squaring off against Tri-Cities coach Doxie Moore. "It was quite a fight, the worse fight I remember," Cooper said of the violent melee that broke out between the two teams. Significantly, Cooper had approached Auerbach before the fisticuffs began to inform him he was not going to take any further verbal abuse regarding his racial heritage. "Then don't take it," Auerbach responded. These were exactly the kind of words the beleaguered Cooper needed to hear.[54]

Going on the road with the Celtics had always been particularly difficult for Cooper. "I wouldn't necessarily call it hell," Cooper commented. "But yes, the worst part was traveling. It was those separate hotels and restaurants and cabs. In Baltimore, I had to stay in a black hotel. Hotels in some other towns—like Washington and St. Louis—said, 'OK, you can stay here but keep out of our dining room.' To soften the hurt, Red always told me I could stay in my room and charge my meals on room service if I wanted—and teammates always joined me." Indeed, his fellow Celtics always offered a welcomed buffer to the hostile forces of society that lurked beyond the sheltered reaches of the basketball court. "There were never any racial problems within the team," Cooper said. "Oh, once in a while somebody would get overanxious in letting me know they'd 'grown up with blacks and had been best friends,' the kind of stuff that gets stale after hearing it over again. But their intentions were good. In fact, I had good support in terms of acceptance by my white teammates and, most of all, by Red and Mr. Brown. I felt a strong relationship with them all."[55]

Sadly, this kind of moral support was lacking after Cooper left the Celtics in the mid-1950s. "Later, with the [St. Louis] Hawks, I wasn't allowed to stay with the team in Miami or Shreveport. I had to stay in a reform school in Shreveport. And they wouldn't let me play in Baton Rouge. Red Holzman was our coach and asked me if I wanted him to take a stand. I got angry because I don't think his offer was sincere—and told him so. I knew they were not going to cancel with 7,000 people in the stands."[56]

By way of comparison, when confronted by a similar situation in Raleigh, North Carolina, during the 1952 season, the Auerbach-led Celtics refused to play, thus pressuring the local powers-that-be to lift the ban. The subject of race "was no problem at all for the Celtics to handle," Cousy said. "We didn't handle it I guess. We just let it flow. Any minority wants, and what they deserve and demand, is simply to be treated like everyone else. I guess that's what we did. We simply didn't focus on the fact that ten of us were white and Chuck was black."[57]

Race wasn't a problem on the Celtics because Auerbach refused to make it so. He made a special point of building a harmonious team atmosphere where blacks and whites could work and thrive together. "I treated them with respect," he explained. "I never believed in handling players. You handle animals. I treated my players like people. I respected their intelligence. I was straight with them and they were straight with me. I didn't lie to them and they didn't lie to me. There was no double standard."[58] To be sure, the Celtics were more than a collection of professional athletes sharing the same locker room space; they were members of a unique brotherhood who pooled their collective energies toward the common goal of winning. In many respects, they embodied the liberal values the 1960s were supposed to be about—equality, diversity, and inclusion. They were a vivid reminder of what lofty heights a then racially divided society could reach if every citizen pulled together and treated each other with mutual respect and forbearance. Without intending to, they became role models for a better America, one where people's deeds were far more important than their skin color or particular social background. This prejudice-free approach became popularly known as "Celtic Pride," a metaphor for what Bill Russell later called personal integrity, imagination, and collaborative decision making.

As Hall of Fame guard K.C. Jones once observed, "Being a Celtic is being with the ball players that play on the club. Seeing how they mesh, seeing how they help one another. Seeing everything that went into making this team win all those championships. It's the same old bit— pride, determination to win, things like that. Any guy who's been on the club has this attitude. We all have a different way of playing the game, but we complement one another. Any rookie who joined the club could see this. He might be wide-eyed and halfway scared. The veterans would advise him and help him. He'd have to see the air of togetherness. He'd see us play and be amazed at the way we went at it. He'd see how we'd want to win a scrimmage that doesn't mean anything."[59]

And no one was more committed to winning than Red Auerbach. It was the sine qua non of his existence. "Many men love victory," offered one magazine writer. "But Auerbach loves it and respects it, and, toughest of all, understands it. He comprehends better than most men that winning is its own reward. The cheers, the silver cup, the gold coins, the bowed head and upraised hand—these come after the fact. The fact itself, the only fact is winning."[60] Without question, Auerbach went to great lengths to find an edge, any edge, that would aid his team in securing victory.

"He's always thinking, no matter what he does out there," Cousy told a journalist early into Auerbach's coaching tenure. "He has a reason for just about everything. A couple of years ago, he started rushing in a big man when a little man had a jump. He would have the little man stop to tie his shoelace to give enough time for the substitution. The other coaches laughed at this at first, but quickly adopted it when they saw it worked. They used it so much, the league finally had to rule it out."[61] In truth, Auerbach always seemed to be running afoul of NBA officialdom, in particular referees. There was nothing that personally offended him more than what he perceived as a blown call against his team. He would work himself into a furious rage and verbally accost the referee with a string of invectives that would cause even the hardest bitten of individuals to blush. Game officials like Earl Strom, Norm Drucker, Sid Borgia, and Charley Eckman were hardly amused by these bullying antics. They often complained of the constant abuse leveled in their direction by Auerbach. "Red always wanted the edge," remembered Strom.[62]

"What you've got to understand is that he's a good-natured fellow, a very capable coach and a man who knows how to deal with his ballplayers," claimed one Celtic. "But because he feels he has to be aggressive all the time, sometimes he goes too far. Especially with the referees. He's always pushing them too hard. We all do somewhat. But Red doesn't let up. And the refs hate his guts because of it. Lots of them have told us so. When we get in a situation where a ref has to call a split-second decision, you know that you're not going to get the break. The ref doesn't do it consciously; there isn't enough time to think about it. But it's just at those times—when a snap decision has to be made—that what is bothering him will show up. And Red bothers the refs."[63]

In his best-selling 1966 memoir, *Winning the Hard Way*, Auerbach self-servingly tried to justify this outrageous behavior by arguing it was done to uphold the integrity of the league. "I battled the referees all these years because I believed the NBA desperately needed more uniformity in the officiating. I mean, let every referee call the charge, let every referee enforce the three-second rule, let every referee call walking whether it affects the play or not. . . . Let them call all the infractions or none of the infractions but play it one way, night after night. You can't imagine how much good that would do for the sport."[64]

A less charitable explanation, however, is that Auerbach was just trying to secure an advantage for his team through old-fashioned intimidation of officials à la a John McGraw in baseball or a Woody Hayes in football. "He's got that baiting of his down to a science," apprised Los Angeles Lakers coach Fred Schaus in 1965. "He knows just how far to go."[65] Auerbach's scare tactics did not stop with referees. He was not above confronting other coaches or team owners as was the case during the 1957 NBA finals against the St. Louis Hawks. Before Game 3 in St. Louis, Auerbach angrily demanded that the height of one of the baskets, the one the Celtics were warming up on and the one the Hawks would be using in the second half, be checked. He argued it was well under the required league height of ten feet. Hawks owner Ben Kerner took personal umbrage at this accusation, especially when officials determined there was no problem with the basket. Kerner growled that Auerbach was trying to show him up in his own building and that he was nothing more than a "bush league ———." "What he called me was unprintable," Auerbach told reporters afterward. "I wasn't going to take it." To demonstrate his displeasure, Auerbach punched Kerner "squarely in the mouth" and might have done greater bodily harm had players, police, and ushers not intervened to break it up. "I just called him a bush-leaguer, and what else is he?" Kerner said. "That's a bush-league stunt. . . . He just wanted to show off before everybody and I told him what I thought. So I took his best punch, so what?" For his actions, Auerbach received a $300 league fine and the lasting enmity of St. Louis fans, but in the end the Celtics came away with their first championship.[66]

"That man did everything he could to provoke me every time he came into our building," Kerner later complained. "He wanted to run the whole show. You'd think *he* was the home team! He'd yell at the scoring table, run up to the PA announcer, bark at the officials, incite the fans, stomp around—hey, anything was possible when Red came to town."[67] But what was perhaps most galling of all for opponents was the ungracious way Auerbach punctuated Celtic wins. "He'd get us down, then rub salt in our wounds with that damn cigar," groused Fred Shaus of the Lakers.[68] The cigar. When lighted by Auerbach near the conclu-

Red Auerbach shows his victory smile while chomping his victory cigar
Copyright 1965 Globe Newspaper Company, Inc. Republished with permission of the
Globe Newspaper Company, Inc.

sion of a basketball contest, it signified that victory was indisputably at hand. "He'd like to embarrass an opponent that way," claimed Hall of Fame forward and Rhodes scholar Bill Bradley.[69] Former Syracuse Nats star Earl Lloyd was equally condemning. "It was tough to dislike Red, but *that* hurt, seeing him sit back, cross his legs and light up. Oh yes, that incensed more than a few people. I can assure you."[70] In his defense, Auerbach said he smoked on the bench to relax and to promote a cigar he was endorsing. "Why stop a guy from making a buck?" Auerbach reasoned.[71] All the same, Celtic players like Bob Cousy and Bill Russell preferred their coach to kick the habit when it came to games. To them, it served no purpose to needlessly rile up the opposition by what could be interpreted as a monumental display of "arrogance." This concern, however, failed to register with Auerbach. He saw the gesture as harmless fun. After all, there were no recorded instances when he lit a cigar on the bench and the Celtics didn't win, so why get upset? "The image of this cigar is unbelievable," he marveled. "A guy in Quincy, Mass., won the thousand-dollar first prize from the Cigar Institute of America for a photograph of me blowing smoke."[72] Indeed, the cigar would eventually become an iconic sporting image forever associated with Auerbach, just as the pearl gray fedora would come to be synonymous with football coaching legend Tom Landry of the Dallas Cowboys.

If Auerbach's players were made uncomfortable by his cigar smoking, they were truly terrified of his driving ability, or lack thereof. "He was cuckoo," Cousy said in a 1985 interview. "I haven't ridden with him since 1951. That was my first year. The penalty for being a rookie was that you rode with Auerbach on exhibitions. We used to play 19 games, and we drove all over New England. He's wrecked more cars than Evil Kneivel. I remember once a little town in Vermont. We were driving through it around 80 miles an hour, and the damn thing just exploded. We sort of glided to the side. When the other guys came along, we picked up our stuff and left. For all I know the damn thing is still there. We'd go to Bangor [Maine] and he'd literally start out two hours after us. Then, he'd boast about beating us there. We'd get to the hotel, and he'd be sitting there puffing on his cigar."[73]

In the end, such eccentricities were overlooked as Auerbach was able to instinctively meet the needs of every individual player on the Celtics roster and meld them into a powerful collective that beat all competition. "He never made any pretensions about treating players the same," Bill Russell told *Sports Illustrated.* "In fact, he treated everybody very differently. Basically, Red treats people as they perceive themselves. What he did best was to create a forum, but one where individuals wouldn't be confined by the system. And he understood the chemistry of a team. People tend to think teamwork is some mysterious force. It isn't. It can, really, be manufactured, and he knew how to do that, to serve each player's needs. And people always say you need to know *how* to win. But that's not enough if you want to keep winning. You also have to know *why* you win. Red always knew that, too."[74]

The roots of Auerbach's rage to succeed can be traced back to his childhood when he was growing up in the ethnically diverse Williamsburg section of Brooklyn, New York, in the 1920s. The son of a Russian Jew who had started a successful dry-cleaning business, Auerbach learned early the value of hustle and grit. He would often help his father late at night in the shop, pressing suits and pants until the wee hours of the following morning. He also learned a painful lesson about knowing when to fend for himself. Once, another boy from the neighborhood picked a fight with him and Auerbach made the mistake of "letting him swing first." After recovering from this "sucker punch," Auerbach vowed he would never permit another human being to get the jump on him again. Henceforward, he would be the one throwing the first punch in fights, something St. Louis Hawks owner Ben Kerner came to learn the hard way in 1957. But it was basketball, not fighting, that became the dominant passion of his youth. I "learned my basketball at a gym built outdoors, on the roof of Public School 122," Auerbach later reminisced. "Unless it snowed or rained, we played. In high school, I made the all-Brooklyn second team, and my players kid me about it now. What they don't know is that we had more good basketball players in Brooklyn in those days than there were in all the rest of the United States."[75]

Auerbach showed enough promise to earn a basketball scholarship to George Washington University in Washington, D.C., and to come under the tutelage of pioneering hoop coach Bill Reinhart. It was from Reinhart that he learned the fundamentals of the "modern fast break," a style of offense that was predicated on rebounding and quick precision passing. Reinhart "first conceived the idea of taking the rebound, turning to whip the pitchout to the guards and then coming down the lanes at top speed with the ball constantly going from man to man in the air without any dribbling," Auerbach noted approvingly.[76] Auerbach would later employ these principles with great success when coaching his champion Celtics teams of the 1950s and 1960s. Before becoming a professional coach, however, he had to first pay his dues.

Following his graduation from GW in the spring of 1940, Auerbach entered a master's degree program at GW and coached high school basketball in the D.C. area. During the Second World War, he was made a third-class petty officer in the U.S. Navy and assigned to the Norfolk Naval Base in Norfolk, Virginia, as a physical education instructor. Displaying the same kind of tireless energy and initiative that would mark

his tenure as Celtics boss, he organized thirty separate athletic tournaments on base and coached a team of former college hoop stars that
included future New York Knicks coach Red Holzman. By the time he
received his naval discharge papers in 1946, Auerbach had developed a
strong confidence in himself and his ability to lead other men. Such confidence came in handy when he learned the Washington Capitols of the
new Basketball Association of America had an opening for a coach. He
immediately went about convincing the team's owner, Mike Uline, that
he was the best available man for the job. As Auerbach recalled, "I was
29 and just out of the Navy when I walked in on Mike Uline and told
him I was the guy to coach his Washington team. . . . I don't know why
but Mike bought my bag. I recruited my team in a phone booth, calling
all over the country to players I had known in the Navy."[77]

The brash young coach made an immediate impact on the pro circuit,
directing Washington to a division title and a 49–11 regular season record.
Though the team was upset in the playoffs, Auerbach won kudos for his
work ethic and fiery determination. "A lot of players on that team . . .
knew as much about coaching as Auerbach that first year," remembered
Caps guard Fred Scolari. "He sure learned well, didn't he? I attribute his
success to the fact that from the start he had the ability to control a club.
He was the boss."[78] A contract dispute forced Auerbach to leave the
team two years later, but he did not find himself unemployed for long.
Snapped up by the Tri-Cities Blackhawks of the newly constituted NBA,
Auerbach attempted to mold a roster of raw and inexperienced players
led by former Illinois All-American Dick Eddleman into a winner. The
task proved beyond even his considerable abilities, however. Tri-Cities, a
public relations artifice referring to the communities of Moline and
Rock Island, Illinois, and Davenport, Iowa, finished the season below
the .500 mark. It would represent the only "losing campaign" in Auerbach's storied 20-year coaching career. Disagreement with ownership
over team personnel policy would prompt another early job exit by season's end. "I was crushed," Auerbach later maintained.[79]

Yet within two weeks he was back on his feet again as Walter Brown
invited him to take over the vacant Celtics coaching post for the
1950–51 season. To suggest that Auerbach wasn't initially bowled over
by the offer would be an understatement. The team had just finished in
last place, attendance had fallen, and the financial losses were mounting.
Job security, needless to say, was something thought of only in the dis-

tant abstract. Brown admitted as much during their initial meeting. "So if we hired you and you didn't get us moving[,] you wouldn't have a job in Boston next year because there wouldn't be any team here," he said. Impressed by the Celtics owner's forthright honesty, Auerbach uncharacteristically made a snap decision. He agreed to take on the challenge of rebuilding the team, provided he was given "complete authority" to "run the show."[80] Feeling that he had nothing to lose, Brown consented to these terms, thus setting the stage for one of the most remarkable turnarounds in modern sports history. With Auerbach now calling the shots, the team posted its first winning record in franchise history and made the playoffs. Though the team was eliminated by the Knicks in the first round, an important corner had been turned. The Celtics became perennial challengers for the NBA championship in the 1950s and 1960s while never posting a losing record. At the same time, the team was able to turn a modest profit, thereby saving the franchise from financial ruin. Auerbach, in other words, had managed to pull off a minor miracle.

"I know now he started something that I don't think will ever exist again," claimed Paul Silas, the All-Star forward who played against Auerbach-coached teams in the 1960s before becoming a starter on two Celtic championship squads in the 1970s. "He could mold players who came from the outside into that [winning] tradition. Only he could do it."[81] Indeed, Auerbach had a special knack for picking up players other teams had given up on and transforming them into All-Star-caliber contributors. Don Nelson, Larry Siegfried, Willie Naulls, and Clyde Lovellette are but a few of the standouts the Celtics coach rescued from the NBA scrap heap. "I believe he sees things in certain players that no one else sees, or maybe no one else bothers to look for," Nelson said.[82]

In actuality, the criteria Auerbach used for finding players to fit into the Celtics system were quite simple. "Mostly," he told the *Christian Science Monitor* in an expansive 1962 interview, "I look for attitude. Actually, a lot depends on what a pro coach needs. I'm willing to pass up a better ball player, for example, and go for a lesser player if that man is going to help maintain the balance of my team. Four great forwards won't do you any good if you haven't got anybody who can play the backcourt. As I said, the idea is to maintain perfect balance. When I scout a player, I like to watch him up close. A lot of coaches prefer to sit high up in the stands where they can get a better over-all view of the floor. But I don't. I sit near to the court as I can, and I listen to see if the player I'm scouting talks on defense—a must in pro ball. I try to judge his timing, speed, and reactions—whether his hustle is real or false, and whether or not he has educated hands. Good hands are extremely important in basketball. I also try to find out all I can about him personally. I do this by talking to his coach, his friends, players who have competed against him, and rival coaches. Usually you can tell right away whether a kid is a selfish or a team player. And then, of course, there's the obvious: Is he big enough, is he strong enough, and can he stand the kind of a travel schedule we have in the NBA?"[83]

As with any successful enterprise, however, luck sometimes played a crucial role, particularly when it came to making key personnel decisions. Take, for example, the circuitous path Auerbach trod to secure the services of backcourt ace Bob Cousy. Initially disdainful of Cousy's basketball talents, Auerbach went out of his way to deride the Boston media as "local yokels" for even suggesting the team acquire him. "The only thing that counts with me is ability, and Cousy hasn't proven to me he's got that ability," he sniffed.[84] Fortunately for Auerbach, he would soon be given the opportunity to revise his opinion. For the team that held Cousy's NBA draft rights, the Tri-Cities Blackhawks, fell into a bitter contract squabble with the former Holy Cross star. Unable to come to terms, Cousy soon found himself traded to the Chicago Stags, just in time to see the team fold three weeks prior to the start of the 1950–51 season. All the Chicago players, save for sharpshooter Max Zaslofsky, playmaker Andy Phillip, and Cousy, were parceled out to other clubs around the NBA. The trio that remained were considered the defunct franchise's best players, but league owners could not agree on how to divide them among Boston, New York, and Philadelphia, teams yet to receive anyone from the special dispersal draft. To break the deadlock, NBA president Maurice Podoloff ordered that the names of the players be written on three separate slips of paper and drawn from a hat. New York and Philadelphia picked ahead of Boston and came away with Zaslofsky and Phillip respectively, leaving Auerbach with the player he least desired: Cousy. Thus, through an unlikely series of events, Auerbach was "stuck" with a Hall of Fame point guard who would go on to revolutionize the game with his acrobatic passing skills. "I was hoping we'd get Phillip, but [we] drew Cousy's name," Auerbach later admitted. "Cousy was better than I thought he was. He was such a competitor."[85]

As far as being a game strategist was concerned, Auerbach liked to keep things simple. "You've got a basketball," he liked to say. "It's round.

The floor's even. If you bounce it, it's going to come straight up. You don't have to watch it. One of the most important things in basketball is the position of the head. The game is not played down there. It's played up here."[86] Consonant with this less-is-more philosophy, he used only seven basic plays during his entire coaching tenure in Boston. Even though rival teams could readily identify the plays as they were being called from the bench, it made little difference in the final analysis. That is because Auerbach had so thoroughly drilled his charges on the fundamental execution of these plays that opponents were powerless to stop them on a consistent basis.

Tied into game preparation was the importance of physical conditioning. As All-Star guard Bill Sharman remembered, "By opening night, we were the best conditioned team in the league and Red believed that we'd steal 3–4 games early—especially on the road—because we were in better shape than anybody else. Even today, some coaches and players believe that you come to training camp and 'play yourself into shape.' That was the prevailing attitude years ago, but not with Red. So every year, he'd get us off to a great start and that would bolster our confidence."[87] The record indicates this approach proved to be extremely effective, as Auerbach teams usually started very fast out of the blocks. The 1959–60 season was a prime example. The Celtics jumped out to an incredible 30–4 start, including 11 victories in their first 12 games. Overall, they finished 59–16 on the year, en route to winning their third championship in four seasons.

Despite this obvious success, Auerbach took pains not to get too carried away with his own importance. "A man thinks he's infallible, he's ridiculous," Auerbach said. "I admit it if I had a bad day on the bench. You let them know you're human too, that you can't be up for 80 games. Otherwise how can you keep patting them on the behind?"[88] Indeed, he never lost sight of who put him in a position to win so many championships. "I wouldn't be standing out here today," Auerbach confessed in a special 1985 Boston Garden ceremony commemorating his career, "if it weren't for all those [players] out there. I just sat on the bench and said, 'Cooz, get the ball downcourt; Russ, get the rebound,' . . . it's great. Tommy [Heinsohn]? I didn't have to tell Tommy anything, he knew how to do it. . . . They're all so great and special to me."[89]

To an unusual degree, Auerbach also went out of his way to solicit the views of his players, especially when it came down to "crunch time" in the final two quarters of a game. "He allowed input from Cousy and Russell

Celtics "Big Three" (left to right): Bob Cousy, Walter Brown, Red Auerbach

right down to the 12th man," K.C. Jones said. "He allowed players to use their imagination and creativity on the court. . . . No other coach I've ever seen in college or in the pros had the grasp of a team the way he did."[90]

"See, when I coached, I always had every ballplayer tell me if he felt there was a good situation on the court," Auerbach said. "Like if his man was overplaying him, we could backdoor him, things like that. Or I'd say, 'Hey, so and so is knocking himself out. He's jumping all over you. He's overreacting. Before you make your move, fake and he'll foul you everytime. Let's take it to him.' Simple as that. But you can't do that till the game is in progress. You see, there have been a lot of great coaches in this game but there haven't been a lot of great bench coaches. By a bench coach, I mean a guy that can get in the flow of the game and make adjustments as the game is progressing."[91]

With Walter Brown's untimely death in 1964, Auerbach took on even greater responsibilities within the Celtics organization. No longer just a coach, he was a general manager, draft coordinator, team spokesman, and traveling secretary all rolled into one. Eventually the pressure of performing so many club functions took their toll on Auerbach. He was physically worn down and weary of the constant travel his coaching duties imposed. He decided to retire from the bench and devote his energies full-time to the front office at the conclusion of the 1965–66 season. Typically, he went out a winner as the Celtics bested the Los Angeles Lakers in the finals for the team's record eighth straight championship and ninth in ten years. "I feel drunk and I haven't had a drink," Auerbach exclaimed in the riotous postgame celebration that followed. In a more reflective moment back in his ninth floor suite at the Hotel Lenox in downtown Boston, he told a reporter that the victory represented the high point of his career. "Relax," he said. "How can I? This is the greatest thing a man can do—go out this way. . . . I've fulfilled my life in basketball. I've not only the record to prove it, but I've got the respect of the ball club and that's the most important thing."[92]

As to who would be his coaching successor, Auerbach considered several possible candidates, including former players Frank Ramsey, Bob Cousy, and Tom Heinsohn, before settling on Bill Russell. "The idea of Russell as coach came to me about a month ago," Auerbach told an April 1966 press conference announcing the decision. "I think we were in Detroit. I asked Bill to come up to my hotel room. I told him what I had in mind and he said he'd think about it. I was impressed because I wouldn't have made a snap decision—either way. I'm glad he took plenty of time to consider every angle. He's sure now."[93]

Auerbach chose Russell because he thought the five-time league Most Valuable Player needed a fresh challenge to keep his competitive basketball fires burning. "You know when a pro athlete reaches his thirties, the way Russell has, he loses some of his motivating power," Auerbach explained. "He has trouble getting himself up for games. But as coach he won't have that problem."[94] In point of fact, Russell had grown "bored" after winning eight straight NBA titles. He discovered he was no longer able to bring himself "mentally and emotionally to the arena every night." His appointment as player-coach thus gave him the opportunity to refocus his competitive energies for the good of the team. "I consider this one of the most personalized challenges I have had in the past ten years," Russell said. "My first thought was that I must be getting too old for even considering such a thing. Actually, my first consideration was the team. I also had to consider the aggravation involved. I've seen firsthand most of the things Auerbach has had to go through for the past 10 years and they're awful. But being somewhat of a nut myself, I finally decided it might be fun."[95]

Pertaining to the issue of being the first African-American to helm a major professional sports team, Russell made it clear he did not see it as an issue at all. He was named player-coach, he said, because he had earned the title. Responding to a reporter's question that his leadership might lead to a "prejudice in reverse" situation regarding the white players on the Celtics, the big center dismissed the speculation outright. "No," he said evenly. "The most important factor is respect. In basketball we respect a man for his ability, period." Indeed, Russell wanted to be judged not on the color of his skin, but strictly on his win-loss performance as coach. "I got to succeed or fail on this job not as a black man or a white man or a green man, but as a coach," he said. "I wasn't offered the job because I was a Negro." Nor did he feel comfortable with being mentioned in the same category as Jackie Robinson, who integrated major league baseball in 1947. "This doesn't even come close to the Robinson case," he scoffed. "At that time there were no Negroes in any big league sports. Now there are so many, you don't even know who they are. But this is part of the thing Robinson did. It is part of the same story. Now maybe there will be some more Negro coaches and managers in sports."[96]

Years later, Russell could still not get over the intense public interest his elevation to Celtics' player-coach generated. "When I took the job as coach, we had a press conference," he recalled. "I remember a couple of questions vividly. One question was what does it feel like to be the first black coach in the NBA and how is it important to you? I said, 'today really isn't important to me. It would be important to me when coaches are hired and fired and you don't know their race.'"[97] As for Auerbach's own personal motives in hiring him for the position, Russell was equally adamant. "If I thought for one second that Red offered me a job [as a coach] for social breakthrough, I would have stopped talking to him. His only motivation for doing this was what was best for the team. He put the best person in that place because [I] was the best person for the job. All of the extraneous things have no place in it."[98]

Reaction to Russell's job promotion was generally positive. "This was a smart move by the Celtics," *Boston Globe* columnist Bud Collins wrote. "Does Arnold Auerbach make any other kind? It was eminently bright because Russell the coach will never allow Russell the player to retire. Russell the coach—loose jointed enough to kick Russell the player in the fanny—will be able to yell at his No. 1 player: 'Listen No. 6—start hustling. It's my job you're fooling around with.'"[99] Howard

Iverson of the *Boston Sunday Herald* offered that Russell's move to the coaching ranks should not have come as a surprise. "When it comes right down to it, when has this bearded basketball genius ever turned his back on a showdown?"[100] Players like John Havlicek similarly chimed in with upbeat thoughts. "He's a team player, and that's a great thing in a playing coach," he said.[101]

If there was a sour note, it was delivered by the *Globe*'s acerbic sports reporter Clif Keane. He speculated that Russell might have problems as player-coach due to what he considered the "glum, morose, moody character" of the Celtics star. "This Russell will have to stop—and maybe he really wants to," Keane wrote. "He knows he has to in his new job. He can no longer think of himself as a coach, he is in the public relations business. He must build up the game, show people he has warmth. The game of basketball, weak as it is, compared with other sports, needs this kind of help. And Russell in his new job will have to give it."[102]

As events developed, the transition to player-coach went anything but smoothly for Russell that first season. He had trouble keeping track of time-outs, making game substitutions, and knowing when to rest his players. In addition, his Celtic teammates had difficulty accepting him as Auerbach's successor, despite their obvious respect for him as a player and as a person. Veteran guards Sam Jones and Larry Siegfried, in fact, openly questioned his ability to handle both coaching and playing jobs. As was his wont, Russell let such criticism roll down his back. "I would be a hypocrite if I ever clamped down on one of my players for sounding off," he said. "I always spoke my mind as a player, so I couldn't criticize anyone for doing the same thing."[103] The growing discontent on the team soon caught the attention of Auerbach, who was monitoring the situation from his perch as Celtics general manager. "At the beginning [the players] came running to me," he said, "if they didn't like what Russell was doing. But I set 'em straight. I told them he was coach."[104] Still, Auerbach did not hesitate to publicly upbraid Russell when the latter failed to show up for a scheduled tip-off against the San Francisco Warriors during a blizzard. "The rest of the ball club made it and people like John Havlicek (he ran over the River Bridge when his car became jammed up) and Bailey Howell (he commandeered a train) had trouble getting there," Auerbach said. When Russell finally made an appearance in the closing moments of the contest, Auerbach exploded in anger. "I called him everything I could think of and I did it in front of the players.

He knew how mad I was and he played it perfectly. He didn't object, he didn't make excuses, he didn't answer me back."[105]

Instead, Russell took responsibility for his actions and moved on. "I made mistakes at first," he said, "mostly in recognizing when a man needed a rest. Also, you know, not all players can play together—styles clash, some combinations don't work. Well, I prepared myself for that, spent all summer thinking about it. But still adjustments had to be made. And you have to understand what it's like on this club. There are no prima donnas and there never were. Walter Brown, who owned it and built it, was a tremendous influence. And then Red—he simply wouldn't allow anyone to get too big. And I wanted to be the same way. In fact, I've had to tell the other players, 'If you've got something to criticize about me or how I'm playing, get it out—tell me off, don't hold it back. I'm not above it.' We've been close as players. We still are close. I can still go to a party with the rest. I don't have to prove my manhood to anyone. I just have to be myself and be right."[106]

Despite all the difficulties, Russell guided the Celtics to 60 victories on the year, the second most in team history and six more than Auerbach had achieved the previous season. Unfortunately, this was not enough to displace a powerful Philadelphia 76ers squad led by Wilt Chamberlain, which finished eight games in front of the Celtics for the best record in league history. In the playoffs, the 76ers continued their domination by rolling over Boston, 4–1, in the Eastern Division finals. "The best way to be a good loser is to shut up," Russell said afterward. "And I'm not sure I want to be a good loser."[107] Critics, however, were quick to condemn him for the club's second place showing, some before the season had even concluded. "The Celtics do not deserve to win the playoffs for the ninth year in succession because in cold-blooded premeditation they handicapped themselves by making Russell, their meal ticket, handle two big jobs," wrote *Globe* columnist Harold Kaese. "As a result the Celtics have not given their fans the coaching they have had from Auerbach or the playing they would have from Russell if he were a player only."[108] Friendly rivals like Wilt Chamberlain were not shy about expressing their skepticism either. "The stupidest thing he ever did was to coach," Chamberlain said. "He ought to quit and go back to being just a player."[109] Russell was unmoved by such criticism. "The Celtics are not dead like a lot of people think," he contended. "They are not even mortally wounded. Personally, I expect a better won-lost record next season and I expect to get past the Eastern Division playoffs. I kid you not."[110]

The 1967–68 season made Russell out to be a prophet. Though the team won six fewer games than they had the previous season and finished a distant second to Philadelphia again, the Celtics came alive in the playoffs. Overcoming a three games to one deficit in the Eastern Division playoffs, they rallied to beat Philadelphia in seven. "Yes, this is the most satisfying victory of my career—so far," Russell said. "But we haven't won anything until we win the championship."[111] He need not have worried. The Celtics upended the Los Angeles Lakers, 4–2, in the finals for Russell's first championship as player-coach. "Russell did a fine job of coaching this year," assessed Philadelphia coach Alex Hannum after the Celtics had ousted his team from the playoffs. "He is more aware of situations. Some things he did last year—well, I just had to scratch my head at them. There was none of that this season."[112]

Indeed, Russell had set a winning tone in training camp when he gathered together all the veterans on the ballclub for a special airing out session in his hotel room. "There is a century of basketball experience in this room," he told them, "and I expect you fellows to help me." The message was received loud and clear. From this point on, old pros like Sam Jones and Bailey Howell made sure that Russell did not shoulder the coaching burden all by himself, especially since he refused the luxury of an assistant coach. "This was the biggest thing to come out of camp," John Havlicek later wrote in a *Sport* article chronicling the season. "The year before, Russell's first as coach, we didn't want to interfere. He was the coach and we didn't want to interfere. He was the coach and he had certain ideas. If I had a judgment that I didn't think was agreeable to him, I didn't say anything. It's not that I was afraid. It was just *his* job. That's the way it had been with Red Auerbach. That was the way it was with Russell. The second year was different. The ballplayers could get on Russell and tell him what he was doing wrong. That was the big factor. Sam [Jones] told him so many times: 'After you get a rebound, you've got to get down court. The offense revolves around you. If you don't get down, we're playing four-on-five.' Russell listened and he responded, which was not surprising. Russell is a unique personality. If he has to play for any person other than Red, who was the only coach he'd ever play for as a pro, playing for himself is the best. Playing and coaching isn't ideal. But one of Russell's biggest incentives is winning. He has pride. He gets himself up for more games than any other coach could. This is important."[113]

Though Russell had surprised sports pundits and prognosticators by guiding his team to the championship, doubts still remained about the

Celtics' long-term ability to sustain the dynasty. The average age of the team was already approaching a creaky 29, and with several younger, quicker, and deeper clubs on the rise like the New York Knicks, it seemed unlikely the Celtics would repeat as champions. Yet as long as Russell stood in the pivot, there always remained a chance, albeit an increasingly remote one, that the team could hold on and win another title. For in Russell the Celtics possessed what one national sports publication later called the "Twentieth Century's Greatest Team Player." "We're not talking just about a player who got a lot of points and rebounded well and passed well," longtime teammate and standout defensive forward Tom "Satch" Sanders said. "We're talking dominance. You have to remember that Russell dominated the NBA."[114] Whether Russell could extend his "dominance" another year would be the Celtics' greatest question mark entering the 1968–69 season. To understand his importance, one needs to first examine the formative events and experiences that shaped his life and superlative Hall of Fame playing career.

The Eagle
with a
Beard

William Felton Russell, the "eagle with a beard" as one awestruck opponent called him, was born on February 12, 1934, the second son of Charles and Katie Russell. He grew up in Monroe, Louisiana, a rural southern town that bore the twin scars of segregation and the Great Depression. "William," his mother once told him, "you are going to meet people who just don't like you. On sight. And there's nothing you can do about it, so don't worry. Just be yourself. You're no better than anybody else, but no one's better than you."[1]

Russell tried to take heed of his mother's advice, but the reality of the situation sometimes proved too overwhelming. Put simply, Louisiana in the 1930s and 1940s was not a hospitable place for persons of color. "I remember that my mother and father loved me, and we had a good time, but the white people were mean," Russell said. "But I was safe. I was always safe. In all my life, every day, not for one second have I ever thought I could have had better parents."[2]

Less endearing was the behavior of the local black elite. "The so-called Negro leaders were continually sending down people to tell us that things were changing," Russell bitterly told Ed Linn of *Sport* in 1963. "I say 'so-called' because they were picked by the white community, and so they did what the white community wanted."[3] Russell's father, whom he affectionately referred to as "Mister Charlie," had little use for such people. He did not believe in bowing or scraping to the dominant white power establishment. If anything, he confronted it head-on with surprising results. "He never let anyone embarrass him in front of his kids," Russell later revealed to television interviewer Darren Duarte. "So one time we got in the car and we went to this ice house to buy some ice. We pull up and the attendant was talking to a friend of his in the office or whatever. We could see it through the window. We sat there five or ten minutes and he never stopped his conversation. So then another car pulled up with a white person in it. [The attendant] stopped his conversation and went out and took care of them. So my father started the car to leave. The guy walks up to the window and says, 'Boy, don't you ever do what you started to do.' And my father politely got out of the car and ran the guy off. Made him leave his job. It's like my father, you know, [said] 'You're not going to treat me with disrespect.'"[4]

Hoping to find a better life for himself and his family, Charlie Russell relocated his wife and two sons to Oakland, California, where both he and Katie found work in the local shipyards. In 1946, however, tragedy struck. Russell's mother died of a kidney ailment, leaving a gaping emotional void in young William's life that he was unable to fill for several years. Shy and introspective, Russell retreated to the stacks of the Oakland Public Library for escape. There he would spend many an afternoon reading about such historic figures as Henry Christophe of Haiti, a nineteenth-century military dictator who had constructed a magnificent citadel in his name on the island. Though a tyrant, Russell appreciated the fact that Christophe was a leader of considerable ability and energy. "For he was the first hero of my youth," Russell later wrote. "A black man who became a dominant force in a power structure."[5]

Russell's involvement with basketball came about almost by accident. Wanting desperately to shine like his older brother Charlie, who was an athletic standout at Oakland Tech, Russell tried out for the local McClymonds High School hoop team as a sophomore. Woefully uncoordinated, he failed to make an impression and was cut. He took the rejection hard and was ready to drop the sport for good when he caught the eye of junior varsity coach George Powles. Sympathetic to Russell's plight, Powles bequeathed him the final roster spot on the junior varsity team. A condition for his participation, however, involved sharing a uniform with another player low on the depth chart. Happy to finally belong to a team, Russell voiced no objection to this arrangement. While hardly an auspicious beginning for someone destined to become arguably the greatest player ever to lace up a pair of high-tops, it was a

Bill Russell scoring over Walter Bellamy
Courtesy of the Sports Museum of New England

start nevertheless. Henceforward, Russell devoted all his waking hours to playing basketball, despite having a body so skinny, he later joked, that he had to "keep moving in the shower to keep wet."[6]

By his senior year he had shown enough improvement to move up to the varsity level and become a fixture at starting center. Mother Nature provided a welcomed assist here as Russell had sprouted to 6 feet 5 inches, 160 pounds. Still, there remained glaring deficiencies to his game. "He couldn't even put the ball in the basket when he dunked," insisted teammate Frank Robinson, who went on to have a Hall of Fame baseball career with the Cincinnati Reds and Baltimore Orioles. Luckily for Russell, the one game where he scored as many as 14 points occurred when a local college scout named Hal DeJulio attended an Oakland High–McClymonds contest in 1951. Impressed by the unexpected show of offense, DeJulio contacted University of San Francisco coach Phil Woolpert and told him he had a lead on a raw unknown talent. A week later, DeJulio approached Russell at his home with an offer of a full athletic scholarship to USF, a small Jesuit-run college without a gymnasium. "We had nothing to offer a high-school boy in a competitive bidding situation," Woolpert later admitted. "Our scout reports were largely from volunteers in the area. Our only inducement was a sincere approach that the boy would get an excellent college education and that he would be able to play on what we hoped would be an excellent basketball team."[7] Having no other scholarship offers forthcoming, Russell accepted with unbridled enthusiasm. "To me, San Francisco was my one chance," he said. "The one chance I'd ever get. I was determined to make the most of it."[8]

Fortune smiled on Russell again following his high school graduation in January of 1952. He accepted an invitation to join a group of California schoolboy all-stars on a monthlong tour of the Pacific Northwest. What transpired over the next several weeks was nothing short of magical as Russell elevated his game to unimagined new heights. Closely observing how opposing offensive players moved on the court, he devised elaborate defensive strategies in his mind on how to stop them. When the opportunity arose in games to translate these strategies into action, Russell found to his amazement that they actually worked. For the remainder of the trip, he became "nearly possessed" by basketball, as he would talk "incessantly" with teammates about perfecting the finer points of his game. His confidence level, never high to begin with, was now

The Eagle with a beard
Copyright 1969 Globe Newspaper Company, Inc.
Republished with permission of the Globe Newspaper Company, Inc.

positively soaring. "I was in my own private basketball laboratory, making mental blueprints for myself," he enthused.[9]

By the time he arrived on the USF campus that fall, Russell had added enough defensive skills to his repertoire to capture the imagination of Dons coach Phil Woolpert. "My God," Woolpert told a magazine reporter, "the first time I did see him in a workout, I couldn't believe my eyes. He could jump—oh, how he could jump—but he was *so* ungainly. Still, there was something about Bill then that you couldn't ignore. He had that rare wonderful confidence in himself. Not braggadocio, but good honest confidence."[10] This self-assurance came through during Russell's first meeting with Woolpert and his coaching staff. "Gentlemen," he announced, "I want you to know that I am going to be the University of San Francisco's next All-American." Significantly, Russell *did* become the school's next All-American representative, and this is what most impressed his new coach. He could back up his brash words with deeds. "He was as fiercely competitive, as proud as any athlete as ever appeared in any sport," Woolpert said.[11]

All the fiery competitiveness could not transform USF into a winner, however. Though the team was blessed with enormous individual talents like playmaking guard K.C. Jones of San Francisco, Russell's roommate, the Dons could not perform up to their collective capabilities. The reason was not hard to fathom. "The Jesuits at the University had very progressive attitudes about racial matters," Russell explained in *Second Wind*, "but not all the students took them to heart, especially on the basketball team."[12] Indeed, relations between black and white players grew so strained by Russell's second year on the squad that he was barely on speaking terms with several of his teammates.

In the middle of this tumultuous sophomore season, Russell came to a realization about himself and the game that would forever change the course of his life. He decided to become a great basketball player. "Everything inside me poured itself into that decision," he confessed, "all the anger and wonder joined together in one purpose, and energy was coming out of my ears."[13] The results spoke for themselves. Over the next two years, he developed into the most fearsome collegiate player in the nation, averaging over 20 points and 20 rebounds a game, while leading the Dons to 56 straight victories and two back-to-back NCAA championships. "With his incredible sense of timing," praised one rival college coach, "he'd leap with you and jam your best shot down your throat. The next time you raced to the basket, you looked over your shoulder, wondering 'Where's Russell?' . . . and missed your shot." So dominant was Russell's performance near the basket that collegiate basketball authorities felt compelled to pass a rule preventing big men like Russell "from touching the ball on its downward arc and guiding in shots."[14] Goaltending, in other words, would no longer be tolerated.

Helping Russell make the transition to great player status was the improved team atmosphere around him. Most of the "biggest jerks," as Russell called them, had graduated, leaving behind a USF team that was committed to one goal: winning ballgames.[15] Equally refreshing was the makeup of the Dons' starting lineup, as Russell and fellow African-Americans K.C. Jones and Gene Brown comprised three of the top five roster spots on the team. Not until Texas Western fielded an all-black starting five in 1966 did an NCAA champion boast as many African-American starters. "Texas Western," *Sports Illustrated* writer Frank Deford has argued, "was the end product of what Russell inspired—and what he had suffered through—a decade earlier."[16] To be sure, Russell and his black teammates attracted a considerable amount of negative attention for their pioneering ways. One USF alumnus openly complained, "They [blacks] are scarcely representative of the school. Perhaps a rule should be established that only three can be on the court at one time." An angry Phil Woolpert responded, "Anyone who claims there should be discrimination toward a Negro or a Protestant or a bricklayer's son on an athletic team or in a classroom is not representative of this school either."[17] Despite such strong rebukes, incidents of an ugly racial nature still persisted. In a practice held in Oklahoma City before a tournament, the local citizenry saw fit to shower the African-American players on the team with coins "as if they were clowns in the circus." Without complaint, Russell collected all the offending objects from the floor and handed them over to Woolpert. "Save this money for us, Coach, and we'll spend it on a victory party," he said in a voice loud enough for everyone to hear. "Then," remembered K.C. Jones in his 1986 biography *Rebound,* "he took it out on the opposition."[18]

Russell's success as a collegian did not go unnoticed by Red Auerbach of the Boston Celtics. Auerbach's old college coach and mentor, Bill Reinhart of George Washington University, had first brought Russell to his attention after watching the USF star perform as a sophomore at the 1953 All-College tournament in Oklahoma City. "He told me, 'Red, I just saw a kid who's going to be something,'" Auerbach later recalled. 'Set your sights on him. He's just what you need.'[19] Indeed, the Celtics of the early 1950s were an exciting, shoot-the-lights-out kind of outfit that usually led the league in scoring and in spectacular plays. Yet for all the high octane offense, they were unable to win consistently in the playoffs, as befitting a team that also led the league in points allowed. Auerbach hoped to undo this woeful trend by bringing Russell aboard to provide some desperately needed leadership on the defensive end.

But Auerbach had to be completely sold on Russell's talents if he was going to mount any kind of concerted effort to attain his services. He contacted a number of former players and college coaches he had become friendly with over the years to determine Russell's true worth as a basketball player. How physically tough was he? Could he stand up to the bruising style of other NBA centers? Could he consistently get rebounds in traffic? Was he a legitimate first round draft pick? These were some of the questions that Auerbach posed to his makeshift network of basketball experts. One former Celtics player, Fred Scolari, nicely summed up what would become the standard hoop opinion of Russell. "Red," he said, "this kid can't shoot to save his ass. He can't hit the side of the basket. He's only the greatest basketball player I ever saw."[20]

When Auerbach reminded Scolari that he had played against the likes of Hall of Famer George Mikan during his pro career, Scolari held firm to his conviction. "I'm just telling you Bill Russell is the greatest basketball player I ever saw. You want somebody to get you the ball, he'll get you the ball."[21] Thus assured, Auerbach began wracking his brain for ways of getting Russell into a Celtics uniform. Given that Boston was en route to a second place finish in the then eight-team league, the Celtics would be picking seventh overall in the 1956 NBA draft. This reality posed a serious problem for Auerbach because in his estimation, no conceivable scenario existed where Russell would be available that late in the selection process.

A trade therefore had to be worked out to acquire Russell's drafting rights, but this would be no easy transaction. The teams picking first and second respectively, the Rochester Royals and St. Louis Hawks, had already begun making noises that they too were interested in Russell. Pragmatic business considerations and what would later be described as "Celtic luck," however, conspired to carry the day for Boston. Unwilling to meet Russell's reported salary demand of $25,000 a year, Rochester dropped out of the running early. To make sure the Royals stayed out of the running, Auerbach got Celtics boss Walter Brown to promise Rochester owner Les Harrison that he would schedule "a couple of weeks" of the Ice Capades at the latter's arena if he agreed to pass on Russell. Brown could make such a pledge because he was president of the popular and financially successful skating show. Nevertheless, there was some element of risk involved. Rochester "could have double-crossed us," Auerbach pointed out. "[Harrison] did not have a reputation you could count on."[22]

As it turned out, Harrison kept his word and exited from the Russell sweepstakes. Next up was St. Louis under the shrewd ownership of Ben Kerner, but the Hawks had no desire to give away so valuable an asset unless they were suitably compensated with a star player. Realizing this, Auerbach offered starting center and six-time NBA All-Star Ed Macauley for the number two pick. The proposed deal was very appealing to Kerner, since Macauley was a popular St. Louis native who had played his college ball at St. Louis University. It also didn't hurt that Macauley was white, given the Jim Crow atmosphere that permeated St. Louis and the rest of the South at the time. White stars were simply more appealing to the team's white fan base than standout African-American athletes like Russell.

Kerner gave initial approval of the trade, but reversed himself when he learned of Harrison's Ice Capades deal with Brown. Sensing he could get more out of the Celtics, Kerner demanded that Auerbach throw in the rights to Clif Hagan, an All-American forward out of the University of Kentucky that Boston had rights to and who was then completing a two-year hitch in the U.S. Army. Reluctance now settled in on the Celtics' side. It was one thing to give up one established player for "an untested defensive specialist," but two?[23] Auerbach thought the price for doing business with St. Louis had grown prohibitively too high. Yet his team's obvious need for a defensive stopper could not be ignored, especially if the Celtics planned on advancing beyond the first round in the playoffs. "You had to remember why you were doing it," Auerbach explained. "You had to feel it was worth it or why bother? We thought he was worth it."[24]

The trade went forward, but Auerbach and the Celtics were still not out of the woods. There remained the possibility that Russell might not sign with the club. For waiting in the wings with a sizable checkbook

was Abe Saperstein of the Harlem Globetrotters. Once the premier basketball team on the pro circuit, the all-black Globetrotters had since
taken a precipitous dive in stature. Under Saperstein's direction, the
team eschewed serious athletic competition for elaborately staged hoop
exhibitions that emphasized "clowning entertainment" and "racial
stereotyping."[25] White audiences were delighted and basketball purists
appalled. To the latter the Globetrotters represented a complete defile-
ment of everything the game stood for.

While self-pride prevented Russell from wanting to become part of
this traveling minstrel show, he could not easily turn his back on the
$50,000 a year salary that Saperstein was reportedly prepared to tender
him. When they met to discuss terms, however, the offer put on the table
was more in the vicinity of $15,000. To make matters worse, Saperstein
refused to negotiate with Russell directly, preferring instead to hash out
contractual details with Russell's college coach, Phil Woolpert. Feeling
that Saperstein was treating him like "this poor dumb Negro boy," Russell vowed at that moment he would never play for the Globetrotters.[26]

He ended up signing with the Celtics for $19,500, a substantial bar-
gain even at the modest salaries most top professional athletes were making in the 1950s. Russell just wanted to play ball and prove his worth as
an NBA center. "When I signed my first pro contract," Russell later
recounted, "Red [Auerbach] asked me whether I was concerned about
my scoring. I had a reputation as not being much of a scorer in college,
and I said I was a little worried. So he told me, 'From this day on, every
time we talk about contracts we will never discuss statistics. I want you
to think about winning, not about scoring.' That took the pressure off
me."[27] Yet before he could embark on a pro career, he had to first fulfill
an obligation to the U.S. Olympic basketball team, which was competing for the gold in Melbourne, Australia. Stocked with some of the finest
amateur talent the American college ranks had to offer, including Russell's USF teammate K.C. Jones, the U.S. team ran the gauntlet of international competition with relative ease. They went, 8–0, and defeated
opponents by an average margin of 30 points a game.

Russell did his part in contributing to the gold medal victory by
crashing the boards, setting picks, and playing tenacious defense. In the
showdown contest against the Soviet Union, Russell simply took over,
scoring 13 points and denying the Russians any semblance to an inside
game. "As a result," the *New York Times* reported, "the Soviet players

were forced into a weaving pattern which sought to set up goals from outside." The final score: U.S. 89–USSR 55. "It was one of the biggest thrills in my life," Russell revealed. "I had a wonderful time. We all mingled together, even the Russians, whom we beat by [34] points."[28]

Basketball was not the only item on Russell's personal agenda during these hectic days. In early December he married Rose Swisher, the niece of one of his old McClymonds High teachers, at the Taylor Methodist Church in Oakland. Russell had been introduced to Rose at a local dance, and a romance immediately blossomed. "I loved her, and I have never since felt that it was a mistake to marry her, because it felt so right at the time," Russell wrote.[29] The marriage would dissolve after 1969, but not before producing three children, Bill Jr. in 1957, Jacob in 1959, and Karen in 1962.

The combination of the Olympic experience and the wedding caused Russell to miss the first three months of the 1956–57 NBA regular season, a period that saw the Celtics vault to the top of the league standings. With Rookie of the Year Tom Heinsohn and the dynamic backcourt of Bob Cousy and Bill Sharman leading the way, the team seemed poised to make a serious run at the championship. The question now became whether Russell would upset this delicate winning balance. Such concern evaporated when Russell made his NBA debut against the St. Louis Hawks three days before Christmas in a nationally televised Saturday afternoon game at Boston Garden. Though he missed all four shots he took from the foul line, he managed to give fans and teammates a hint of things to come by grabbing 16 rebounds in 21 minutes and blocking three successive shots from Bob Petit, the league's leading scorer.

"Right now," veteran Celtics frontcourt man Arnie Risen told reporters after the game, "he'll block any shooter in the league who shoots straight over head and turns and shoots straight from the pivot, because he's so tall and can get up so . . . and he'll murder them on the defensive board."[30] Jack Barry of the *Boston Globe* was even more effusive in his praise. "Bill Russell may revolutionize the game of basketball," he predicted. "Up until now great scorers like Petit and [Minneapolis Laker center George] Mikan or playmakers like Cousy have been the type of players to draw crowds for professional basketball. Yet Russell could be the first player to become a drawing card on his defensive ability."

Russell's heroics continued throughout the remainder of the regular season as his defensive prowess and rebounding helped spark the Celtics

The Eagle in flight
Copyright 1966 Globe Newspaper Company, Inc.
Republished with permission of the Globe Newspaper Company, Inc.

to an NBA-leading 44–28 record, the team's best finish in franchise history up to that point. While it is true that the Celtics were in first place when Russell arrived, there can be little doubt that he kept them there. "He won me a championship ring," contends Risen, who also earned a ring with Rochester in 1951. "I knew right from the first practice that he was going to be something special. We ran through the plays with him and he showed he could jump over the moon and do it quickly. The first couple of scrimmages, why, I was eating every other shot that I threw up there and that hadn't happened to me very much in my career."[31]

If Russell had a weakness as a rookie, it was his offense. "He could shoot but he wasn't a great shooter," recalled longtime teammate Jim "Jungle Jim" Loscutoff. "On free throws he was a lousy shooter. But funny thing. In a tough situation, when we needed a free throw or two free throws, the damn guy would always make them. He had the guts of a steer."[32]

This mettle was in evidence during the playoffs when Russell formed the hub of an aggressive team defense that ground opponents into fine dust. In the finals against St. Louis, the team that relinquished its rights to him, Russell was everywhere, blocking shots, pulling down rebounds, and generally disrupting the Hawks' offensive game plan. "He was a lion," remembered Tom Heinsohn, who had played against Russell as a collegian at the 1955 Holiday Festival tournament in New York. "The greatest competitor I was ever around. He refused to lose."[33] As the series came down to a climactic Game 7, Russell was nothing less than spectacular. Hauling down a game-high 32 rebounds and scoring 19 points, the former All-American made several key defensive stops, including five blocked shots. The Celtics won in double overtime, 125–123, to earn their first NBA title. For Russell the occasion marked the third time in thirteen months that he had been crowned a champion, an unprecedented accomplishment in modern sports annals. "This one scared the hell out of me," he confessed to reporters. "I never was so scared in my life. I was shaking all over. Did you see my legs when it was over? I felt like jumping all night I was so happy."[34]

To celebrate the victory, Russell gleefully allowed Auerbach and fellow rookie Heinsohn, who scored 37 points before fouling out with two minutes remaining in the contest, to shave off his trademark goatee amid the postgame locker room revelry that ensued. "Well, there it is, boys—I mean, there it isn't," a clean-shaven Russell joked. "It's gone down the drain. I promised they could do it if we won the title, and now nobody can ask me about the thing any more."[35]

There would be nine more championships to follow over the next eleven years, including a record eight straight between 1959 and 1966. And the one constant running through all of them was number 6, Bill Russell. "You can say what you want about individual players in any sport, but when it comes to winning, there is no one like Bill Russell," Los Angeles Lakers guard Jerry West told a reporter. "I know some of those guys in other sports, like baseball and football, are great. But I don't think there ever has been anyone, in any era, who could compare to Russell. . . . I play this game myself and I know what [winning championships] means. I've been through it all—broken bones, the rough stuff, the pressure, the big shots that went in and the big shots that didn't, and I know. Really, you have to play against this man to appreciate him. Only another athlete could possibly know what I mean."[36]

One nonathlete who *could* appreciate what Russell meant to basketball was nationally syndicated sports columnist Jim Murray. "No one at no time has dominated the sport as W. F. Russell has," he wrote in 1965. "He is Henry Ford at an assembly line. Abraham Lincoln at a platform. Babe Ruth with a bat. Jim Brown with a football. He is genius in his BVDs. He has shaved a thousand points a year from a court game which was on its way to breaking down every adding machine in the country. If he gets any better, they may make him play blind-folded. Even then, he will be 6-to-5 to block 90 percent of the shots. Even then, the registered super-stars of the game will still go around scouring the floor on their hands and knees and demanding irritatedly of the referee, 'Did you see a ball around here some place? I had it only a moment ago?' . . . He is Bill Russell and he owns the game of basketball in fee simple. As no one ever has before and as no one ever will again. He is as all alone for his time and his specialty as Shakespeare, Caesar—or Bridget Bardot."[37]

Unlike most professional athletes of his era, Russell was not averse to taking stands on controversial political topics, especially when they had to do with racial equality and constitutional rights. A case in point was heavyweight world champion boxer Muhammad Ali's refusal to register for the military draft in 1967. Ali argued that his Muslim faith prevented him on religious grounds from engaging in such activity. For this principled stance, Ali was stripped of his boxing title and threatened with imprisonment by federal authorities.

Though not saying whether he agreed with Ali's decision to forego the draft, Russell publicly defended the boxer's right to adhere to his religious beliefs as he saw fit. "I don't think he has been treated fairly or justly," Russell maintained. "There is nothing that says the heavyweight champion of the world must belong to a particular religion or not be a conscientious objector to war. Muhammad's right to be a Black Muslim—or a Catholic or a Protestant—is guaranteed by the Constitution."[38]

Russell's outspokenness on such hot-button issues seemed to fit in with the times. Indeed, his rise to NBA superstar status occurred almost simultaneously with the most significant social movement of the century: the drive for civil rights among African-Americans. Beginning with Rosa Parks's brave refusal to move to the back of the bus in Montgomery, Alabama, in 1955 to Martin Luther King Jr.'s call for social justice and equal opportunity during the 1963 March on Washington to the intoxicating promise of 1964's "Freedom Summer" in the sweltering heat and dusty back roads of Mississippi, the civil rights movement fundamentally transformed America in ways thought inconceivable only a generation before.

"We can never be satisfied as long as our children are stripped of their selfhood and robbed of their dignity by signs stating 'for whites only,'" Dr. King informed a nation in his stirring "I Have a Dream" speech of August 1963. "We cannot be satisfied as long as a Negro in Mississippi cannot vote and a Negro in New York believes he has nothing for which to vote. No, we are not satisfied until justice rolls down like waters and righteousness like a mighty stream."[39]

Russell knew firsthand the racism and prejudice that Dr. King spoke of in American society. He had, after all, spent his formative years growing up in the heart of the "separate but equal" Jim Crow South and had endured taunts about his skin color at almost every stage of his life. Not even his celebrity status or the increasing number of NBA championship rings on his fingers could shield him from the harsh reality that persons of color were second-class citizens in white America.

"I was a world champion," he complained bitterly after taking his children on a 1962 car trip to visit their grandfather in the Deep South. "I was a man. Yet, from Washington, D.C., to Louisiana, my children could not stop to eat [due to segregated facilities]. My children could not stop to sleep. They rode in the back seat of the car driven by their father, who was their father and a man and a world champion and we could not stop because we were black. Were I the lowest white trash in the world, I would have been able to stop. But I was black. And I had to keep going. My children had to keep going with the wonder in their eyes that things could change, with the not understanding pleas from the back seat: 'Daddy, can't we stop? Daddy, I'm hungry.'"[40]

The previous year, Russell grew personally indignant when two of his teammates, Sam Jones and Tom Sanders, were denied service at a hotel coffee shop in Lexington, Kentucky, on account of their skin color. The Celtics were in town to play a scheduled exhibition game against the St. Louis Hawks, but Russell saw no reason to stay and compete. To do so, he thought, would be tantamount to surrendering to bigotry and injustice. He booked a late-night flight out of Lexington, along with fellow blacks Jones, Sanders, K.C. Jones, and rookie Al Butler. "For a great number of years," Russell said, "colored athletes and entertainers put up with those conditions because we figured they'd see we were nice people mostly and, in some cases, gentlemen, and they'd say, 'Those people aren't so bad.' I'm not insulted by it, I'm just embarrassed. I'm of the opinion that some people can't insult me. But it was the greatest mistake we ever made because as long as you go along with it, everybody assumes it's the status quo. I couldn't look my kids or myself in the face if I had played there. A man without integrity, belief or self-respect is not a man. And a man who won't express his convictions has no convictions. I feel the best way to express my convictions is not to play. If I can't eat, I can't entertain."[41]

Nor was Russell's experience with racism confined to below the Mason-Dixon line. In the predominantly white town of Reading, a middle-class suburb north of Boston, Russell had his home vandalized while he was away for a three-day weekend. The intruders destroyed his trophies, spray painted the term "NIGGA" on the walls, and defecated in his bed.[42] To add further insult, a petition was circulated within the community to prevent him from purchasing a home in a nicer section of town. "I didn't really care what they thought," Russell later claimed. "I saw a house. I liked it. I bought it. I was the one making mortgage payments. It didn't matter to me what anyone thought."[43]

"When he first came to Boston, he was very naïve," close friend Harold Furash told the *Boston Globe*. "He reacted to what is regrettably public antipathy to the black people. There's just a lot of prejudice around. He reacted to it, and resented it, as I think anybody would."[44] Even the simple act of driving an automobile could arouse unwarranted hostility. "Hey, nigger, how many crap games did it take you to win that car?"[45] shouted one bigot to Russell, as the latter was tooling around the streets of Boston in his convertible. Such unpleasant encounters did not deter Russell from becoming active in the civil rights movement. If anything, it reinforced his desire to change the world for the better. "I get irritated when people ask me what the Negro wants," he said. "I'll tell you what he wants—opportunity and choice."[46]

In August 1963, he journeyed to Jackson, Mississippi, at the request of Charlie Evers, the brother of slain civil rights leader Medgar Evers, shortly after the latter had been gunned down at his doorstep while returning from a local NAACP strategy session. To ease the racial tensions that threatened to boil over into violence from the incident, Russell was asked to conduct basketball clinics throughout the community. "I can use some help right now," Charlie Evers had told him. "But you may be killed." For Russell there was little doubt as to what course of action he would take, despite pleadings from his wife and several close friends to remain in Massachusetts. "A man must do what he thinks is right," he explained. "I called Eastern Airlines and ordered my ticket."[47]

Though he felt "about as big as a target range," Russell dutifully went about teaching Jackson's youth the intricacies of basketball and did much to reassure nervous civil rights workers about the importance of their mission. "He was talking to everybody, encouraging us, and his mere presence literally lifted the mood . . . that day," lifelong civil rights activist and defense attorney William M. Kunstler later remembered. He added that Russell was the only professional athlete "who demonstrated enough interest in the deep South civil rights struggles in the early Sixties to come take a look at what was happening in that arena."[48]

Former teammate and Georgetown University basketball coach John Thompson would later credit Russell for bravely embracing his black heritage at a time when such behavior was considered a societal taboo. "This was when it was an insult to call a man 'black,' when it was similar to calling a man a 'nigger,'" he revealed to writer Tony Kornheiser. "Bill Russell called himself a black man. He was one of the first men I ever saw to truly acknowledge the fact that he was black, and to identify very strongly with his roots in Africa."[49]

At the same time, Russell was under no illusion that the sometimes preferential treatment he received as a star athlete was in any way indicative of the real treatment blacks were receiving throughout American society. "Unless you walk around in a fog," he said, "and I did when I was younger, there are some things you have to come to grips with. Here's the way I look at it. A lot of places I go now I'm acceptable because—well, look, I play golf. I don't belong to a country club, but I play a lot of them as a guest. As Bill Russell of the Celtics, I'm acceptable. If I tried to join as Bill Russell, citizen, I'd have no chance. I'd have to be awful foolish to believe in what is fondly known as 'The American Dream.'"[50]

In Boston, Russell was an early proponent of desegregated schools, a controversial issue that would tear the city apart along racial lines the following decade. He also was not shy about expressing his opinion on the worsening state of black-white relations in Boston, warning presciently of the racial violence to come in the late 1960s and 1970s. "The fire that consumes Roxbury [the city's predominantly black section] consumes Boston," he told the graduating class of Patrick Campbell Junior High School in 1966. "The fire will spread."[51] Regarding his own profession, Russell showed no trepidation about criticizing the NBA for having what he considered discriminatory hiring practices. In the early 1960s he claimed that a rigid racial quota system existed in the league that barred many qualified African-American players from securing spots on team rosters. "Blacks have to be better players than whites to make the team," he contended. African-Americans "have got to make the white population uncomfortable and keep it uncomfortable because that is the only way to get their attention."[52]

Russell *did* make many white Americans "uncomfortable" in 1958 when he said the following: "I don't like most white people because they are white. Conversely, I like most Negroes because they are black. Show me the lowest, most downtrodden Negro and I will say to you that man is my brother."[53] To his credit, Russell soon admitted that he had "slipped into the error that many people make"—he began pigeonholing individuals into convenient racial groupings.[54] He, in effect, apologized for blaming the entire white population for the unfair conditions that most blacks had to labor under in American society.

In the cramped confines of the Celtics locker room, where writer Frank Deford once stated "equality reigned," Russell's teammates did not seem to pay such outbursts any serious mind. "He would get defensive and have a chip on his shoulder," Bob Cousy recalled. "The indignities he had to suffer, such as people defecating on the wall of his home. People would be celebrating what he did one moment and then they didn't want him to play at the local country club the next. It's easy to say, 'Turn the other cheek.' But realistically, any of us would have fought back."[55]

Russell himself harbored no ill feelings toward his white teammates. Shortly after Don Nelson joined the Celtics as a free agent in 1965, he found himself in a lonely predicament. "Russ came up to me the day before Christmas, and said, 'Where are you going tomorrow?' I had no place to go, really, because my family was back in Illinois. 'Come over and spend the day with me and my family,' he said. I felt funny, like I was intruding, so I said no. But Russ insisted, and I went to his home and had a beautiful day. I'll never forget Bill Russell for that. Nobody can ever tell me a bad thing about that man."[56]

John Havlicek had a similar experience during his rookie season. "When I first came to Boston, he was very nice to me," Havlicek said. "He spent one whole day showing me the city. Another time, when he heard I was looking for top stereo equipment, he drove me all over town until I found just what I wanted. And then he made sure the man I bought it from gave me a good deal." To Russell such selfless acts came naturally, without need of any outside prodding. "We were part of a team, and it's a team sport," he said. "That's why we were so good. The Celtics played together because we knew it was the best way to win. We always recognized that and understood it. You quickly realize all the other things aren't that important." These were words Russell took seriously in an era before big salaries, free agency, and huge endorsement deals conspired to undermine the whole concept of team unity by emphasizing individual star performers. As Russell later wrote, "The Celtics teams I played for were a model of how a successful enterprise can operate. . . . From the owner, Walter Brown, to Red Auerbach, our coach, down to the guy who swept the locker room, there was first and last an unspoken understanding that all of us were there for one purpose: winning."[57]

The emphasis placed on team cohesiveness was put on display at the conclusion of Russell's triumphant second year as player-coach. As team trainer Joe DeLauri recalled for *Sports Illustrated,* "After we won the championship . . . [Russell] kicked everyone who wasn't a Celtic out of the dressing room. . . . The press was pounding on the door, furious about deadlines and all, and Russell turned around and looked at us and he asked [Bailey] Howell to lead the team in prayer. He knew Bailey was a religious man—it was also his first year on a championship team—and he knew Bailey would appreciate it. Russell's not a religious man himself. Sam Jones said, 'You pray?' And Russell said, 'Yeah, Sam.'"[58]

According to longtime college and Celtic teammate K.C. Jones, Russell never once in his experience put himself above the team despite being the undisputed "heart and soul" of the club with his superior shot blocking, rebounding, and overall defensive skills. "Russ had struggled in high school as a basketball player," Jones related in his autobiography. "He sat on the bench for three years and only got in to play his senior year. He received his scholarship to USF primarily because of the efforts of Hal DeJulio, a USF graduate who sensed Bill would be an asset to the team, not because he was a highly talented high school star. Yet without being known as a great basketball player or looking like a movie idol, Russ somehow managed to sustain a self-confidence and an ego that were bigger than all of us. It was strange, but we were all better because of his confidence. We fed on it and increased our own sense of self."[59]

Even young, impressionable basketball fans sitting in the stands picked up on this playing confidence. "I mean, you'd watch him shoot free throws—he was kind of awkward," said former Philadelphia 76er star Julius Erving, who observed Russell while growing up on Long Island, New York. "And the way he passed. He couldn't dribble the ball. You look at a whole lot of things with basketball skills, basketball talent. But by the end of the game they've got 120 points and the other guys have 106. It's his focus, his tenacity. Never when I saw him play did I look at him as the most talented player on the court. But he would be the best player because of what he could bring to the table and how he could make everyone better and how he was in the clutch and how he was always a step ahead."[60]

Another New Yorker who went on to a Hall of Fame playing career in Milwaukee and Los Angeles concurred with these sentiments. "I wouldn't know how to play if it weren't for him," confessed former center Kareem Abdul-Jabbar. As a youngster Abdul-Jabbar, then Lew Alcindor, would visit the old Madison Square Garden to root for the Knicks when it was common practice in the league to hold doubleheaders with different teams. "The Celtics played in many opening games," he said. "I would have to say I saw them play 25 times and the man I studied was Bill Russell. I learned so much. The next day my coach would say, 'How many of those guys scored 20 points?' and the answer would be 'none.' But everybody would have something to do with it, most of all Bill Russell. Watching him I learned the dynamics of the game, and how to win. Being a Knicks fan in those days was agony."[61]

Agony was a good way of describing how Celtics opponents felt playing against Russell. "In big games, no one was better," contended former St. Louis Hawks owner Ben Kerner, who unwisely traded away Russell's draft rights in 1956. "In the fourth quarter, he'd get every defensive rebound. How are you supposed to win when you get only one shot and there's Russell sweeping the backboards?"[62] "The Celtics dynasty was built around Russell," offered Ed Macauley, whose trade to St. Louis made possible Russell's coming to Boston. "Take away one of the great players Red [Auerbach] had then . . . and the Celtics still could have done what they did, though it would have been more difficult. But take away Russell and it never would have happened."[63]

Macauley received no argument from his old Celtics running mate, Bob Cousy, who roomed with Russell on the road in the late 1950s. "It was a perfect fit," he affirmed. "All of us together was a perfect match. We keyed on Russ and his skills that he had defensively as well as rebounding. He added a component that none of us had to a degree. He literally revolutionized the sport with his defensive prowess, with his shot blocking. He was the most extraordinary athlete to play that position so far."[64]

To give an example of Russell's extraordinary athletic skill, Cousy recalled Game 7 of the 1957 finals against the St. Louis Hawks at Boston Garden. "It was in the last few seconds of the game and we were down by a basket," he told the *Boston Globe*. "We got a fast break going and I led Russ down the floor on a breakaway basket. The momentum of the basket sent Russ into the crowd. While that was happening, the Hawks had a player named Jack Coleman, a good working-man's forward, who had stayed at halfcourt on the breakaway. They took the ball out quicker than we had anticipated and we got downcourt with Coleman staying halfcourt and no one near him. By the time I looked around, I knew I had no chance of catching him." Yet Russell somehow managed to do so by first extricating himself from the Garden crowd and then racing by Cousy in the manner a speeding car would a pedestrian. "How many strides it took to cover those 94 feet I don't know, but just as Coleman was going in for the winning layup, Russ just took off from the foul line," Cousy explained. "The ball had left Coleman's hand, but Russ had banged it against the backboard and we went on to win the game in double overtime. It's the most amazing physical display I have ever seen."[65]

Physical skills were one thing, but Russell's main weapon was his ability to get inside the heads of his opponents and anticipate almost preternaturally how plays would unfold on the basketball court. "He was smart in a lot of ways people couldn't see or didn't realize," John Havlicek said. "He would try to play his man a different way every time. One time he'd stay off. Another time he'd put a body on him. He'd say to himself. 'What did I do before that I can change?' The one thing he would do every now and then when we had a game under control was allow a player to complete a play. Then, if that same play came up again in a close situation, the player might be thinking he'll make it when in comes Russell out of nowhere. It was uncanny the way he did that."[66]

Without question, Russell transformed the playing court into a chess board every time he stepped onto the floor. Basketball became the ultimate intellectual challenge as he developed into a kind of surreal grand master of the hardwood. "In our league I promise you that any team can beat any other team on a given night," he wrote in a *Sports Illustrated* cover piece in 1965. "The difference a lot of the time is all psychological. We use every little trick, every pressure, every mental gimmick we can. And there are certain rules we live by."[67]

He called them "Russell's Laws," and his first commandment was to always make sure the players on the opposing side did what he wanted them to do. "You must start him thinking," he said. "If he is thinking instead of doing, he is yours. There is no time in basketball to think: 'This has happened; this is what I must do next.' In the amount of time it takes to think through that semicolon, it is already too late." Russell's "Second Law" involved exercising what he called a "killer instinct": "the ability to spot—and exploit—a weakness in your opponent."[68] This point was of crucial importance.

In later years Russell could not resist needling arch rival Wilt Chamberlain for his performance against center Willis Reed of the New York Knicks in Game 7 of the 1970 NBA finals. Reed had suffered a serious hip injury earlier in the series against the Chamberlain-led Los Angeles Lakers, which forced him to sit out Game 6. Now he came dramatically limping onto the court before a wildly cheering Madison Square Garden crowd. Chamberlain never recovered. He was placed in a state of "benign perplexity" throughout the contest, which the Knicks went on to win for their first world championship. "If I'm the one playing when Willis comes out limping," Russell suggested, "it only would have emphasized my goal to beat them that much worse."[69] In other words, he would have "mercilessly" challenged the crippled Reed at every opportunity until the latter was either removed from the game on a stretcher or had displayed some ability to stop him. With such a "killer instinct" in evidence, chances are the Lakers and not the Knicks would have been the NBA champions if Russell had been allowed to take Chamberlain's place that day.

This leads to Russell's "Third Law"—"Be cute but not cuddly, I mean, you should be nice at all times, but there is a lot to be said for an elbow in the chops when all else fails."[70] Translation: Do whatever you feel is necessary to get the job done on the playing court without shedding too many tears about how your opponent may feel. A basketball player's primary consideration should always be about winning. "To be the best in the world," as Russell later put it.[71] Those who jumped center against Russell in his playing days and those who followed in his footsteps shortly thereafter never quite figured this out. "If there is a machine that could measure talent," Cousy postulated, "Kareem would come off that machine as the most multitalented. Maybe Wilt was the strongest. Kareem was the most well-rounded, but he didn't have Russ's intensity. If he had played the way Russ did, he would have been burned out by 31. And that's what lifted Russ above all the centers. It's an animal-like intensity that he brought with him to the game. In terms of quality, with 11 championships in 13 years, he is the most productive center that ever played the game."[72]

Russell's "Final Law" had to do with recognizing basketball as a game of habits. If you disrupt an opposing player's habits by "psyching him," he said, then you have won the round ball battle of wits. This could only be accomplished through some artful subterfuge. "Say they're rolling in toward me," Russell revealed, "and I want to go to their right. First, I've got to get them thinking instead of playing naturally. I fake directly toward them with my head, and with my left arm extended—pointed straight toward their chest—and my weight on my left foot. This is not exactly the prettiest posture in all the world, and immediately they think, 'Ah hah, Russell has his weight on the wrong foot.' And, sure enough, they swerve right every time to go around me. Now, I can whirl completely around quickly enough off the left foot (which turns out to be the right, or correct, foot, after all), plant all my weight on my right foot, leap up, and when I'm at the peak of my jump, guess who has the shot—if my timing is correct. If I want them to move left, I swing my left arm over a little bit more to their right. You follow me here? I have very long arms, and they've got to move left."[73]

By having Russell play the defensive stopper role, his Celtics teammates could "gamble a bit" on defense by overplaying their man to the outside without fear of getting beaten inside to the hoop. They could do so because Russell provided an impregnable second line of defense that could extinguish the offensive threat as it developed. More times than not, Russell would end up with the rebound, which he would then use to ignite the famous Celtics fast break with a made-to-order outlet pass to an open teammate downcourt.

The end result would be two points and total humiliation for the opposition. "His whole being concentrated on stopping his man's shot, on intimidating and getting the ball after the shot," K.C. Jones maintained. "No one should ever forget that Bill's purpose in getting the ball was to give it to his teammates. . . . His goal was aiding his teammates and denying the other team victory."[74]

Russell's shot-blocking talents alone were enough to give fits to opponents such as veteran 6-foot, 8-inch center Neil Johnston of the old Philadelphia Warriors. Johnston had been the NBA's leading scorer for three consecutive seasons prior to Russell's entering the league. His specialty was a sweeping hook shot that allowed him to average 19.4 points a game over an abbreviated eight-year career. "Right from the start, Russ didn't even have to jump to block Johnston's shot," Bob Cousy later wrote. "He would be there quicker than poor Neil. Neil went from being scoring champion to being out of the league. In short order. Neil Johnston not only couldn't play his game against Bill Russell, he also couldn't play it against *anybody*. It was incredible the effect Bill Russell had on a man who had been such a scoring machine."[75]

For his part, Russell was always matter-of-fact about this important aspect of his game. "Look, I can block shots," he told Jeremiah Tax of *Sports Illustrated* in 1958. "But if I tried to block all the shots my man takes, I'd be dead. The thing I got to do is make my man *think* I'm gonna block every shot he takes. How can I do it? O.K., here. Say I block a shot on you. The next time you're gonna shoot, I *know* I can't block it, but I act exactly the same way as before, I make exactly the same moves. I'm confident. I'm not thinking anymore, but I got *you* thinking. You can't think and shoot—nobody can. You're thinking, Will he block this one or won't he? I don't even have to try to block it. You'll miss."[76]

"Look, everybody's got shooters," Red Auerbach once explained. "But the business of matching baskets in this game is a dangerous delusion. You have to stop the other side because it is your defense that triggers your offense. That's why Russell was so important. He made the other teams rewrite their offense patterns. He forced them to find new ways to score. And he did this with the most remarkable sense of timing I've ever seen. . . . He introduced [the blocked shot] to pro basketball as a brand-new weapon of defense, something like the antimissile missile the Pentagon is always talking about. I'm not saying that nobody ever blocked a shot before Bill. I'm talking about a man blocking shots against players bigger than he is and then taking the ball away from them."[77]

This demonstrated unselfishness on the defensive end also served to inspire those around Russell to play better. With the "big man" neutralizing the opposition to the point of helplessness, his teammates could swoop in like great birds of prey and relentlessly pick away at the carnage left on the floor. "Energies we once had to expend on defense were now almost totally concentrated on offense," Tom Heinsohn said. "We began crashing the offensive boards with abandon, which meant we were now taking more shots than ever, and our fast break became truly devastating."[78]

But Russell's talents were not limited solely to defense. He had other less noticeable abilities on the court that only sophisticated hoop fans and sportswriters could appreciate. "People remember him for his rebounding and his shot-blocking," John Havlicek offered, "but in my mind he could have averaged 20 points per game if it had been necessary for the teams he played on at the time. But Bill understood how he could be most valuable to the team, which was by defending the only way he could while allowing his teammates to score the bulk of the points. . . . He knew what it took to win."[79]

As it was, Russell averaged a credible 15.1 points a game over his 13-year career. While he initially had difficulty scoring from beyond the immediate vicinity of the basket, Russell in due course developed an effective hook shot and an underrated outside jumper to keep defenses honest.

"The first year after I retired," Russell recalled, "John [Havlicek] said he missed me more on offense than defense, and that was very gratifying. I could have run any of our plays from any spot on the floor. That was very important to me, and it came in very handy when I coached, because if one of the guys were having difficulty I could understand the problem. Also, if I knew all the plays from any spot on the floor, the coordination *had* to be better."[80]

Observed 13-year Celtics veteran Tom "Satch" Sanders, "We were the players we were because of Russell. We also rose higher because of him. A quick man like Havlicek could make four to six more lay-ups because of him. Russell made people more effective. We all added to our games because of him."[81]

Maintaining these high performance standards did not come without a price. Before big games Russell became so emotionally worked up that he felt compelled to vomit in the locker room, sometimes while the national anthem was being played. "He used to throw up all the time before a game; or at halftime—a tremendous sound, almost as loud as his laugh," John Havlicek told writer George Plimpton in 1968. "He doesn't do it much now, except when it's an important game or an important challenge for him—someone like Chamberlain. Or someone coming up that everyone's touting. It's a welcome sound, too, because it means he's keyed up for the game, and around the locker room we grin and say, 'Man, we're going to be alright tonight.'"[82]

The mounting pressure to win got so acute during the 1963–64 regular season that Russell feared for his own sanity. "I felt the world coming to an end for me," he confessed. "I was on the verge of a nervous breakdown. I could feel everything slip away from me."[83] Luckily, this depression "ebbed" at the start of the playoffs and, as he later put it, he began feeling more like "Bill Russell" again. Yet self-doubts continued to linger. Who was he really? Was playing what he increasingly regarded a child's game really that important? Would he be better off pursuing some other line of work?

Russell would struggle with these questions his entire playing career. The soul-numbing monotony of being constantly on the road did not help matters. Russell described the NBA season as being seven months of unrelieved loneliness. To relieve the solitude, Russell, by his own admission, partook of extramarital affairs, just as many of his teammates and countless other professional athletes of his era did. When the Celtics were scheduled to play the Knicks in Madison Square Garden, for example, he would usually pay a nocturnal visit to a New York stripper he later referred to as Kitty Malone. Unlike most of his athletic contemporaries, however, Russell took the opportunity to expand his intellectual horizons as well as satisfy his physical needs. He and the well-read Malone would stay up until the sun rose the next morning debating contemporary political issues and discussing history. They also could just as easily be found roaming the streets of Greenwich Village and stopping by local coffee houses to listen to the 1960s protest songs of Joan Baez and Bob Dylan. "I didn't really understand it until I talked with Kitty," Russell confessed in his second autobiography, "but those coffee houses showed me that whites were capable of protest and sadness too. . . . Those coffee houses opened up a new way of thinking for me, because I saw that at least some white people got the blues, were irreverent and weren't tight-assed."[84]

Uptight was hardly the term his teammates would use to describe Russell within the complex inner workings of the Celtics. To them he was a fellow jokester, someone to laugh at and with depending on the given set of circumstances. "Just make sure you stay *inconspicuous*," they mockingly advised him when he took his hard-to-miss 6-foot, 9-inch frame to Jackson, Mississippi, to help civil rights leader Charlie Evers diffuse a tense racial situation in 1963. Russell's taste in clothes was also open to ridicule, as he liked to be seen in the latest fad, whether it was Nehru jackets, love beads, or caftans and sandals. He would step out of the shower, only to find his teammates "parading around" the locker room in his "trendy wardrobe." Indeed, Satch Sanders could be counted on to mimic his teammate's often brooding tendencies by striking a locker room pose that was deliberately evocative of Rodin's *The Thinker*. Russell's reaction to such needling invariably involved an ear-piercing laugh that he once likened to a giraffe's, if the latter were capable of laughter.[85]

Russell gave as good as he got, however. Before a big semifinal game of the playoffs one year, he took the opportunity to remind a married teammate who had a girlfriend on the side that he had better play well or else he would be back home with his wife sooner than expected. The teammate tried to affect an air of measured disgust, but as he went to light a cigarette, he could no longer contain himself. A loud belly laugh erupted from his body, sending the unlit cigarette flying across the room. Like falling dominoes, the rest of the Celtics joined in on the hysterics as the "compressed inner tension" of the room oozed out of them "like heat waves rising off the desert."[86]

Needless to say, the Celtics won the playoff game.

The cutup image was in direct conflict with Russell's public persona. To the outside world and especially to the fans of Boston, he was cold, aloof, and downright unpleasant. This unflattering representation, in fact, was fueled by a largely hostile and unsympathetic white Boston press corps that seemed more interested in seeking sensationalistic headlines than taking the time to find out the type of person Russell really was. The writers, many of whom were of Irish descent, could be culturally insensitive and downright racist toward athletes of color. Indeed, one bigoted *Boston Globe* scribe went so far as to refer to the game of basketball as "African handball" in the press box.[87] "There were sportswriters," Tom Heinsohn later said, "who told me personally, who covered basketball, that they didn't vote for [Russell] for MVP of the All Star Game because they wanted it to go to Jerry Lucas. They didn't want a black guy getting the MVP of the All-Star game."[88] Russell was certainly cognizant of the backward racial attitudes emanating from the local media. He believed they helped perpetuate a negative image of African-American ballplayers in the city, which had all sorts of unfortunate consequences, not the least of which was financial. White players like Bob Cousy, for instance, could be counted on to have greater earning opportunities outside of basketball than blacks of similar stature. "He was a good friend of mine, a great player," Russell once fumed, "but did you know in the early '60s, Cousy made more money from endorsements than all the other black athletes in all the other sports combined? You can check that. This is discrimination."[89]

If this was not enough, reporters began calling Russell "Felton X," in mocking reference to his middle name. Russell received this moniker after he had made an offhand remark to a local reporter in 1959 that he was thinking of moving to Liberia to "get away from you, anyway." The writer, he later ruefully noted, elected to leave out the part of wanting to put distance between himself and his interviewer. The story that eventually ran suggested that he was deserting his homeland. "No one could understand that a man can be caught between two worlds," Russell explained. "West Africa is my ancestral home. The United States is my native land."[90]

Instead, it was generally assumed that Russell was forsaking the United States and embracing the radical ideology of Black Muslims. The only problem with this characterization was that it was patently untrue.

Russell had never embraced the Muslim faith, but this did not prevent members of the Boston media from trying to keep this intelligent and articulate professional athlete in his place. After all, there could be no "uppity" blacks on the plantation that was the provincial Boston sports scene of the 1950s and 1960s. "In Boston we won 11 championships and after the last championship all I could hear was there were too many black guys on the team," he said.[91]

Russell, of course, did not help his own cause by refusing to sign autographs for fans and making comments decrying the image consciousness of modern professional athletes. "What I'm resentful of," he told the *Saturday Evening Post* in 1964, "is when they say you owe the public this and you owe the public that. You owe the public the same thing it owes you. Nothing. Since I owe them nothing, I'll pay them nothing. I'm not going to smile if I don't feel like smiling, and bow my head, because it's not my nature. I'd say I'm like most people in this type of life. I have an enlarged ego. I refuse to misrepresent myself. I refuse to smile and be nice to the kiddies. I don't think it's incumbent upon me to set a good example for anybody's kids but my own."[92]

Despite the public uproar generated by these comments, Russell refused to back down and recant his statements. He had spoken what he thought needed to be said. He refused to play the usual public relations game practiced by indiscreet politicians and sports superstars and claim he was misquoted. He was standing by his words. "In the future," he promised, "I'll never fail to speak my piece when I believe I'm right. In the past, I haven't been able to sleep after games because I couldn't get unwound."[93]

Whether the public understood him or the underlying motives behind his behavior was irrelevant. "I don't make it easier for them to understand me," he once admitted. "I avoid that as much as possible. People who are realistic are non-conformists because they do what they want to do without caring what others think. I'm that way."[94]

His relationship with Boston was more complicated. Though he would later make peace with the city and claim it was a "tough town" for athletes of all races to play in, the feeling that Boston had unfairly treated him because of his race had always gnawed at him. He told his wife he would never be accepted as a "legitimate sports hero" like Ted Williams or Bob Cousy because he was a "Negro."[95] "For me, [the city] had very little to offer," he once claimed. "I came here as a rather naïve young man, as a professional athlete. An extraordinary professional athlete. And I lived in a situation where I realized quite rapidly that if I were to be a major athlete in this town it would be in spite of everybody and not because of everybody. I realized in my first year this town was basically a racist town, and not very subtle about it."[96]

Given Boston's troubled history of racial conflict, this was understandable. But in the years after his retirement as a player, Russell went a step further. He derided the community as the most "rigidly segregated" in the country and said he would rather be "in jail in Sacramento than be the mayor of Boston." "You know," he told the *Boston Globe,* "I remember when [Carl] Yastrzemski was a rookie [for the Red Sox]. One of the writers said, 'Too bad he ain't one of us.' This is what made Boston different for me. It really went past black and white. They would be into 'Is he a Jew?' 'Is he Irish?' 'Is he Polish?' 'Is he Italian?' And it seemed all the ethnic groups were contemptuous of each other. It wasn't just that the whites were contemptuous of the blacks, or vice versa.

"You know, when I came to Boston, as a 22-year-old I didn't know what a Jew was. But I became aware of it here, because people here make a distinction based on ethnic background, race, religion or whatever."[97]

This myopic cultural attitude embraced by the city's less than progressive elements forever colored Russell's view of Boston, which he once hailed as the place where Paul Revere had ridden for freedom. As he wrote in the late 1970s, "If Paul Revere were riding today, it would be for racism: 'The niggers are coming! The niggers are coming!' he'd yell as he galloped through town to warn neighborhoods of busing and black homeowners." He concluded that he had never been to a place where people were more involved in trying to "dismiss, ignore or look down on other people."[98]

Still, not even Boston in all its shameful provincialism could ignore the athletic feats of accomplishment that Russell would achieve during the 1968–69 season.

CHAPTER 3

Getting Under Way

As the Celtics prepared to open training camp in September 1968, one of the bitterest presidential races in modern memory was heating up. Both Democratic and Republican nominees were busily jockeying for position on a wide range of issues, including Vietnam, civil rights, student protests, military defense, crime, and urban riots. But it was the all-encompassing "law and order" issue that seemed to garner the most attention and debate. "I do not believe that the American people are bitter or filled with hate," Democratic candidate Hubert H. Humphrey maintained. "I do not believe that they're racists. I intend to appeal to their basic good." Republican candidate Richard M. Nixon offered a more cynical take on the situation. "The quiet Americans, the silent Americans," he said, "who have not been the protesters, who have not been the shouters—their voice is welling up across the country today. The great majority of Americans are angry. They don't like what's been happening in America these last four years."[1]

One person particularly incensed with the trend of recent events, but for an entirely different reason, was African-American radical Eldridge Cleaver. He saw an invitation to deliver a series of lectures at the University of California staunchly opposed by a group of right-wing conservatives headed by former actor turned governor Ronald Reagan. "I have never liked Ronald Reagan," Cleaver said. "Even back in the days of his bad movies—bullshit flicks that never turned me on to any glow—I felt about him the way I felt about such nonviolent cowboys as Roy Rodgers and Gene Autry: that they were never going to cause any action or allow anything to happen. They were just there, occupying space and wasting my time, my money and my sanity. One knew that movies were into a make-believe bag, but the unreality exposed on the screen by the flat souls of such pabulum-fed actors as Reagan reflected to me—black ghetto nigger me—a sickening bag of humorless laughter and perfect Colgate teeth."[2]

On the international front, Czechoslovakians were still defying the Red Army's occupation of their country in the wake of events following the Prague Spring, when an indigenous popular democratic movement was crushed by Russian tanks and soldiers. "It is a country gone mad with anger," reported two correspondents working for *Life* magazine. "Partisans have painted over every road sign that might help the Russians. Omnipresent posters ask the invaders, 'Why?' Russian troops everywhere, clutching Pravda to their dirty khaki uniforms, look aghast at the jeering people they come to save. Huge crowds hoot down Soviet propaganda loudspeakers—which broadcast mistakenly in Russian. 'Ivan,' the crowds of young Czechs shriek, 'you are like Hitler, you are worse than Hitler—get out.'"[3]

On a lighter note, a gothic soap opera called *Dark Shadows* was causing a considerable stir in daytime television. Set on an ancient estate in the fictionalized town of Collinsport, Maine, the campy ABC-TV show focused on the nocturnal doings of a 173-year-old vampire named Barnabas Collins, who was played by veteran stage actor Jonathan Frid. Originally written as a villain, Barnabas soon developed into a sympathetic, even romantic character who did constant battle against a host of witches, ghosts, warlocks, werewolfs, and other supernatural creatures of the night. The show was a ratings hit and was rumored to have been a favorite of former First Lady Jacqueline Kennedy. "It was so silly and so scary and so unpredictable, and at the same time, you could not watch a show that you didn't see somebody make a mistake, so it was a howl," cast member Lara Parker later commented. "And everybody who watched it either got scared, or they could be sensually or sexually aroused or they could giggle."[4]

Good cheer was also in order at the start of Celtics training camp. During a September 23 press conference held at the Hotel Lenox in downtown Boston, the team announced the signing of Bill Russell as player-coach for an additional two seasons. Exact terms of the deal, which had a reported monetary value of $200,000 a year, were not revealed, but, judging from the upbeat mood exhibited by Russell, they could not have been unfavorable. Yet money appeared to be distant from Russell's thoughts on this particular day. He preferred to talk instead about the prospects his team had for the upcoming 1968–69 basketball campaign. "We were in first place most of the entire season last year and I look for us to be a better ball club this year," he enthusiastically told the media gathering. "In fact, I think this will be one of the best teams we've had in the last four or five years." As for players to look out for, Russell singled out the performance of team captain and all-purpose forward John Havlicek, who was known around the NBA for his legendary endurance. "John thinks he can't get tired," Russell joked, "and I want to take advantage of that." Regarding his own performance expectations, Russell was cryptic, saying only that as coach he had "a fat center" that he needed to do something about. "Guess I'll have to run him for awhile," he said.[5]

While Russell spent the next few weeks shedding pounds and getting his club ready for the regular season, he and the Celtics front office also had to contend with a problem that threatened to jeopardize the team's chances of repeating as champions. Starting point guard Larry Siegfried, a key performer during Boston's 1967–68 title run, had refused to report to training camp at Tobin Gym in Roxbury, due to the unhappiness he felt over his contract. This bold act, which represented the first contract holdout in team history, was just the kind of thing Russell and the rest of the Celtics had come to expect from the scrappy former Buckeye.

For Siegfried had always marched to the beat of his own drummer. Russell even took the liberty of nicknaming him after an orbiting earth satellite called *Telestar*, because of the "way out" behavior he displayed.[6] "Siggy was a flake, all right," he later said.[7] Indeed, the 6-foot-3-inch, 192-pound guard was different. Stubborn, intemperate, unpredictable, and self-absorbed, Siegfried often worked himself into an emotional lather over the most innocuous of things. As Red Auerbach recalled, "One night he took a couple of bad shots in the game, and one of the guys grumbled at him. These things happen all the time, but you don't dwell on it. Larry did. He let it bother him. He went into a shell and wouldn't shoot, so I got mad at him for being so sensitive. You can't be [sensitive] in this game." But not even a great motivator like Auerbach could always get through to Siegfried. "Larry has always played a sound, hustling defense," Auerbach said. "But when you've the ability to be a brilliant shooter like he has, you have to make the most of it. He wouldn't though. He'd have a bad game and he wouldn't shoot for a couple of weeks."[8] Things didn't improve under Russell's coaching watch. The Celtics leader repeatedly clashed with Siegfried over his role on the team. Like Auerbach, he wanted the former Ohio State playmaker to shoot the ball more, but Siegfried was not always receptive to the idea. "It reached the point," Tom Heinsohn later wrote, "where Siegfried was going to solve the problem for everyone by quitting. He was going to join the ministry. He was going to get next to God. He had to get away from the emotional turmoil he was experiencing with the Celtics."[9] True to his iconoclastic nature, he never followed through on the threat, but this didn't stop him from complaining. Eventually, Russell would throw up his hands in disgust and conclude, "I can't talk to that kid."[10]

Nor was Siegfried ever shy about expressing an opinion on topics other than basketball. Once he was asked by a reporter to give his views on modern women. His reply went as follows: "They're too independent. You meet a girl and right off she tells you she's about to go to Europe for six months, moving to another state, or buying a sports car. Then there are the girls who are too caught up in their careers. Girls try to give the impression they're perfectly content and busy with no room in their lives for some guy."[11] He continued along this vein, decrying the competitiveness of the opposite sex in many social and professional situations. "Some give the impression, 'Anything you can do I can do better.' It makes a man feel important if he can maybe teach a girl how to ski or fish. But most girls act as if a sports date is a tryout for the Olympics. If they acted just a little more feminine and a little less independent, a man would do just about anything for them. Follow me?"[12]

While many professional athletes of his era shared these unenlightened sentiments, few were so bold as to publicly disclose them. But then Siegfried was never one to hold back, whether it was in the court of public opinion or on a basketball floor. At the height of his game, Tom Heinsohn would usually select Siegfried to scrimmage against in practice "[b]ecause Larry offers everything a player needs for opposition, scrap, ability, maneuverability, courage and shooting ability."[13] And it was in the area of all-out hustle that Siegfried particularly excelled. "A loose ball was my ball," he later claimed. "It's as simple as that. Every free ball you get is a big plus for your team, a matter of four potential points—two your team can get, two the other team can't get. Diving for loose basketballs is the way I learned basketball. If that stands out as an abnormality in pro basketball it's because most guys won't bend over to pick up the ball. But that's what the game is all about. And that's the way I played it. You've got to hustle, really hustle."[14]

Larry Siegfried learned basketball while growing up poor in the small rural farming community of Shelby, Ohio. "We didn't have a whole lot," he said of his family upbringing. "I probably would say basketball gave me a lot of opportunity."[15] Indeed, opportunity came knocking in the form of an athletic scholarship from Ohio State after Siegfried became a star player at Shelby High School. For a self-professed "farm boy" who possessed little in the way of worldly sophistication, the prospect of playing before sell-out Big Ten crowds with such standout teammates as John Havlicek and Jerry Lucas proved exhilarating. "We had an awesome club," he said. "It was a combination of a lot of people, and I think that was the beauty of the team."[16] He averaged 15.7 points per contest during his college career and was one of the main catalysts behind Ohio State's successful NCAA title drive in 1960. "He could shoot, play defense and he was a great playmaker," Havlicek said. "He really showed us a lot."[17]

Given the level of success he enjoyed at Ohio State, it hardly came as a shock when the Cincinnati Royals made him the third overall pick in the 1961 NBA draft. But in a move he lived to regret, Siegfried turned his back on this opportunity. "I played ball at Ohio State," he later explained. "There was always a lot of bad blood between the University of Cincinnati and Ohio State. There was no way I was going to Cincinnati. . . . It was a really bad situation."[18] Instead, Siegfried tried his luck with the Cleveland Pipers of the new American Basketball League. Unfortunately, the upstart league folded after two lackluster seasons, leaving Siegfried unemployed and in need of a team. After sitting out a year, he tried hooking up with the St. Louis Hawks, who had obtained his NBA rights in a trade, but he got cut in training camp due to the surplus of guards on the roster. "It didn't matter how well I played," he later said, "I had no chance."[19] He was coldly informed of his fate when the team bus pulled out of the parking lot. St. Louis coach Harry Gallatin told him, "So long, Siegfried. It was nice to know you."[20]

Devastated by the news, Siegfried thought his basketball career was over. "My confidence was completely ruined," he later confessed. "I was finished." Then the unexpected happened. On the recommendation of former Ohio State teammate John Havlicek, the Celtics claimed him on waivers for $1,000, and Siegfried suddenly found himself competing for a roster spot on the defending world champions. But making the team wasn't easy. His playing skills had eroded as a result of being away from the game for a whole season. He appeared light-years away from the All-American form he had displayed so spectacularly at Ohio State. Still, Celtics coach Red Auerbach decided to take a chance on him. For in Siegfried he saw an unselfish, hardworking player who could run the floor on the break and make intelligent decisions. "The thing about Larry," Auerbach later said, "is that he's a thinker. In fact, he has one of the sharpest basketball minds I've ever run across, but sometimes it gets into a little bit of trouble. He'll think in a situation rather than simply reacting. And the opportunity will be gone."[21]

Siegfried became the twelfth man on a veteran squad that boasted such Hall of Fame talent as Russell, Havlicek, K.C. Jones, Tom Heinsohn, and Frank Ramsey. Used primarily as a practice session player, Siegfried saw action in only 31 regular season games that first season, while averaging a paltry 3.3 points per contest. While other former star players might have become hopelessly discouraged by such a turn of events, Siegfried refused to wallow in self-pity. He continued to work on his game, going so far as to practice with a local high school team when the Celtics didn't bring him along on road trips.

All this hard effort began to pay off during the 1965–66 season, when Siegfried posted double figures in scoring and became a valuable contributor off the bench. Indeed, he displayed a versatility that allowed Auerbach to use him in a variety of game situations. "When Sam [Jones] is in and I'm subbing for K.C. [Jones], then I have to go strong on defense," Siegfried explained. "I just change my game and dig. If Sam is out and I'm playing with K.C. then I switch to shooting. I try to pattern myself a lot after K.C. He gives wonderful tips to me. I learn a lot from all of them." Perhaps the greatest lesson of all learned was that he could still play and play well. "They gave it all back to me," he said of his Celtics experience. "Willie Naulls came up to me once and said: 'You'll make this team because you're a good hungry ball player. You can play this game.' You'd be surprised what a thing like that means."[22]

When K.C. Jones retired following the 1966–67 season, Siegfried's importance to the team only grew. Now a starter, Siegfried played some of the best ball of his career. He tossed in 12.2 points a game while dishing out 289 assists. Moreover, only Oscar Robertson of the Cincinnati Royals could boast of having a higher free throw shooting percentage. Siegfried finished with a .868 average, thus missing what would have been his second free throw crown by only .005 percentage points. He had led the NBA with a .881 average in 1966. Still, not everything came up roses. He severely injured his back in the middle of the season and had to sit out 20 games. "That injury was serious enough so I had to be hospitalized," he said. "Inactivity is something I don't handle too well and for a while I began to wonder if I'd ever get back. And if I did get back, how much I could play. Several times I thought of quitting. This was going to be my big year and instead they've got me in a bed. Now I'm glad I didn't quit."[23] Indeed, with Siegfried returning to the fold and playing a crucial role down the stretch, the Celtics were able to bull their way to another NBA championship that spring. It represented the kind of winning effort that Red Auerbach had come to expect from Siegfried. Auerbach "was always a stickler for the team concept and I was a team player," Siegfried told an interviewer in 1984. "I think Red picked me because of that. It seems the hardest thing to do these days is to get a player to give of himself to the ballclub. That's what we did, and that's why the Celtics were always winners."[24]

But winning was not enough to satisfy Siegfried in the early autumn of 1968. He wanted more money and an assurance that he would not be traded to another team, especially after he got wind of a rumor he was going to the Atlanta Hawks for guard Lenny Wilkens. "I wanted to play for the Celtics, but that was out of my hands if they wanted to trade me," Siegfried said. "I had no say in the matter. I would have played for less money in Boston than I would in Atlanta. So I figured if I was going to Atlanta, I'd hold out for every penny."[25] Auerbach hit the roof when he learned of the no-trade demand. "Larry is no different from anyone else who signs a Celtics contract," he fumed. "Whether that player will be traded is up to the club to determine, not him. I'd have to be out of my mind to let a player dictate that. Sure, I can sympathize with a man not wanting to be traded. But anytime we can be helped by a trade, we'll make it."[26]

Further raising Auerbach's ire was the fact that Siegfried tapped an attorney, Bob Woolf of Boston, to negotiate terms for his contract. Woolf "went in to see Auerbach, and Red blew up," Siegfried later recalled. "He figured it was illegal or something. Before that, a player would just go in himself, talk with Red and kind of herky-jerky a figure. Now this lawyer business was something new to Red. It was unheard of. And so I was the bad guy. Well, if I was a troublemaker, what are these guys today?"[27] Woolf, who would go on to become one of the most powerful and successful sports agents in the country, had his work cut out for him. For Auerbach had a well-earned reputation for being a tough, shrewd, and resourceful negotiator. As Celtics general manager, he had consistently imposed tight restrictions on player salaries, even for steady producers like Satch Sanders and K.C. Jones. Whenever they protested their relatively low wage scales, Auerbach always had a handy response ready. "You wanna go to another team?" he once asked Jones. "You can't shoot. You're short. Where you gonna go?"[28] To be sure, outside of Russell, who commanded top dollar both as a player and as a coach, there were few Celtics who were paid what they were truly worth. And the reason for this had less to do with Auerbach's own parsimonious nature and more to do with the harsh fiscal realities confronting the team. Put simply, the Celtics were a financial basket case due to a perennially unstable ownership.

Since the death of Walter Brown in 1964, the team had changed hands several times. With each new ownership group, however, came the same problems. Because of poor home attendance and the enormous price tag associated with renting Boston Garden, the Celtics had to struggle to turn a profit each year. The financial situation got so bad, that National Equities, Inc., the corporate entity that had owned and operated the franchise since 1965, decided to sell out to Ballantine Brewing of New Jersey in August, after realizing an annual return profit of only $30,000. Their initial investment in the team had been $3 million.[29] "People kept comparing us to the Yankees," Auerbach later told biographer Joe Fitzgerald, "but there was a big difference. After every season the Yankees would go out and buy someone like Johnny Mize. The Celtics couldn't do that. We had to depend upon what we got out of the draft and on any old players we could convince to postpone retirements. The most I ever spent for an older player was the $6,000 I paid to get Wayne Embry. We simply didn't have any cash reserves to go to if we came up short. Believe me when I say we were winning world championships some years when we didn't have a goddamned dime in the bank."[30]

For this reason, Auerbach was extremely reluctant to give in to Siegfried's contract demands. But the thought of the Celtics starting the season without an experienced point guard, coupled with an already thin backcourt situation, forced Auerbach's hand. On September 26, he came to terms with Siegfried for a substantial undisclosed salary increase, thus ending the historic eight-day holdout. Curiously, the final agreement made no mention of a no-trade clause, though Auerbach apparently assured Siegfried and Woolf that he had no intention of making such a deal. "Larry must have heard rumors that he was going to be traded, or something," Auerbach commented. "Nothing could be further from the truth."[31] No one was more relieved by this outcome than Siegfried. "It felt great to be back with the guys again," he said shortly after rejoining the team. "I can't say I'm in top shape yet. I've been working out alone at the Cambridge YMCA . . . it will take me a few games to get me in proper condition."[32] As for Woolf, he added his own spin to the situation. "Red was most amicable and we got along just fine," he said of the final negotiations. "Larry received what he wanted and Red knows now more than ever that Larry wants to be a Celtic and remain a Celtic, and will give his usual 100 percent."[33]

Siegfried's holdout cast a spotlight on the shifting balance of power that was then taking place between management and ballplayers. After years of timid submission, NBA players were finally standing up for their collective bargaining rights and challenging management at every turn. Eventually their agitation would result in landmark economic concessions from the owners: wide-ranging free agency, a majority share of league revenues, and guaranteed salary levels. Indeed, NBA players would become the "envy" of all professional athletes. But the road to labor emancipation was a long and difficult one. Players didn't even bother to form a union until 1954, when Celtic great Bob Cousy saw the crying need for such an organization and proceeded to do something about it. "I had no desire to form a red-eyed union, complete with demands for higher pay, shorter hours, longer vacations and elaborate pension setups," Cousy later wrote. "But I had been listening to player gripes and making a few of my own for nearly four years, and I had a pretty good idea of what improvements should be made. I had had no experience with unions and had never belonged to one. I had a fuzzy idea of what should be done to form one and was also skeptical as to how some of the players, to say nothing of the owners, would react to the idea. But I was sure most of the players would go along with me."[34] As it turned out, Cousy was correct in his assumption, and the National Basketball Player's Association came into being.

While this development represented a major breakthrough, the Player's Association possessed little or no influence in these early years. The NBA didn't even see fit to formally recognize the organization until 1957, and then only because it feared the NBPA would affiliate itself with a powerful union, such as the teamsters. A modicum of respect was finally achieved in 1964, when the Player's Association threatened a boycott of the NBA All-Star game, which was being staged for the first and last time at Boston Garden. At issue was a proposed pension plan that would give retirement benefits to all players. Up to this point, management had arrogantly refused to engage in any meaningful discussion on the subject. But that was all about to change. "I was coming in with the St. Louis contingent," remembered guard Lenny Wilkens, now an NBA coach. "When we got to the hotel, we saw [NBPA general counsel Larry] Fleisher, Bill Russell and Tommy Heinsohn in the lobby. They came over and said, 'We have a problem. We have to go see the commissioner [Walter Kennedy].' We went to Mr. Kennedy's suite and told him we wanted a commitment for a pension plan. We didn't have one back then and he didn't think the league could do that. We told him that we were going to strike the All-Star game. He couldn't believe it. He asked each one of us if we would strike and we all said we would."[35]

As game time approached, the players turned the screws even tighter. "That evening," Wilkens continued, "we all went into the locker room to tell all the players what we were going to do. We told them we were going to stay in the locker room until we had a commitment."[36] Alarmed by this turn of events, several owners attempted to contact their players and convince them to abandon the boycott—or else. But the union leadership had deftly anticipated this move and took protective measures to preserve unity. "There was this old Irish cop standing by the locker room door and we told him not to let anyone in," Tom Heinsohn later recalled. "He then put his head in and said to Elgin Baylor and Jerry West that [LA owner] Bob Short was out there and wanted to talk to them. They wouldn't go. Short told the cop to tell them that if they didn't come out, then they were through as members of the Lakers. I can still remember Elgin standing up and telling the cop, 'Tell Bob Short he can go [bleep] himself.'"[37] Adding further tension to the situation was the heightened media coverage of the event. "It was the first game to be televised nationally in almost a year," Wilkens said. "ABC was going to begin a series of games with this game. The game was to begin at 8:30 and at 8:15 ABC told the league if we didn't come out in five minutes, they were going to go with another program."[38]

Backed into a corner, commissioner Kennedy gave his word to the players that he would do everything in his power to redress their grievances. Given this assurance, the players voted to play the game, which the East won, 111–107. Shortly thereafter, Kennedy was able to get the owners to agree to a pension plan, thus giving the Player's Association its first major victory. "Nobody took us seriously," Heinsohn said. "I told [Celtics owner] Walter [Brown] about the pension and he said, 'What are you talking about? I don't even have a pension.' That's the way it was. But Kennedy followed through and we got what we wanted. But it was close. We almost didn't play the game that night."[39]

The union would score another major victory in 1967, when the players threatened a work stoppage before the playoffs if the owners failed to come to terms on a collective bargaining agreement. As in 1964, the owners capitulated and gave in to the players' demands. The playoffs took place as planned, but an important corner had been turned. "I think they [owners] realized that the players were going to strike," Larry Fleisher said. "They had to deal with us as an equal or they were not going to have any playoffs. They had to look at the union, the Player's Association, as, if not an equal adversary, at least a strong adversary."[40] The numbers bear it out. Whereas the average salary for a pro basketball player was $9,400 in 1967, this figure rose to nearly $1 million by 2000. Contributing to this upward financial trend was the creation of a rival professional league, the American Basketball Association, in 1967. "By bidding for college players and giving marginal NBA pros an alternative, the new league did, by its mere existence, push salary expenses higher," noted basketball historian Leonard Koppett.[41] Clearly, a revolution had occurred in player-management relations. And Siegfried's holdout was symptomatic of these new changes.

With the successful resolution of Siegfried's contract situation, however, the Celtics were able to approach the coming new season with a high degree of optimism. Indeed, the team had all five starters returning from the previous year's championship squad—Russell, Sam Jones, Bailey Howell, Tom Sanders, and, of course, Siegfried. Combined, this quintet had 45 seasons of pro experience to go with 31 championship rings. Hands down, they represented the most seasoned lineup in the NBA.

Off the bench, the Celtics could likewise rely on the versatile talents of John Havlicek, who was generally considered the finest sixth man in the NBA, and Don Nelson, a fearless rebounder who could spell Russell at center. If there was a major weakness, it involved the lack of quality depth in the backcourt. After Jones and Siegfried, the talent level dropped off precipitously in Emmette Bryant and Mal Graham. Bryant was a journeyman who had been acquired in the off-season from the Phoenix Suns, while Graham was a former NYU star who had never lived up to his immense promise. One potential solution to the backcourt problem, however, was heralded first round draft pick Don Chaney out of the University of Houston. But due to a six-month hitch he had with the Army Reserves, the defensive guard would be unable to play for the first half of the season. Until then, the team was expected to make do with a patchwork guard rotation. Whether this would be good enough to win in the NBA's rugged Eastern Division remained to be seen, however.

For the division had undergone a dramatic transformation over the previous half decade. Instead of being a private hunting reserve for the Celtics, the East had evolved into a competitive free-for-all. Leading the pack here were the always dangerous Philadelphia 76ers, only two years removed from an NBA championship. Despite having shipped superstar center Wilt Chamberlain to Los Angeles in the off-season for three lesser talents, the team continued to look formidable behind the capable veteran leadership of Hal Greer, Luke Jackson, and Chet Walker. Third-year man Billy Cunningham, who had averaged 18 points in his first two seasons with the ballclub, appeared primed for a breakout year in scoring as he possessed one of the smoothest and most accurate shots in the league.

Nipping at the heels of the 76ers were the steadily improving New York Knicks, who harbored aspirations of going deep into the playoffs. The possessors of a talent-rich backcourt in Dick Barnett, Walt Frazier, and Bill Bradley, the Knicks liked to run at every opportunity, provided big men Willis Reed and Walt Bellamy could come up with the rebounds. Adding depth and experience to this All-Star lineup were veterans Cazzie Russell, Phil Jackson, Howie Komives, and Nate Bowman. Just below the Knicks in terms of overall ability and expectations were the young Detroit Pistons, who boasted the dazzling offense of guard Dave Bing and the gritty toughness of forward Dave DeBusschere. Bing tossed in 27.1 points a game during the 1967–68 campaign, while DeBusschere came through with a 13.5 rebounding average. Ably assisting them were Happy Hairston and Terry Dischinger in the frontcourt and Jimmy Walker and Eddie Miles in the backcourt.

If the Pistons appeared to be a team on the rise, the opposite was true of the aging Cincinnati Royals, winners of just 39 games the previous season. Led by the incomparable Oscar Robertson, who always seemed a threat to record a triple double, the Royals were an uneven club that relied too much on the extraordinary skills of the "Big O" to bail them out of late game situations. Robertson did receive some help from All-Star forward Jerry Lucas and center Connie Dierking, but never enough. One ballclub figuring to make things interesting regardless of where they finished in the final standings were the offensive-minded Baltimore Bullets, cellar dwellers in the East during the previous two seasons. Bolstered by the talents of Rookie of the Year Earl "the Pearl" Monroe, the Bullets hoped to improve their team defense as they had averaged an impressive 117.4 points a game in 1967–68, while giving up a less-than-crowd-pleasing 117.8. Rounding out the division were the also-ran Milwaukee Bucks, a first-year expansion team who had little going for them apart from former Celtics backup center Wayne Embry.

As for the rest of the NBA, outside of the Atlanta Hawks, who fielded an outstanding starting frontcourt in Zelmo Beaty, Bill Bridges, and Lou Hudson, there was little in the way of serious competition facing the Los Angeles Lakers, who were viewed as virtual locks to win the Western Division championship. Indeed, with new arrival Wilt Chamberlain teaming up with all-time scoring greats Jerry West and Elgin Baylor for the first time, the sky appeared to be the limit for the traditionally star-crossed franchise. Anything short of a league title in the spring would be considered a failure of epic proportions.

Failure was the farthest thing from the minds of Bill Russell and the Celtics as they prepared for their October 18 season opener on the road against the Detroit Pistons. While some preseason publications such as *The Sporting News* could not resist pointing out that the defending world champs were getting somewhat long in the tooth and therefore less likely to repeat, the ballclub collectively shrugged off such unflattering labels. "We expected to win, that was the key," Tom Sanders later said. "That we expected to win, not that we were expected to win."[42] Even a dismal exhibition season record of 2–8 could not shake the team's confidence. "We're ready," Auerbach told reporters. "Russell has done a good job with the team's training program. The only reason we lost all those games was because Russell was playing himself into shape instead of trying to win ball games. That's what exhibitions are for."[43]

Russell subsequently went out and proved his old coach correct as he grabbed 36 rebounds to lead the Celtics to a convincing 106–88 victory over the Pistons. After trailing 40–38 at halftime, the Celtics broke out in the third period, outscoring the Pistons, 22–3, in the first four minutes. Larry Siegfried, a game-high 26 points, and Sam Jones, 24, provided the bulk of the offense during this stretch, connecting on six big hoops. "The Celtics," reported the *Boston Herald-Traveler*, "kept pouring it on and with five minutes left in the game they had a 25-point lead and were content to run out the clock at the expense of the stunned Pistons, who were rattled by what happened in the early minutes of the half." Indeed, the overall magnitude of the Celtics "explosion" was such "that they scored one more point [39] in the third period than they did in the entire first half."[44] For the Pistons, Dave Bing was scoring leader with 20 points.

The Celtics continued their offensive rampage the following evening in Chicago with a 106–96 dispatching of the Bulls. Once again, Siegfried was the main scorer with 26 points, while Bailey Howell and John Havlicek contributed with 24 and 20 points respectively. The Celtics achieved the win despite being without the services of Russell, who fouled out with 6:15 to play. The team led by only 3 points at the time, having blown a 12-point lead in the first half. But Don Nelson, filling in admirably for Russell in the pivot, induced Chicago's 7-foot rookie center Tom Boerwinkle into foul trouble and the team took off from there, rebuilding their advantage to double figures. The loss was the first of the season for the Bulls, who had entered the contest with an unblemished 3–0 mark. While no one was issuing orders for new championship rings just yet, the 2–0 Celtics were showing signs they were as competitive as ever. "It's still a bit early to predict how the season will go," Auerbach told reporters back in Boston. "There's no doubt our chances of repeating depend on Bill Russell. If there is one trouble with this team, it's the idea in the minds of players that Russell can compensate for all the mistakes of other players. But when the others decide to help themselves by blocking out, this club is going to be as good as any we've had."[45]

Boston fans got a chance to see for themselves how good the Celtics were when the team played host to the Cincinnati Royals in its October 23 home opener at Boston Garden. Built in 1928 by boxing promoter Tex Rickard, the Garden sat inelegantly above North Station, a tangled cluster of railway lines that extended to the city's western and northern suburbs. Long the home of traveling three-ring circuses, prize fights, and

Boston Bruin hockey games, the building possessed a raffish charm that appealed to local fans like John Powers, a prominent sports journalist who grew up rooting for the Celtics in the 1950s and 1960s. Looking back at these early days, he once observed that it was not all the big games and championships that left him with the greatest lasting impression, but the colorful sights and sounds surrounding the arena. "Walking along Causeway Street, you belonged to another era," he wrote, "one that seemed perpetually stuck at nine o'clock on some bygone Friday night, that smelled of cigar smoke and was filled with Cadillacs and tweed overcoats and men with flattened noses, ruined voices and big rings."[46] This Runyonesque atmosphere did not dissipate once a person entered the Garden. If anything, it only became more intense. "You could hear the pinball machines stuttering to your right as soon as you entered the lobby at street level," Powers pointed out, "the bells keeping up a steady cacophony. There were always people playing them, kids mostly, with no place else to go. There were always people everywhere. On the left, the stairs to the upper level were stained with urine, and there was usually a derelict sitting on them, swilling from a bottle of Old Grand-Dad. You could smell hot dogs frying on the hole in the wall grill a few feet away. Around the corner, where North Shore commuters waited on old wooden benches for their trains, you bought your tickets, looking up at the marquee overhead that told you everything Walter Brown had planned."[47]

After passing through an ancient turnstile, patrons would move to their seats via an intricate maze of ramps and stairs, all the while listening to the sonorous tones of organist John Kiley belting out such standards as "It's a Great Day for the Irish." Once seated, a person could not avoid gazing upward and seeing the many green and white championship banners hanging from the darkened ceiling, a view that one writer compared to the "inside of a bat cave."[48] But perhaps the most distinctive feature of all was the gleaming white parquet floor that was laid out checkerboard style atop the ice surface the Bruins skated on. Installed for the munificent sum of $10,000 in 1946, the parquet floor achieved notoriety around the NBA for its "dead spots," sections of the court where the ball could not bounce as a result of cracks from the uneven ice underneath. Needless to say, this gave the Celtics a tremendous "home court advantage." As K.C. Jones recalled, "It meant something to play in the Garden from the minute we won that first championship in 1957. The Garden would be worth 10 points to us to start the game. I mean, teams were intimidated to play us there. The floor added to it."⁴⁹

While Celtics players extolled such advantages as being part of a general, hard-to-define Garden mystique that helped them win, opponents were less sanguine. They viewed the building as a dilapidated pit where the only thing worse than the substandard lighting and air ventilation were the ramshackle visiting dressing rooms where the showers always seemed to run cold. "The locker rooms in Boston Garden are the worst in the league, as every player in the NBA knows well," Hall of Fame center Kareem Abdul-Jabbar later wrote. "They're small, old, and tired. Like the building itself. The plumbing is antiquated throughout, and rats now inhabit the back corners of this proud survivor from another era."⁵⁰ Interestingly, Auerbach never seriously disputed this characterization. "The truth was that the Garden hated us [Celtics]," he claimed. "They never did anything to help us. If you got cold water and a hot locker-room, so did we."⁵¹ Still, this fact did not prevent many opponents from thinking that their plight was due to some sinister plot concocted by Auerbach to soften them up. The Celtics GM did his best to encourage such paranoia. "But, if that's what the teams thought, I let them," he said. "I felt the distractions could help us win."⁵²

No such diversions were believed to have played a role in the Celtics' subsequent 108–101 downing of the Royals, as the home team won its twelfth consecutive Garden opener before a small but enthusiastic gathering of 10,036. To mark the opening night festivities, Russell came up with 30 rebounds and 12 blocked shots. "He was just unbelievable . . . unbelievable," Auerbach gushed. The Celtics had built an imposing 20-point lead only to see it cut down to 6 in the fourth quarter as the team went "ice cold" from the field, connecting on only 2 of their first 14 shots. The team rallied in the closing moments, however, to put the game safely out of reach. Tom Sanders provided most of the damage here, as he tied Bailey Howell for the team lead in scoring with 21 points. "I worked him hard in practice and he's in good shape," Russell said.⁵³

For the Royals, Connie Dierking, a game-high 25 points, and Adrian Smith, 21, provided the scoring punch as team leader Oscar Robertson did not get to play due to a leg injury he had suffered the night before in a game against Los Angeles. Robertson did, however, get to coach the final 17 minutes of the contest when Cincinnati headman Ed Jucker was assessed two technical fouls by referee Earl Strom for arguing a call. "I didn't say a thing to him when he gave me the first one," Jucker said. "Then I just waved my hand at him and he gave me the second one. It's the first time I've been tossed out of a game in this league."[54] Robertson, who was dressed in street clothes, filled in capably, but to no avail. "A couple of baskets we missed would have made a difference," he concluded. Russell was equally brusque in his comments. "We were O.K.," he said. "We'll get better when the schedule tightens up and calls for us to play at least three times a week. Game experience just can't be learned in practice. You gotta be there."[55]

Broadcasting the game "high above courtside" was Johnny Most, the longtime "voice" of the Celtics. Proud, colorful, bombastic, and driven, Most approached each game as if it were his last. "If I bring pleasure to people," he once told writer Joe Fitzgerald, "if I make them laugh a little, give them a couple hours of enjoyment, then I've done my job. Basically, I'm an entertainer, and I have to believe people really want to listen to me. It is egotistical, yes, but if you don't feel that way, you can't go on. I want to believe people listening to me are really enjoying themselves."[56] There was never any danger of unhappy listeners as long as Most was around. He kept Celtics fans of all ages glued to their radios for over three decades. "You'd be surprised," noted one impressed Celtic, "how many persons regularly turn off the sound when we appear on TV and listen to Johnny Most's play by play. My wife has been doing it for years."[57]

Born and raised in the Bronx section of New York City in the 1930s, Most attended DeWitt Clinton High School and Brooklyn College where he played football and basketball. Like many young men of his generation, his education was interrupted by World War II when he entered the Army Air Corps and served as a waist gunner aboard a B-24. He participated in 28 combat missions with the 15th Air Force out of Italy and was awarded the Purple Heart and Distinguished Flying Cross. Following his discharge, he became interested in radio as a career and picked up a diverse assortment of broadcast jobs, including one as a substitute host for a minister on a Sunday morning religious show. "The guy phoned in and suggested I play religious records," Most later recalled. "So I went to the library and brought some out. It sounded like the best way to fill. Anyway, when I went on the air, I was very solemn and proper and I said 'Reverend so-and-so couldn't make it today. Instead, we'll play a collection of sacrilegious records.' I knew what I had done the minute I said it, and I just about fell over I was so embarrassed."[58]

Most had better luck performing a hoodlum's role in the popular *Dick Tracy* detective series of the late 1940s. But frustration at being repeatedly cast as a thug caused Most to eventually sour on dramatic work and instead take up play-by-play announcing. "Who knows, maybe I could have been Telly Savalas," Most once said wistfully.[59]

His first "real break" in sports broadcasting occurred when he beat out 300 other aspirants for a job with the Brooklyn Dodgers announcing games for a network of rural stations. His responsibilities included doing telegraphic recreations from a studio when the Dodgers were on the road. "Branch Rickey [the Dodgers' owner] was a frugal man," Most remembered. "He didn't want to pay me to travel. So we'd go to the ballpark and record crowd noises—boos and hisses, popcorn vendors, guys selling beer. I'd open the game by saying, 'This is Johnny Most with a recreated account of the Dodgers-Pirates game coming to you directly from Forbes Field, Pittsburgh.' . . . You told them the truth, you just didn't make a big deal out of it. And I'd forget myself. This was drama, this was acting. I'd do doubleheaders sitting in a little room for eight hours with headphones on. I thought I was in the goddamn ballpark. I could smell the hot dogs."[60]

Most soon branched out to do New York Knicks games with legendary play-by-play man Marty Glickman and was taught an invaluable lesson about broadcasting basketball games on the radio. "Marty Glickman influenced my rapid-fire description of ball-handling, playmaking, shooting," Most said. "The medium is sound, not sight; the fans can't see it, but they can sense as well as hear the game, if the announcer's voice speeds with the pace of the court action."[61] As for Glickman, he was duly impressed by his young broadcast partner's obvious flair behind the mike. "We did all kinds of basketball in those days and had a lot of top announcers, but Johnny was the best of them," Glickman claimed. "He was crisp and objective, too."[62]

Learning the Celtics had an opening for a lead announcer in 1953, Most tossed his name into the mix and experienced an unexpected stroke of good fortune. "I survived an audition that called for 60 applicants to describe play-by-play of a silent Celtics game film," Most said. "There were six applicants left, and it just happened the Celtics were undertaking a six-game exhibition trip. Each of us was assigned to do one of the games. I was to do the sixth game. The big break was that the Celtics were playing the Knicks when my turn came, and my familiarity with the Knicks didn't hurt me. Walter Brown, the late Celtics owner, heard my broadcast. After the game, Walter phoned Red [Auerbach] and told him to call off the auditions. I had won the Celtics job."[63]

Most quickly established himself as a local sports fixture, winning over Boston fans with his staccato delivery and exuberant style. Once he got so worked up over a Boston-Syracuse playoff game in 1959 that his set of false teeth came flying out of his mouth in midsentence. As Most remembered, "The Celtics were roaring from behind and I really was into it. That morning a clip on my partial plate had broken and my teeth were wobbling all over the place during the broadcast. Finally, after some big play, the teeth just flew out my mouth. I caught the damn things in mid-air and turned to Al Gernert, who was helping me with the broadcast and asked him: 'How do you like those hands?'"[64]

While his energy and wit were major assets, they were nothing compared to the richness of his deep, resonant voice, which he jokingly claimed to have achieved by gargling with Saniflush. "God what a voice," sports columnist Bob Ryan later reminisced. "Johnny had the most piercing vocal instrument known to man. It was not an announcer's voice. . . . It was a voice more suited to announce the arrival of an ocean liner. In the fog. To hear that voice coming through your radio is one thing, but to hear it in person was another matter. You could be seated in Row 1 of an airplane and still hear Johnny, in his normal conversational mode, back in Row 47."[65]

Unfortunately, Most's voice was about the only thing one could "hear" during Celtics home games in the 1950s and 1960s as few fans bothered to patronize the often half-empty Garden. "It was frustrating to see the [hockey] Bruins, with lousy teams, sell out night after night, especially after the Celtics began to win," Most admitted. "Five minutes before a Celtics game, you could always get a good seat. That was part of the reason I developed such a personalized style. I had to keep people interested for two and a half hours, to entertain and explain the game at the same time."[66]

One way to keep local audiences from turning the dial was to portray the action as a kind of morality play on hardwood. The Celtics were always the knights in shining armor charging to the rescue, while opposing teams represented perfidious villains to be vanquished. "I told him I didn't want [him] to be impartial," Red Auerbach explained. "I wanted him to be a fan. Later it used to make me laugh when I heard him. I'll admit he carried it to the extremes."[67] Among the extremes was tagging opposing players with unflattering nicknames such as "Trash Mouth," "Laughing Boy," and "McFilthy" and questioning a referee's personal integrity when the latter made a call against the Celtics. Nor did the verbal abuse necessarily end between the lines. Future Celtics executive vice president Dave Gavett discovered this when he chatted with fellow Dartmouth graduate and Laker Rudy LaRusso before a 1962 Boston-Los Angeles playoff game. "In those days," he said, "the [visiting] teams used to dress in the old Hotel Manger, and they'd put on their warmups and walk through North Station to the Garden. Rudy and I were walking along and Johnny came around the corner and he kind of nodded at me and said, 'What are you doing with him? Roughhouse Rudy, you're a dirty player,' and he really got on him and wouldn't stop. Well, Rudy turned to me and said, 'Who's that guy?' and I said, 'It's Johnny Most, he does the Celtics games.'"[68]

For his part, Most never apologized for taking this admittedly biased stance. "I believe when you're with one club, objectivity is a lot of baloney," he revealed to the *Boston Herald* in a 1979 interview. "You can't tell me anyone working with a bunch of people year after year who doesn't develop affections isn't kidding himself. I believe you should broadcast what you feel. If I were doing network games, I could be objective because I would not have formed close ties with anyone whose games I'm doing. When the Warriors were still in San Francisco, their broadcaster couldn't do one game and I filled in. It was totally even-handed. In '75, we did some of the Buffalo-Washington playoff; the winner would play Boston. Well, I had no stake in either team, the broadcast was objective, and we had a great time."[69]

Though he called many a crucial contest, Most's greatest moment as a broadcaster occurred during Game 7 of the 1965 Eastern Division finals between the Celtics and the Philadelphia 76ers. With time running out and the Celtics leading, 110–109, John Havlicek dramatically intercepted an inbounds pass from Philadelphia's Hal Greer to save the victory. "Havlicek stole the ball!" Most screamed into his microphone, thus creating one of the most memorable catchphrases in sports history. "It gave me some of the healthiest publicity I ever got in my life," Most said. "It was something to be remembered for, something to hang my hat on. It gave John and me a sense of 'foreverness' I couldn't have had otherwise."[70] Most underestimated himself. Even if he had never made the famous call, he still would have occupied a special place in the hearts of basketball fans everywhere. As former Celtics player Tom Heinsohn once commented, "He made heroes of us all and I dare say there aren't many people today with pen or word of mouth that could portray it any better than Johnny did."[71]

As the Celtics finished up their October schedule and moved into November, the team continued to roll on, winning 8 of their next 11 and giving every sign they were serious contenders for the NBA crown. Indeed, they possessed the third-best record in the league at 12–4. Only the Lakers in the West and the surprising Bullets in the East had better overall marks. In perhaps their most dominant outing during this stretch, the visiting Celtics demolished the playoff-contending Atlanta Hawks in a 123–103 laugher on November 3. The Celtics never trailed in the contest as John Havlicek, 28 points, Sam Jones, 20, and Larry Siegfried, 20, came up with big scoring efforts and Bill Russell handled matters on the defensive end as his shot-blocking prowess helped induce Atlanta into making 32 turnovers. "I know I've used this term before," exclaimed Auerbach afterward, "but it was a team victory all the way. They played great defense against a team that was sky high for us since it was our first visit to their [arena]. For example, Satch Sanders [13 points] played a great game against [forward] Lou Hudson, who is usually very effective against us and while Bill Russell scored only one point, people in Atlanta realize what he did defensively. He was brilliant. . . . We stole the ball and made them lose it often."[72]

Playing a key role as always during this successful run was John Havlicek, who Russell once wrote was so good and durable as a swingman "that if I were playing in an imaginary pick-up game among all the players I've ever seen, he's the first one I would choose for my side."[73] The son of a grocer, Havlicek had a typical middle-American childhood while growing up in Lansing, Ohio, in the 1950s. His life consisted of church, family, school, and sports. Among his early friends, he could count Phil and Joe Niekro, who lived across the street and who would go on to have distinguished pitching careers in major league baseball. "We were like brothers," he said.[74] And just like the Niekros, Havlicek demonstrated an early proclivity for athletics. "I don't know how John got interested in sports," his mother once said. "I just know he was always coming into the room, going to bed, throwing his balled-up underwear in the air and catching it, like it was some kind of game."[75]

In high school he played every sport in season, including a memorable turn as the starting football quarterback. "Our line averaged 135 pounds," Havlicek later recalled. "The opposition regularly outweighed us by as much as 80 pounds per man. But we were quick. We were tricky. I was real good at faking the ball on the belly series. . . . Once I faked to a back going into the line, then pulled away. He was tackled and the referee blew the whistle. The referee was still looking for the ball when I walked over and handed it to him."[76] Although he excelled on the football field, once throwing three touchdown passes in a game, his true love was basketball. As a senior, he averaged 30 points and 20 rebounds a contest, while earning All-State honors as a forward. Owing to his varied athletic talents, he received scholarship offers from some 80 colleges and universities.

While flattered by the deluge of interest, Havlicek had already made up his mind on what sport he would play and where he would play it. During his senior year, he had become a member of an Ohio basketball All-Star team with Larry Siegfried and future Hall of Fame center Jerry Lucas. "We all became real close," Havlicek said. "We decided to go to Ohio State together."[77] It was a decision that he never lived to regret as he teamed up with Siegfried and Lucas to make the Buckeyes one of the most successful clubs in college basketball. In his three varsity seasons at the school, his teams compiled a 78–6 mark to go with three Big Ten championships, three Final Fours, and one NCAA crown in 1960.

Along the way he developed a deep understanding of what it took to win. Just before the 1960 championship season began, for instance, Havlicek strode into Ohio State coach Fred Taylor's office and "respectfully" told him he was going to sacrifice his individual offense for the good of the team. "At the time," Taylor later commented, "we were trying to sell our kids on offense. Defense is hard to sell, but here was John literally jumping at the chance. I never saw anything like it. And of course I never saw anything like John. By midseason I was usually assigning him to the opposition's best player automatically, whether it was a frontcourt man or a backcourt man."[78] This unselfishness quickly drew the attention of Red Auerbach. "The first time I ever saw Havlicek I was scouting Ohio State and while I had heard about John, I had no idea of all the things he could do," the estimable Celtics general manager said. "Although he obviously was defense oriented, he looked as though he could be taught to shoot. And when he streaked up and down the floor without taking a deep breath, I was stunned. All I could think of was: 'Wow! Have we got something here. Is this guy ever going to make a great pro. Are people going to think I'm smart after I draft this guy.' But then I began to worry that maybe somebody else would take him before the Celtics' turn came in the draft."[79] Fortunately for the Celtics, the latter scenario didn't materialize as the rest of the NBA judged Havlicek's concentration on defense as having more to do with a fundamental lack of scoring talent than any personal commitment to winning. The team subsequently grabbed him in the first round of the 1963 college draft, but an unforeseen development soon arose to cast doubt on whether he would ever play a minute in a Boston uniform.

For despite the immense prestige associated with being drafted by the defending world champions, Havlicek was not at all enthusiastic about making pro basketball a career. He instead pinned his hopes on playing in the National Football League. "I did things in basketball that pro football coaches thought would carry over to football as a wide receiver," he later explained. "I was quick, had good moves and good hands. Several pro teams sent me questionnaires. I began to think I might like to play pro football. I figured that if I could play for the [Cleveland] Browns, who had drafted me, I'd stay in Ohio, and I like Ohio. And the football season is short, the pay was the same as basketball, and football is not as demanding as basketball. And I knew that if I didn't make the Browns, I could go back to basketball."[80] True to form, Havlicek gave his all in attempting to crack the Browns star-studded lineup, running 40-yard sprints in 4.6 seconds and catching the ball "as well as anyone in [tryout] camp," outside of standout Cleveland receivers Gary Collins and Ray Renfro.[81]

Nicknamed "the Spear" by his Browns teammates, Havlicek made his pro football debut in an exhibition game against the Pittsburgh Steelers. "The crowd gave me a big hand," he remembered. "They were curious to see if a basketball player could play football. Somehow I made my block, on the cornerback, I think. A perfect block. Jim Brown ran a sweep 48 yards to the Pittsburgh 2. Somebody in the huddle said, 'O.K., Spear, do it again.' I was feeling pretty good. This time it was an off-tackle play. I lined up looking into the face of [defensive end] Big Daddy Lipscomb." Lipscomb, who stood at 6 feet 7 inches and 260 pounds, was not so easily moved, however. As Havlicek recalled, "Well, at the snap, I kind of blasted straight ahead, or at least that's what I intended to do, except that Big Daddy started grabbing everyone in sight, including me, throwing us around until he got to the runner. I ended up at the bottom of the pile. I wasn't sure if he'd knocked off just my helmet, or my whole head."[82]

Still, Havlicek was not without his moments on the gridiron. In the same exhibition contest, he managed to showcase his own physical toughness while on the receiving end of a broken pass play. "The ball was way over my head, and I never had a chance," Havlicek said. "But I had been trained to keep running and watch out for blind-siding. A corner back and I were on a collision course, and I was much taller and had the leverage. I really unloaded on him. When I got back to the bench, veterans like Bernie Parrish and Don Fleming congratulated me for laying the guy out."[83]

While established stars like Jim Brown, Jim Houston, and Gene Hickerson went out of their way to praise Havlicek as a player, Cleveland coach and team founder Paul Brown decided that he was already too "loaded" at the receiver position to warrant keeping the former Ohio State standout on his roster. He was thus unceremoniously dumped to ponder what might have been. "Of course, I was crushed at first," Havlicek said. "I felt the Browns had really made a mistake. I felt I could really play. An [American Football League] club, Houston, made me an offer, but after I thought it over, I decided that if I was cut by the Browns, then the Good Lord was trying to tell me something. I decided to stick to basketball."[84]

Arriving in Boston to play for the Celtics, however, required some major personal adjustment. Used to the laid-back, down-home atmosphere of the Midwest, Havlicek was not quite prepared for the gritty urban landscape he encountered in Beantown. People were less friendly, and the pace of life seemed too harried. "I hated Boston when I first got there," he later confessed.[85] Adding to his initial personal doubts was the apparent makeshift manner in which the Celtics organization was run. "Coming from Ohio State," he once told author George Sullivan, "where the locker room was just so, I thought [the Celtics clubhouse] would be very open and spacious; what I saw was a dungeon. There were no lockers, just hooks and nails in the wall where you hang your clothes above a long bench, which you sat on and put your shoes under. There was one coat rack where everybody including some of the sports writers hung their overcoats. . . . The uniforms were not the caliber I thought a world champion team's would be like, either. It was a mix 'n match sort of thing as compared to Ohio State where everything was new. And in college there were equipment people, laundry people, a person for everything. Here it seemed like one man—Buddy LeRoux, the trainer—was running the whole thing."[86]

Despite these misgivings, Havlicek worked hard to fit in with the veteran team and to make a positive impression. He succeeded on all counts. "He's going to make the old boys work," an approving Red Auerbach told reporters during Havlicek's first training camp. "He's really a good one. He can run, pass, shoot, he's great on defense, he can play the backcourt and defense, too. Nobody's job is sure in the corner this year. This kid is better than we ever thought he was. His attitude is great, just great."[87] As if to prove his coach correct, Havlicek went out and had an outstanding rookie season, averaging 14.3 points, 6.7 rebounds, and 2.2 assists per game. "He is so smart for a rookie," observed Sam Jones. "He feeds the pivot better than many veterans in our league. He gives that ball to Bill [Russell] just where Bill wants it. All Russ has to do is extend his arm and tip Havlicek off and he's got the ball in the right spot. He's also wonderful in our pressing defense."[88]

While he did experience initial difficulty protecting the ball on the dribble, the 6-foot-5-inch, 210-pound Havlicek nevertheless exhibited a maturity on the court that belied his rookie status. "Red could afford to put him in right away because he never made any mistakes on defense and he was a lot better offensively than we were led to believe," said backcourt star Bob Cousy, who was performing in his last campaign as a Celtic when Havlicek came aboard. "He always played bigger than his size—which was 6 ft. 5 in.—and eventually he made the tough shots almost as well as he made the easy ones."[89] Bill Russell chose to remember a less-discussed side of Havlicek that first year. "He was a country boy when he joined us, and I mean country!" Russell later said. "You have no idea how country he was. He was genuinely a good person who had as close to a perfect temperament as I've ever seen in any athlete. And he wanted to win more than most. I don't know what went on inside him, but John never seemed to get flustered or upset. He was like a sponge: He learned as fast as any player I ever met. Things which make for winning were things he absorbed rapidly."[90]

This ability to mentally break down the game came as no accident. "I'd listen in practice, then go back to my room and diagram the patterns and plays until I knew them by heart," Havlicek said. "Knowing your own job wasn't enough. You were expected to know the responsibilities of everyone else on the court, too, so that if the game boiled down to one last play or one last shot, there would be no breakdown in execution. No one wanted to be the weak link that made us fail."[91] To this end, Havlicek demonstrated an uncanny ability to handle pressure situations in the tense, final moments of games. "Havlicek is one of the most complete players in the game," Knicks guard Walt Frazier said. "He can play guard, he can play forward, he can shoot and he can pass. He's the type of guy you can't relax on. And he's great under pressure. In a tough game. You don't want to see him with the ball."[92]

In Havlicek's case, such behavior became as much second nature to him as brushing his teeth or putting on his pants each morning. "Pressure is a mental thing," he once explained. "I've never allowed it to affect me because I have confidence. I don't get upset or panic if I make a mistake or take a bad shot. I've always lived by the percentages. I know they'll even out over the course of a game or a season. Whenever I've been in a slump—and I've had several in my career—I do other things, like working harder on defense or setting picks. I never press or force shots during a slump because I realize they are part of the game. I don't totally ignore shooting slumps. When they happen, I usually take extra practice. There's always a reason. It's usually the rhythm, so I'm confident the problem will disappear as quickly as it arrived. The worst thing a player can do is think about his mistakes and shooting slumps when he's on the court."[93]

For this reason, Havlicek contended he never had to get himself "mentally ready" for a game. He instead focused his energies on keeping his body in peak physical condition for the long haul of the NBA season. "I have a very simple routine during the season—plenty of sleep and a lot to eat," he said. "Not too many people like to accompany me when I go out to eat, because they know it will cost them a lot of money trying to keep pace with my intake. I'm not into health foods, but I'm conscious of the right things to eat. I have to eat four or five times a day in order to play 40 minutes a game."[94] Indeed, the large food intake helped fuel the hyperkinetic style he displayed so prominently on the basketball floor. As syndicated sports columnist Milton Gross wrote, "There is an injection of Krypton in John as he hurtles toward the basket with the ball or goes up for the rebound. He doesn't have the fluid grace of Oscar

Robertson or the speed of Jerry West or the water bug maneuverability of Walt Frazier or the pile driving strength of Rudy LaRusso, but there is no other in pro basketball who can play the front or backcourt with such an admirable blend of brute force, bouncy fancy and unrelieved stamina."[95] Knicks forward Bill Bradley concurred: "He's always in motion. The Celtics look for him constantly. He's a very good shotmaker, he drives, he plays defense exceptionally well. He's by far the most difficult player I have to play against."[96] For his part, Havlicek liked to boast that he had never felt exhausted during a contest. "Playing an entire game isn't that big a deal to me," he said. "I move about the same whether I'm in the frontcourt or the backcourt, so that it really isn't a factor. What you have to remember is that there are a lot of chances to rest during a game. For example, it takes nearly two hours to play 48 minutes of basketball, so for 70 minutes I'm actually resting. Maybe it would be tougher if I couldn't sleep on the road. Some players can't, you know. They have to be in a hotel room or at home to sleep. But me—I can sleep anywhere—in planes, buses, taxis, anywhere. The only difference for me over the years is that the longer I've stayed around the more difficult it's been for me to concentrate."[97]

Given the explosiveness and versatility of Havlicek's game, it seemed only appropriate that he was used primarily as a "sixth man," a role that entailed coming off the bench and providing his team with an instant spark on either offense or defense. "I could start him if I had to," Auerbach once said. "I don't start him because to me he's more valuable coming off the bench. He lights a fire under the team. He's the ideal swingman. Besides, I never thought it was too important which five players started a game. I figure it's the five guys you have in the end of the game that counts."[98]

As the seasons progressed, Havlicek became more and more of a major contributor to his team's success. He posted regular season averages of 19.9, 18.3, 18.8, 21.4, and 20.7 points between 1963 and 1968, while helping the Celtics capture four NBA titles during that span. In addition, he acquired a reputation for being a gutsy defender, one who could come up with the big defensive stop late in a ballgame. This was certainly the case during the deciding game of the 1965 Eastern Division playoffs, when Havlicek stole an inbounds pass from Hal Greer with 5 seconds left to preserve a one-point Celtics victory over the Philadelphia 76ers at the Garden. "I was guarding Chet Walker,"

Havlicek later recalled. "Now I know Chet isn't going to cut towards the basket. There are three of their men behind me, because I can see just one other 76er standing on a line with Chet. The man who has the ball out of bounds has 5 seconds to send the ball into the court. I wasn't counting aloud, but I sensed that there were three seconds elapsed and the ball hadn't come in. Now I figure that I can take a peek back at what's going on. . . . At the same time I can watch Walker out of the corner of my eye. I had both the man passing in and Walker pretty much in sight. So now I sense something fast is going to happen. And it does. Greer throws the ball in. My hands were in the air. I flicked at it with my right hand towards Sam Jones who was behind me guarding John Kerr. And then I saw Sam catch it and away I went towards the other end, and Sam after me dribbling the ball. So that's what happened. I was very lucky. But I'm glad I came through at the end that way."[99]

The unforgettable play, which Celtics broadcaster Johnny Most made famous with his timeless "Havlicek stole the ball!" call, marked a turning point in Havlicek's career. No longer would he be looked on as just another role player on a team of superstars. Henceforward, he would be seen as a superstar in his own right, whose offense and defense could collectively spell the difference between victory and defeat for the Celtics. Bitter rivals like Wilt Chamberlain sensed this immediately after Philadelphia's gut-wrenching loss to Boston. "That kid is a great ballplayer, and I mean great!" Chamberlain gushed. "He's made for the Celtics, and tonight was just the right type of game for guys like him. . . . He's great when it's hell-bent-for leather because he's not afraid to mix it up, and he can kill you both ways."[100]

Havlicek's rising status was confirmed two years later when newly appointed Celtics player-coach Bill Russell named him team captain, an honor that only Russell, Bob Cousy, and Frank Ramsey had ever enjoyed. "He deserves it," Russell said. "It will give him even more chances to show his leadership abilities. I expect him to do a lot, including yelling at referees. Havlicek plays just about as much as I do and I see no reason to any longer keep both the job of coach and Captain."[101] Havlicek took his new responsibilities seriously and provided more than his share of inspirational leadership. Perhaps the most conspicuous example of this occurred during the 1968 Eastern Division playoffs, when the Celtics found themselves down three games to one to the defending world champion Philadelphia 76ers. Prior to Game 5, a determined Havlicek marched into the locker room and wrote "Pride" on the blackboard in large letters. "That's very important," Havlicek said. "Pride might be just that little thing that can push you to get the [play-off] money."[102] This motivational tour de force apparently had its intended effect. For while no NBA team had ever recovered from a 3–1 playoff deficit, the Celtics defied history and the odds by coming back and taking the series in seven games. "The things other people laughed at," Tom Sanders said, "the Celtics believed in."[103] And no one was a truer believer than John Havlicek.

This winning attitude, however, appeared to desert the Celtics when they faced off against the Lakers in Los Angeles on November 19. The Lakers administered a 116–106 drubbing of the Celtics before a partisan crowd of 15,878 at the Forum. Having built a comfortable 6-point margin at halftime on a torrid team shooting percentage of 64.1 percent, the Celtics proceeded to get blown away in the third quarter as Elgin Baylor, Tom Hawkins, and Wilt Chamberlain reeled off 10 unanswered points to start off the period. Altogether, the Lakers outshot the Celtics, 34–21, for the quarter, as Baylor collected ten of his team-high 30 points for the game. Things continued to go downhill for the Celtics in the final frame as 6-foot-7-inch rookie Bill Hewitt tossed in 10 of L.A.'s first 15 points to give his team a double-digit lead they would not relinquish for the rest of the evening. Havlicek led the Boston offense with a game-high 32 points while Sam Jones chipped in with 17. "That was a good second half," Lakers coach Bill van Breda Kolff told reporters afterward. "We really had had some movement out there in the third quarter and early in the fourth."[104] Russell, who recorded 6 points and 21 rebounds, offered no excuses for his team's performance. "I just think we weren't really crisp with our passes in the second half," the player-coach said. "The poor passing enabled them to get some breakaways and that put us in a hole."[105]

While the game represented only the fourth Celtics' loss of the season, its significance went well beyond the final box score. For it represented the resumption of a personal duel that had come to define the very quintessence of professional basketball in the 1960s.

Nobody
Roots
for Goliath

Bill Russell versus Wilt Chamberlain. It was the seminal rivalry that captured the imagination of the American sporting public in the 1960s and transported the game of basketball to unimagined new heights of interest and popularity. Indeed, to discuss the NBA of this era without mentioning the memorable on-court battles these two legendary talents waged is to do a disservice to the historic record. That is because the Russell-Chamberlain showdowns became the main reason why millions of fans attended games or watched the NBA on network television during these turbulent years of war and rapid political and social change. As writer Tony Kornheiser later recalled, "We gathered in dorm lounges across America to watch the NBA, usually to watch Boston play Philadelphia. More specifically, to watch Bill Russell play Wilt Chamberlain. Actually, to watch Russell beat Chamberlain."[1]

And truth be told, Russell did prevail more times than not over Chamberlain. In 142 regular season games, Russell's teams possessed an 85–57 record when facing squads led by Chamberlain. This dominance carried over into the playoffs as Russell's teams held a commanding 29–20 edge over Chamberlain's in 49 postseason contests, including a perfect 4–0 mark in Game 7 situations. Yet when it came to individual statistics, Chamberlain was by far the clear winner. In head-to-head matchups during the regular season, Chamberlain scored 4,077 points for an average of 28.7 while Russell could muster only 2,060 points for an average of 14.5. In the rebounding department, Chamberlain also

Nobody roots for Goliath (Wilt Chamberlain)
Courtesy of the Naismith Memorial Basketball Hall of Fame, Springfield, Massachusetts

took top honors, pulling down 4,072 for a 28.7 average to Russell's 3,373 for a 23.7 average. Nor did Chamberlain's performance drop off in the playoffs as he averaged 25.7 points and 28 rebounds to Russell's 14.9 points and 23.3 rebounds.

But was Chamberlain undisputedly superior to Russell as a basketball player? That depends, according to those who played alongside each either as teammates or opponents. "I think Wilt has been more versatile and a greater player than Russell, but I think Russell has been a more valuable player because he is more settled-down, is better able to fit in with a team, and most important can rise to the heights far better when it is needed," opined Los Angeles Lakers guard Jerry West in his book *Mr. Clutch: The Jerry West Story.* "For one series or one game, Russell is superior, and in pro basketball the final laurels of each season usually rest on what happens in one last series or even just one last game."[2] Former Russell teammate and longtime NBA broadcaster Tom Heinsohn agreed with West. While conceding Chamberlain's statistical superiority, Heinsohn contended that no player had a larger impact on the outcome of a game than Russell. "If you could ask anyone [from that era] like a Bob Petit or what have you who was better, Russell or Chamberlain, they'll all tell you Russell," he said. "The reason is not only did [Russell] block shots which they didn't used to count, but he would totally disrupt your offense and make you come up with an offense that could beat him specifically. He was worth 60, 70 points a game for us."[3]

For his part, Chamberlain generally scoffed at such comparisons. "You hear about all those big confrontations between Bill Russell and Wilt Chamberlain . . . there were no confrontations," he said. "I scored more points against the Celtics than anybody else, and there were three and four people playing me, not just Bill Russell. Nobody really cares about that, it's not important. But I care because it's something that's personal to me. We all want to get credit for what we've done."[4] Not one to downplay his own accomplishments, Russell never took undue offense at such remarks. He admired and respected Chamberlain's talents enough to see that they magnified his own importance to the Celtics as a premier defensive player. Chamberlain "was very tall, very strong, very smart, ergo a problem," Russell later confirmed. "I had determined before he got here what I would have to do to beat him. His statistics had nothing to do with my statistics. He felt for his team to have its best chance to win, he'd have to be at his best. I felt I had to work with my

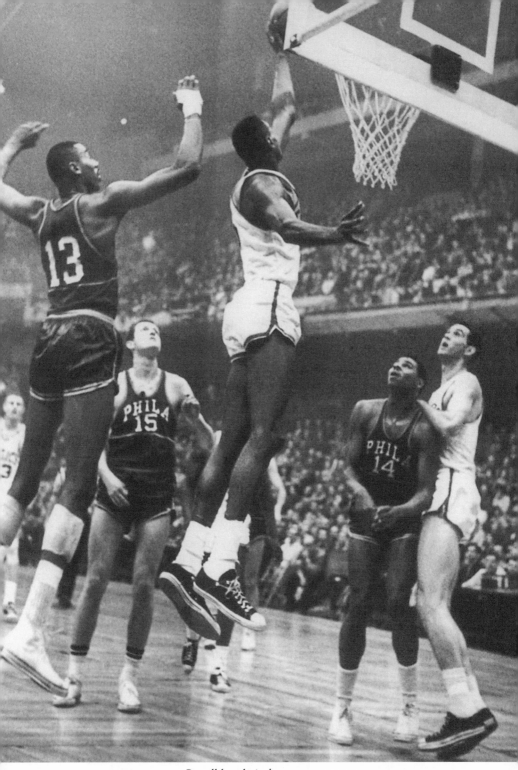

Russell knocks it down
Courtesy of the Boston Public Library

teammates."[5] Indeed, whereas Chamberlain felt compelled to dominate the stat sheet, Russell was more concerned with improving the overall level of play of those around him. "Like our offense," Russell once explained. "It's fast break. The sooner Cooz or [Bill] Sharman gets the ball, the sooner we're in business. They know I'll get them the ball. I use myself as a decoy a lot. I get the ball in the pivot, make a move to the middle to draw somebody else in, and hit the free man, maybe Heinsohn. Tommy's man comes at me, but he's got to go back to Tommy. He's coming back, Heinsohn can drive on him or if he doesn't come back, Tommy's got the shot. In the books that doesn't show as an assist for me, but the last two years I still have been second in assists on our team. I could score only ten points but still help the team win."[6]

Personality wise, there was also a marked difference between the two arch rivals. Russell was an intensely private individual who liked to keep his emotions tightly under wrap and out of public view. Chamberlain, on the other hand, was an outgoing and demonstrative sort who relished being the center of attention. When approached by complete strangers in airports or restaurants, Chamberlain without fail was polite and courteous while Russell was more likely to be cold and dismissive. Ever alert to gaining a competitive edge on the basketball floor, Russell and his teammates used Chamberlain's friendly, laid-back demeanor to their advantage. "He only had one flaw," Russell explained. "He was a nice man. We'd beat up on him. He would never hurt anybody. I would."[7] To be sure, Chamberlain was so solicitous of his opponents' well-being that he would alter his own shot selection rather than risk inflicting a potentially crippling injury on them. "I once tried to guard Wilt near the basket," recalled a rival forward. "And I somehow got my hand up near the basket, trying to block the shot. Wilt started to dunk that ball—but then he stopped and tossed a shot off the backboard. It went in—but I didn't care! I still had my hand attached to my wrist. I'm convinced Wilt changed his shot just to keep from hurting me."[8] This less than hell-bent approach did not please his coaches, especially two-time NBA champion Alex Hannum. "I can't say how many times I wanted him to be more aggressive," he said. "He was afraid he'd break a guy's arm if he really slammed the ball down. I told him, 'You break a guy's arm just once and just see the respect you get.' He'd look at me as if I was crazy."[9] Nevertheless, there were times when Chamberlain did lose his cool. One evening Chamberlain grew incensed at Red Auerbach for arguing with a referee in the middle of a game. "That's enough out of you," Chamberlain menacingly told Auerbach. Russell wasted little time in getting in between them. "If you're going after Red, you've got to go through me," he said. Although angered, Chamberlain backed off. "Bill was madder than hell and Wilt knew better than to push it any further," Auerbach later told biographer Joe Fitzgerald. "I've always maintained Chamberlain is the strongest man in the world, but I wouldn't want to bet on who'd walk away if he and Russell really mixed it up."[10] This occasional unpleasantness on the court did not detract from Russell and Chamberlain's tight personal bond off the court, however. They made a point of sharing meals and being frequent guests at each other's homes throughout their playing days. In fact, whenever Boston was scheduled to play Philadelphia on Thanksgiving, Russell would spend the day eating turkey and mashed potatoes at the Chamberlain family homestead. But once game time arrived, the cordiality and hospitality ended. "He'd go out and kick the [expletive] out of me," Russell said.[11]

Luckily for Russell, the latter was not the case when the two first met in Boston on November 7, 1959, Chamberlain's fourth game as a pro. "I'd been getting information; what works, what doesn't against him," Russell recalled. "No matter how prepared you are, you're not prepared. I decided I'm not going to look up to him."[12] This approach was quickly abandoned, however, when Russell lined up against Chamberlain for the opening tapoff. Instead of staring directly into Chamberlain's eyes, Russell saw only his chest. "So I looked [up]," Russell related. And what he saw was truly frightening from a defender's point of view. Chamberlain was a seven-foot wall of muscle possessing the speed, grace, and endurance of an elite track athlete. "What are you going to do with this?" Russell asked himself.[13] He soon provided an answer by giving one of the best individual game performances of his entire career. While Chamberlain narrowly outscored Russell, 30–22, the Celtics center took half as many shots and held a 35–28 rebounding edge in a convincing 115–106 Boston victory. Defensively, Russell also achieved the upper hand as he repeatedly thwarted Chamberlain's drives to the basket. As *Sports Illustrated* reported, "Every time [Chamberlain] tried to use his chief weapon, a fall-away jump shot, Russell went up with him; Russell's large hand flicked away at his vision, slapped at the ball, once blocked it outright—a shocking experience for Wilt Chamberlain. All told, in this man-to-man situation Chamberlain hit exactly four baskets; the rest of his 30 points were made on tip-ins and a few dunk shots, in which, free of Russell, he stuffed the ball into the basket from above it."[14] Afterward, the two foes expressed nothing but warm admiration for each other. "Man, he sure keeps you thinking," Chamberlain said. "He made me take some awfully poor shots. I figured he'd play my moves. You know, move every time I did. But he didn't. He played my shots—and he seemed to know every time I was going to shoot. . . . [He's] the best I ever played against. Guys told me that you could over-play Bill to his right and that he'd never go left on you. Well, that's wrong fella. He was tougher than I expected."[15] Asked for his own thoughts, Russell replied, "Well, he sure tires you out. And when I say tires I mean mentally as well as physically. You can't relax against him—not even for a second. . . . He's about all I can handle now—the toughest I ever played against."[16]

How Chamberlain got to be "the toughest" is a story of hard work, soaring ambition, and an almost boundless faith in his ability to succeed. He was born on August 21, 1936, in Philadelphia, Pennsylvania, the eighth of eleven children of a struggling working-class family. His two oldest siblings died before they reached the age of two. Chamberlain's father, William, was initially employed as a welder in a shipyard, before moving on to a janitorial position at a local publishing company. His mother, Olivia, worked as a domestic to bring extra money into the household and to generally make ends meet. As a young boy, Chamberlain attempted to supplement this modest family income by delivering newspapers and performing a variety of odd jobs such as shoveling snow, cleaning cellars, and washing windows. "I always hustled, always looked for a way to make a few extra cents," he later wrote.[17]

Despite the obvious economic constraints, Chamberlain and his surviving six sisters and two brothers never went without life's necessities while growing up in the racially mixed Haddington section of West Philadelphia. There was always food on the table, clothes on their backs, and a decent roof over their heads. "We were just raised the way I wish everybody would be raised," Chamberlain once remarked of his tight-knit family. "So that was just a lucky start. We never talked about bigotry. We never talked about anyone being any different than anybody else. We had white neighbors who lived right next door to me. We went to a Jewish store on this corner, an Italian store on that corner. And they all became just people."[18]

Basketball did not enter the picture until his early teen years. Up to this point, Chamberlain was chiefly concerned with running as his main athletic pursuit. In fact, he seriously entertained thoughts of becoming an Olympic Games track champion. He dismissed basketball as a "sissy game." Then, according to Chamberlain, he began to grow. "One summer—I think I was 14 then—I went down to Virginia to my uncle's farm, and I grew about 4 inches in seven weeks or so," he remembered. "When I got home, my mother almost didn't recognize me. I had to talk her into letting me in the front door."[19] By the time he was 14, Chamberlain stood an imposing 6 feet 7 inches, and he would top off at over 7 feet before he graduated from high school. It was during this period that he acquired a nickname that would stay with him for the rest of his life—"the Big Dipper." He literally had to dip under doorways in order to enter a room. As good humored as it was, this sobriquet, along with the even more popular "Wilt the Stilt" later on, seemed to convey on Chamberlain an unwanted status. Indeed, he always felt people were too quick to dismiss his prodigious athletic accomplishments as a product of his height. "I understand being 7-foot tall leaves it hard for people of average stature to understand what it is to be an athlete at that size to begin with," he complained. "It's easy for them to see someone smaller's athletic abilities. In gymnastics, a girl is 4-2 and she is applauded even more when she does her routine well. She has a distinct advantage. Nobody looks at it that way, but she is a giant in her sport. People are mesmerized by size. They always think it's a distinct advantage for the guy who has the most height. That simply is not true. Most of your superstars in [the NBA] have been 6-5, 6-6."[20]

Given the tremendous growth spurt he experienced as a teenager, Chamberlain found himself constantly approached by friends and schoolmates about playing basketball. "Man, as tall as you are, you should play basketball," he was told. Eventually worn down by these entreaties, Chamberlain reluctantly took up the sport and to his great surprise found that he actually loved it. He became so totally immersed in the game that he and his friends would lock themselves in a local gym on many a warm summer day and play until the sun went down. "You could see it when we were in seventh grade," recalled Jimmy Sadler, Chamberlain's junior high and high school teammate. "He would be great not because he was tall, but because he could do so many things. Back then, pretty much everyone who was tall was awkward too. Not

Wilt. He was graceful. He could easily run the floor. And he had great coordination. By the ninth grade—I remember this distinctly—I was thinking, 'He could be in the pros *now*.'"[21]

Chamberlain quickly established himself as the most accomplished schoolboy basketball player in Philadelphia, setting still-standing scoring records for points in a game (90) and points in a high school career (2,206). Ensconced at the center position, Chamberlain became the main reason why his Overbrook High School squad captured two city titles during his three varsity seasons. In those days, high school did not begin until the tenth grade; otherwise more championships and scoring records would have been in the offing for the young hoop star. Suffice it to say, however, Chamberlain made a lasting impression. "The three years I spent [at Overbrook] were the best three years of my life," he later claimed.[22]

In the summer months between high school seasons, Chamberlain continued to hone his basketball skills by playing at Kutsher's Country Club in the Catskills region of upstate New York. By day he worked as a bellhop at the resort while at night he jumped center against some of that era's best collegiate basketball talent. "It was a sort of breeding ground for future professionals," Chamberlain remembered. "Every summer resort up there had its own basketball team made up of college kids who needed jobs for the summer. They worked a little and played a little. And who was the coach at Kutsher's? The man with the cigar."[23] A moonlighting Red Auerbach was indeed his coach, but almost immediately the two strong-willed individuals were at odds over how the game should be played. "Don't you think, Chamberlain," Auerbach roared, "that it might be sort of a good idea to defense your man from *in front* of him instead of *behind* him? What the hell are you doing back there?" While others might have withered under such displays of bellicosity, Chamberlain simply shrugged them off. He went on to cheekily explain to Auerbach that defending from behind prevented an opposing player from wheeling around and getting off a good shot against him. Chamberlain's unusually long arms, which had a tendency to catch opponents in a smothering vise grip, saw to that. "Looking back on it," Chamberlain would recall in 1965, "I think maybe it was my attitude that first touched off Auerbach. You know, I wasn't the most *modest* kid in town, and I had a lot of moves for a high school freshm[a]n playing with the big boys. And when Red would call practice he would sort of talk to me in that voice that catches you right here, right between the ribs."[24]

Despite the personal friction, Auerbach thought enough of Chamberlain's basketball abilities to devise a scheme that potentially could have put him in a Boston uniform. "Why don't you go to Harvard, kid?" he innocently asked Chamberlain one day. "And then we'll be able to pick you off in the territorial draft for the Celtics."[25] A league rule that dated back to 1946, the territorial draft was designed to let struggling NBA teams "piggyback" on the popularity and success of collegiate players performing within geographic proximity to their designated hoop operations. A team was given the exclusive right to sign a player in its territory, in exchange for giving up its first pick in the regular NBA draft, which followed the territorial draft. This allowed moribund franchises like the Cincinnati Royals, for example, to have first dibs on future Hall of Famer and University of Cincinnati backcourt sensation Oscar Robertson. The risk of Robertson entering the regular NBA draft and plying his trade for another city was therefore eliminated altogether. Similarly, by arranging to have Chamberlain attend Harvard, Auerbach was banking on the hope that Boston could land Chamberlain as its own territorial draft pick. Unfortunately for the gruff-spoken Celtics coach, wily Philadelphia Warriors owner Eddie Gottlieb outflanked him. Desperately needing a local box office attraction of his own, Gottlieb used his considerable influence around the league to secure exclusive territorial draft rights to Chamberlain while still in high school. "The league felt sorry for Eddie," Auerbach later explained to writer Terry Pluto, "so they made a special provision for him. We didn't like it in Boston, but back then deals were made all the time."[26]

Gottlieb and his Warriors had to wait several years before they could avail themselves of Chamberlain's unique athletic gifts, however. For Chamberlain became the object of an intense recruiting war by all the major collegiate basketball powers in the country. When the dust finally settled, Chamberlain surprised many observers by choosing to go to the University of Kansas in Lawrence, Kansas. "The main reason was [then Kansas coach] Phog Allen," Chamberlain claimed in 1961. "I wanted to play under the best and I figured he was the man."[27] Allen, who had been instructed in the intricacies of the game by none other than basketball inventor and founder Dr. James Naismith himself, certainly wasn't shy about expressing his interest in the Philadelphia native. "With him, we'll never lose a game," he said, "we could win the national championship with Wilt, two sorority girls, and two Phi Beta Kappas."[28] Left unsaid, however, was the fact that Chamberlain received several under-the-table financial inducements to attend Kansas, including cash payments that eventually added up to between $15,000 and $20,000. Rumors of such a lucrative arrangement prompted New York sportswriter Leonard Lewin to cynically speculate that when Chamberlain eventually entered the NBA, he would have to take a "cut" in salary.[29]

As events proved, Kansas turned out to be an unfortunate choice for Chamberlain. One of only a small handful of blacks attending the conservative midwestern school, Chamberlain was constantly confronted by racism in all its virulent forms. Since he had not encountered much prejudice growing up as a person of color in Philadelphia, he was perhaps not as prepared as he should have been about the pernicious race situation in the heartland. "Well, it took me about a week to realize the whole area around Lawrence, except for one black section of Kansas City, was infested with segregation," he later wrote.[30] After seeking out the advice of some alumni, Chamberlain boldly took it upon himself to integrate various eating establishments surrounding the campus. "I'd just sit there and glower and wait," he recalled. "Finally, they'd serve me. I never got turned down or bad-mouthed or anything, and when I got through, other blacks would follow me."[31] Still, the overall experience must have been discouraging. Chamberlain wanted to be judged not on his skin color, but on his own talents and abilities as a person. Kansas did not appear to afford him that opportunity.

In terms of basketball, Chamberlain was equally disappointed. Phog Allen had to step down as coach before Chamberlain played his first varsity game, due to the university's mandatory retirement age policy. Allen was seventy. His successor, former assistant coach Dick Harp, proved less than satisfactory in Chamberlain's eyes. True, Harp piloted Kansas to an elite nationally ranked status, but he did so on the coattails of his enormously gifted sophomore center. Indeed, Chamberlain was an athletic marvel to behold during these years. "No man in the country can cover him," contended Oklahoma State coach Hank Iba. "We concede him his points and try to blanket the other four men."[32] Statistics bore out Iba's argument. In his first varsity campaign alone, Chamberlain proved an unstoppable force averaging 29.4 points per game, fourth best in the nation. Already the comparisons with Bill Russell were being made. "Wilt shoots better than Bill Russell," maintained one close observer of the national hoop scene. "He's faster, and he handles the ball better. The only place Russell has an edge on him is defensively."[33]

Yet for all his offensive fireworks, Chamberlain could not bring home a national championship to Kansas. The closest he got was his sophomore year when the number one ranked and undefeated University of North Carolina Tar Heels edged out Kansas, 54–53, in three overtimes in the deciding contest of the 1957 NCAA tournament. "We made it a personal challenge," said Tar Heels coach Frank McGuire. "It was North Carolina against Chamberlain. We had three men around him on every play—a man in front, one behind and a third who dropped off as soon as the ball was thrown in."[34] Despite the defensive pressure, Chamberlain still managed to pour in a game-high 23 points. But the image of his "invincibility" as a basketball player was irretrievably damaged. Fairly or unfairly, he was now looked on as someone who could not win the big game. He was, in effect, a loser. "That started it," he later bitterly commented. "A triple-overtime loss to an undefeated team."[35]

After another disappointing season his junior year, in which Kansas failed to qualify for the NCAA tournament, Chamberlain opted for an early exit strategy. Typically, he had his own pragmatic reasons for leaving school so abruptly. "Money," he later told writer Dick Schaap. "I realized that I was going to make my living from basketball. I also realized that my career wasn't endless, that I had to make money while I was young. I felt that another year of college and the college degree weren't going to help me enough to compensate for the loss of a year of earning power. So I turned pro. That was the reason."[36]

At the time of his decision, he stated he would arrange a "big barnstorming tour" around the country, while waiting a year for his NBA eligibility to kick in. Then-existing league rules prohibited undergraduates or dropouts like Chamberlain from playing pro basketball until their college class had graduated. Chamberlain's barnstorming plans, however, were quickly abandoned when the Harlem Globetrotters approached him about playing a year for them for the then princely sum of $65,000. The understanding was that Chamberlain would be permitted to move on to the NBA at the conclusion of the pact, as his first choice was to play for his hometown Philadelphia Warriors. Chamberlain enthusiastically agreed to these terms and later claimed his experience with the famous traveling basketball troupe was instructive, insofar as he learned things about the game that he otherwise would not have had he remained in Kansas. He didn't "clown much," he confessed. "Toward the end of the year with the Trotters, I played outside. I wanted to learn how to dribble, how to handle the ball. I couldn't have done that in college."[37] He also got to witness firsthand the tremendous talent of Trotters' star Meadowlark Lemon. "Meadowlark was the most sensational, awesome, incredible basketball player I've ever seen," Chamberlain gushed. "People would say it would be Dr. J or even Michael Jordan. For me it would be Meadowlark Lemon."[38] Indeed, Lemon possessed an acrobatic flair and shooting touch that few have ever matched. In the strength department, however, Chamberlain had the clear advantage. Once he got Lemon so riled up during an exhibition game that the Trotters' court leader assaulted him in the locker room afterward. "But I saw him out of the corner of my eye, and I grabbed him in mid-air and held him over my head like a barbell until he stopped screaming," Chamberlain recounted.[39]

Such on- and off-court high jinks ended for Chamberlain when he joined the Philadelphia Warriors for the 1959–60 season. He would now be playing in games that officially counted, while attempting to live up to the standards of excellence he had set for himself in college. On the latter score, he was wholly successful as he averaged 37.6 points and 26.9 rebounds a game, to go along with Most Valuable Player and Rookie of the Year honors. "He's tremendous, there's no doubt about it," apprised Carl Braun of the New York Knicks. "But it's not something we haven't seen before—like Russell, I mean. He disorganizes you under the basket the same way. With Wilt, of course, there's that offense on top of it, which is better than Russell's." St. Louis Hawks coach Ed Macauley had been likewise impressed, declaring in the preseason that Chamberlain represented the "greatest single force" to come into pro basketball. "We plan to play him straight and see what happens," he said. "If we're not successful, then we'll do anything. We may try pressing him in the dressing room or deflating the ball."[40]

Chamberlain's only misstep came in the playoffs against Boston. Facing the defending world champions in Game 2 of the Eastern Division Finals, he got into a fistfight with burly Celtics' forward Tom Heinsohn. Upset that Heinsohn was impeding his progress downcourt, Chamberlain snarled, "You do that to me again, I'm going to knock you on your ass." Heinsohn, who was under strict orders by Red Auerbach to stand in the big center's way, foolishly declined to take heed of the warning. An enraged Chamberlain proceeded to deposit Heinsohn on his backside and take an ill-advised swing that in hindsight might have cost his team a world championship. "I slid from the top of the key to midcourt," Heinsohn later said of the altercation. "He goes to level me with a punch, lets it fly, and I'm saying, 'Did I leave a will?' But he hits [Warriors teammate] Tom Gola in the back of his head, and he breaks his hand. He kept playing with the broken hand."[41] Though he managed a record 50 points in Game 5, Chamberlain's hand hurt enough that he was effectively neutralized for the rest of the series, which Boston won in six games. "We might have won that series if I hadn't been injured," he lamented years afterward.[42] Adding to Chamberlain's disappointment was the fact that he was beginning to be unfavorably compared to Bill Russell. "This series proved what a man can do against the odds apparently stacked against him," commented Celtic supersub Frank Ramsey, when asked to appraise the competitive differences between the two centers. "When it was all important in several games that were close," he continued, "it was Russell who was making the big plays."[43]

The combination of the frustrating playoff loss and the constant physical pounding he endured during his rookie season convinced Chamberlain that the time was right to hang up his sneakers. "If I continue I feel it may be bad for me and for my race," he said in a statement released to the media. "If I come back next year and score less than I did last year, I may have to punch eight or nine guys in the face. I may lose my poise and I don't want that."[44] That Chamberlain brought up the subject of race in his decision to retire was not insignificant. Although several blacks had entered the league since Chuck Cooper integrated the sport in 1950, most team rosters remained overwhelmingly white. Popular prejudices against persons of color still carried the day in many quarters of the NBA. Indeed, it was not uncommon for a great player such as Russell to hear an opponent call him a "Black Gorilla" to his face. In remarks to the press following his surprise announcement, Chamberlain confirmed that racial problems had "some connection" with his decision "but they weren't the entire reason."[45]

He gave a hint as to the other reasons why he was leaving the game in a provocative *Look* magazine article he penned at the end of the season. In the piece, which was entitled "Basketball Has Ganged Up on Me," Chamberlain recounted the gross injustices he believed had been perpetrated against him during the recently concluded basketball campaign. "The National Basketball Association has two standards of officiating: one for the league as a whole, another for me, Wilt Chamberlain of the Philadelphia Warriors," he said. "Until they start calling fouls committed against me on the same basis as for everybody else, I'm not going to develop my full scoring potential and team value. And the Warriors are not going to beat out the Boston Celtics for the Eastern divisional championship of the N.B.A."[46]

He argued that teams were setting up illegal zone defenses to limit his scoring opportunities and league officials were deliberately looking the other way. "The only team in the league that plays me with one man is the Boston Celtics with Bill Russell," he wrote. "They can do this because Russell is the game's defensive ace. Bill is 6 feet 9½, with long arms and beautiful timing. He seems to hang suspended in the air almost half the night. He makes me shoot higher than I usually do, and his tremendous reach leaves my hook shot useless." Everyone else in the league, however, chose to defense him by assigning at least two "hatchet men" on him in every game. "They give you a real beating," he complained. "The body contact is rising in intensity, and I'm in the middle of it. There are some great shovers in this league. I start a play in the pivot, end up in the corner and never know how I got there."[47]

Chamberlain attributed the reluctance of league officials to crack down on these offenses to an alleged bias against big men in the sport. "I guess the officials figure this way: 'From a flat-footed stance, Chamberlain can reach 9 feet 6. He can make a standing jump of 3 feet 9. At the top of his jump, he can reach 13 feet 3 above the upper edge of the basketball rim. So we've got to give the defense more than average leeway to cope with him.' I feel it would be just as logical to say that a 250-pound fullback who can run 100 yards in 9 seconds could be tripped and slugged by the defense without a penalty being walked off."[48]

As expected, Chamberlain's retirement announcement rocked the entire basketball establishment. "The unfortunate aspect of the whole matter," remarked NBA commissioner Maurice Podoloff, "is that the boy hadn't even come into his prime. I am sure he would have broken all the records next season that he created during the past one."[49] Warriors owner Ed Gottlieb was equally taken aback. "The move comes as a complete shock to me," he claimed.[50] Not surprisingly, opposing players had somewhat different takes on the situation. "Chamberlain feels he's being pushed around more than anybody else in the league," Celtics' team captain Bob Cousy sarcastically commented. "The guy has only averaged more than 36 points per game, broken the rebound record and had more foul shots than anyone else. How easy does he want it?"[51] Teammate Tom Heinsohn was also unmoved. "Too bad about him," he said.

"He gets away with more on the floor than any player in the league and he's always crying. Let him quit."[52]

Chamberlain did not remain "retired" for long, however. After rejecting an offer by Abe Saperstein to bring him back to the Globetrotters, he had a change of heart and signed a new three-year deal worth an estimated $75,000 a season with the Warriors. "Eddie Gottlieb finally talked me into returning by appealing to both my pride and my pocketbook," he later revealed.[53] Gottlieb told his young superstar that if he continued playing, he stood an excellent chance of breaking every major record in the book. The challenge was one Chamberlain could not easily ignore. The subject of greatness was constantly on his mind. Just as baseball Hall of Famer Ted Williams wanted to walk down the street and hear people say, "There goes Ted Williams, the greatest hitter who ever lived," the same held true for Chamberlain.[54] His burning ambition was to become the greatest basketball player in history.

The only problem was that in his efforts to be the best, Chamberlain more times than not sacrificed the good of the team for individual statistical glory. Indeed, winning never seemed to be high on his list of priorities. Breaking records and grabbing headlines were. And therein lay the central paradox of Chamberlain's illustrious hoop career. He was an individualist in a game that demanded teamwork and personal sacrifice. Sure, a Satch Sanders might have been able to score 20 points a game and achieve All-Star status, but the Celtics never would have won as many championships in the 1960s if he had. Sanders's role on the team was that of a defensive specialist and, in his own words, all it took was "one man crossing over into another man's specialty to spoil the balance of that special machine."[55] Chamberlain was never quite able to grasp this concept as selflessness appeared beyond him. For team success usually took a back seat when individual accomplishments were at stake. A case in point was his stubborn insistence on never fouling out of a game. On the surface this objective seemed laudable enough, but on closer inspection it showed how truly self-absorbed Chamberlain could be on the basketball court. "When he got that fourth foul, his game would change," John Havlicek later observed. "I don't know how many potential victories he may have cheated his team out of by not really playing after he got into foul trouble."[56]

Chamberlain recaptured the imagination of the basketball world on March 2, 1962. It was on this date he set a record that, along with Joe

DiMaggio's 56-game hitting streak in 1941, has never been equaled in the annals of professional sport. Before a sparse but enthusiastic crowd of 4,124, he scored 100 points in a late-season contest against the New York Knicks in Hershey, Pennsylvania. "It was something you couldn't believe," recalled broadcaster Bill Campbell, who called the game. "As he got closer to the 100, he just seemed to will it."[57] Chamberlain's offensive outburst shattered a mark he had set earlier in the season for most points in a game (78). "I wasn't even thinking of hitting 100 but after putting in nine straight free throws I was thinking about a foul shooting record," he told reporters afterward.[58] As if to add an exclamation point to his otherworldly performance, he hit a record 28 of 32 from the foul line and grabbed 25 rebounds. "It was my greatest game," he said.[59] Few would disagree. "Wilt was such a phenom that we took it for granted," game referee Pete D'Ambrosio later confessed to author Terry Pluto. "When he scored 100, it was mentioned on the news and in the papers, but it wasn't the kind of huge event that it would be today. That's because we weren't able to put Wilt in the context like we can now."[60] His Warrior teammates seemed to sense early that something special was unfolding, as they repeatedly fed Chamberlain the ball. But according to an Associated Press account of the game, New York tried to foil this strategy by stalling their offense and mobbing Chamberlain on the defensive end. Neither approach worked as the Warrior center also set league records for field goals (36), most points for a half (59) and most points in a quarter (31). Needless to say, Philadelphia won the contest, 169–147, despite allowing three Knicks to score over 30. "I feel confident to say that 100 points is a record that will not be broken," Hall of Famer and basketball executive Jerry West insisted decades later. "Whole teams don't even score 100 points."[61] In the years to come, Chamberlain would joke that at least 150,000 persons had come up to him to claim they were present at the historic game. "But they don't say Hershey," he said. "Most of them are New York fans who swear it was Madison Square Garden. Just yesterday was like my 19th million time a guy telling me, 'I was at that game. I was a young kid and my father took me to the Garden.' Well, first of all, the guy was older than me. I just said to myself, Oh, no, not another one."[62]

The 1961–62 season would prove memorable to Chamberlain for other reasons as well. He averaged an eye-popping 50.4 points and 25.7 rebounds a game and became the first NBA player to shoot 50 percent from the floor for an entire season. He also set league marks for field goals attempted and made. In sum, he was on a roll to which few players other than Michael Jordan could ever relate. Yet the unfavorable comparisons with Russell continued, especially after Chamberlain's Warriors squad fell to the Celtics in another bitterly fought seven-game playoff series. Early in 1962, Chamberlain took time to publicly vent his feelings on the subject. "It's my honest belief that I could do as well as Russell defensively and he could almost match me offensively if we switched teams," he argued. "What it comes down to is a matter of concentration. You can't concentrate on both defense and offense without losing a piece of each. It's physically impossible under the grind of an 80-game schedule in the NBA. So each of us emphasizes that part of the game that best serves his club." He also claimed that he did not receive any "special exhilaration" from scoring in the high double digits most games. "People don't realize the pressure of being expected to do it every night," he said. "Ask Roger Maris. If the Yankees lose, it's because he didn't hit a home run and how can you expect him to hit one every day? I'd rather score 30 a night and play more defense. I know I can do it and next year hope to do it if we're lucky to come up with a backcourt man who can hit consistently. After all, we don't have any Cousys or Sam Joneses on our team to take a lot of the load off me."[63]

In other words, Chamberlain was saying don't blame him for Philadelphia's playoff failures, blame the supposedly inadequate cast of supporting players around him. In making such a bold statement, he conveniently neglected to mention he was surrounded by formidable talents like Tom Gola, Paul Arizin, Guy Rodgers, and Tom Meschery. Arizin and Gola alone combined for thirteen All-Star game appearances between them during their standout Hall of Fame careers, while Rodgers and Meschery were good enough to make five. Chamberlain's contentions thus have a hollow ring about them. He did have good players surrounding him in the Philadelphia lineup; he simply was unable to successfully blend his talents with theirs. Still, his dismissive public comments about them were hardly a prescription for good team karma, and his remaining years with the Warriors were marred increasingly by controversy and club disunity. Wilting under the intense glare of the media spotlight, Chamberlain felt that nothing he did on the basketball court was ever good enough for the fans, coaches, and front office executives who had initially invested such high hopes in him. The expected championships never materialized, and for this Chamberlain felt he was being unfairly held responsible. "Nobody roots for Goliath," he once said.[64] Not even a dramatic change in scenery improved the situation. Beginning with the 1962–63 season, the Warriors relocated to San Francisco as Ed Gottlieb sold his franchise for $850,000 to a group of local businessmen. Though the team would capture the Western Division title in 1963–64, it came up short again in the playoff finals against Boston, who won its seventh championship in a row. Chamberlain had to deal with being a bridesmaid yet another year.

When San Francisco got off to a miserable start the following season, management singled him out for the team's shortcomings. Chamberlain grew sullen and angry. In a show of defiance, he grew a goatee like Russell, which only served to alienate the Warriors' brass even more. In the early 1960s facial hair of any sort, especially on a tall, physically imposing black man, was considered taboo. Chamberlain paid these attitudes no mind and proudly sported the goatee for the rest of his life. At this juncture the San Francisco front office had collectively made up their minds that Chamberlain had to go. He was sent packing to the newly formed Philadelphia 76ers for three players, Lee Shaffer, Paul Neumann, and Connie Dierking. Chamberlain had perhaps sealed his fate in San Francisco earlier in the season when owner Franklin Mieuli went out of his way to present him with a diamond stickpin commemorating the 1963–64 Western Division championship. "What is this piece of shit?" he scoffed.[65]

His homecoming in Philadelphia, although a relatively happy one, failed to bring him much luck against the Celtics. For the fourth time in Chamberlain's advancing pro career, his team was eliminated by Boston in the playoffs. Typically, it was accomplished in excruciating fashion. In the closing moments of the Eastern Division title game, the 76ers staged a valiant come-from-behind effort that ultimately fizzled as a pass intended for Chamberlain for the potential game winner was intercepted by budding Celtics superstar John Havlicek. Boston won, 110–109, extending its dynasty and dashing Chamberlain's hopes for an NBA championship yet another year. Even before the debilitating finish, however, Chamberlain had announced that the 1964–65 season would be his last. "I've had it," he claimed right after his trade to Philadelphia. "I'm not a selfish player about points and I've never been one. I'm tired of hearing all the blame rest on me. I'm sick of the criticism and people saying I've never played on a winning team. Everything I've done since I started playing basketball I've done under orders. Nobody can get the ball in the hole better than I and that's what every coach I've played for has wanted me to do. This is getting to be a damned joke. Year after year, depending on how the team is doing, that's the amount of abuse I get. Last season, when we won the Western Division in San Francisco, people started saying I'd become a team player. This year, because the team's in last place, I've been selfish. How do you figure it?"[66]

As before, Chamberlain's talk of leaving the game was premature. He signed a new three-year deal with Philadelphia worth $150,000 a year. This made him easily the highest paid player in the NBA, but riches alone did not satisfy him. He longed to shed his loser image, and in 1966–67 he got his wish as he led the 76ers to the promised land of an NBA championship. Though he averaged a career-low 24 points per game, he shot an incredible .683 from the floor and led the league in rebounds with 24 per game, while pacing Philadelphia to a record 68 regular season victories. As a team the 76ers averaged an impressive 125 points per game, thanks in part to Chamberlain's out of character willingness to pass off and share the scoring load with such talented teammates as Chet Walker, Hal Greer, Wally Jones, Luke Jackson, and Billy Cunningham. Indeed, he ranked third in the league in assists with 630. This newfound generosity on the court was instilled in him by new Philadelphia coach Alex Hannum, his former mentor in San Francisco. Hannum let Chamberlain know in no uncertain terms at the start of the season that he wanted him to concentrate less on scoring and more on defense, shot blocking, and rebounding. Put another way, he wanted him to play more like Bill Russell. After some initial disagreement, in which fisticuffs nearly broke out between the two, Chamberlain came around to Hannum's team-oriented approach.

"The Celtics," Hannum told a magazine reporter during the regular season, "changed the game by winning with defense. They showed that a big shot-blocker could keep you in the game. Oh, sometimes there's a weak man in there against Wilt. So we give him the ball. But against Detroit the other night Wilt kept giving up the ball from the pivot and we got a lot of easy baskets. Of course, I understand this is easier to do when you're winning the way we are. Wilt doesn't mind giving up the ball because he sees the results. But suppose we are losing. It's only natural for him not to want to give up the ball to a guard who's shooting 40 percent when he can shoot 70 percent."[67]

Unfortunately for the rest of the NBA, there were not many nights during the 1966–67 season when Chamberlain reverted to old form and tried to be a one-man scoring machine. "He's doing a lot of things he didn't do before," observed former teammate Al Bianchi. "He's pitching the ball out on fast breaks, blocking shots and he's not taking that fall-away jumper. That's the shot you're willing to give him. He's not scoring so much anymore and I don't know if it's good, but they're *winning*. When I was with Syracuse he'd get 70 points and we'd win by 30. If he had played the way he's playing now, well, maybe he wouldn't have won but the games would have been a lot closer. Right now he's playing a more complete game every night. The name of the game is not scoring, it's rebounding and defense, and that's what he's doing now."[68]

In his autobiography, Chamberlain claimed personal vindication for his stellar performance during this banner year. "I felt great," he wrote. "During the regular season, I'd answered all those critics who always said I couldn't do anything but score and that I was a disruptive influence on my team."[69] Opponents certainly concurred with Chamberlain on this point in 1966–67. "He's a lot different," opined Celtic backup center Wayne Embry. "You have to think when you play him. Should you drop off on the guy coming through or should you stay with him? If you stay with him he might pass off. If you drop off he might fake the pass, take it in and he's up there *dunking*. When he was shooting, what the hell, you just tried to keep him away from the basket. This way he's stuffing more on you and there's nothing you can do about it."[70]

In the playoffs, Chamberlain was equally brilliant as he paced the 76ers to an easy first-round victory over the Cincinnati Royals and a five-game dismantling of the Celtics in the Eastern Division final. "Boston is dead! Boston is dead!" became the chant Philadelphia fans used to punctuate the victory, but Chamberlain was strangely subdued in the locker room celebration afterward. He reminded his teammates that they hadn't won anything yet. The surprising San Francisco Warriors led by sensational sophomore forward Rick Barry still awaited them in the finals. But Chamberlain need not have been so cautious, as the 76ers summarily dispatched the Warriors in six games to become what many have considered the greatest basketball team of all time. He was now a champion for the first time in his professional career and the feeling was intoxicating.

Still, Chamberlain could not totally escape the demons of his past. "The press, quite accurately, called the championship a team victory," he later wrote. "They said we had beaten Boston because we were a better team than the Celtics—'not necessarily because Chamberlain was better than Russell.' Of course, they'd never taken that approach all those years Boston beat my team. They never said Boston won because they were a better team—'not necessarily because Russell was better than Chamberlain.' When Boston was winning, it was always Russell who was responsible, Russell who made the Celtics a great team, Russell who beat me. But they wouldn't give me the same credit for our victory."[71]

Not everyone agreed with this assessment. "A lot of people have said that Wilt is a loser, but few of them have been players," wrote Hall of Fame forward Rick Barry in his caustic 1972 autobiography *Confessions of a Basketball Gypsy*. "Few players have the guts to say this about a guy who might be their teammate or might take anger out on them on court. But I'll say what most players feel, Wilt is a loser. He has a complex about this. He thinks the world is picking on him. He resents criticism, but he does not take advantage of his incredible natural ability. . . . When it comes to the closing moments of a tough game, an important game, he doesn't want the ball, he doesn't want any part of the pressure. It is at these times that greatness is determined, and Wilt doesn't have it. There is no way you can compare him as a pro to a Bill Russell or Jerry West. If Jerry West had been a center, his team would have won as many championships as Russell's. These are clutch performers."[72]

The frustration over not receiving the same credit Russell got for his championships would only be compounded the following season as Chamberlain had the "loser" tag hung on him once again. Even before the basketball campaign began, he seemed to sense the intense pressure he and his Philadelphia teammates would be under to repeat. "In a way," he said, "I like it better when we lose. It's over and I can look forward to the next game. If we win, it builds up the tension and I start worrying about the next game."[73] Though they failed to set any record books afire in 1967–68, the 76ers continued to be a solid club, coasting to a 62–20 record during the regular season, a full eight games ahead of the Celtics who were mired in second place for the third consecutive year.

Chamberlain also posted big numbers as he averaged 24 points and 23 rebounds a game to go along with a league-leading 702 assists. Yet the emotional intensity and close team chemistry that existed a year before was missing. Hannum spent the entire season feuding with Philadelphia general manager Jack Ramsey, which resulted in his abrupt departure at

season's end. "You could see [Hannum] was distracted and not concen-
trating—and he later admitted as much to me," Chamberlain later
opined.[74] Nor did Hannum endear himself to black players on the team
when he failed to call a team meeting following the assassination of Martin Luther King Jr. in early April. The 76ers were set to defend their
playoff crown against Boston at home in the opening game of the Eastern Division finals when news came of the civil rights leader's murder.
"Red Auerbach called the Boston players together, and they talked about
whether or not they should play the game or ask for a postponement,"
Chamberlain later wrote. "They agreed to play. The day of the game,
they came to Philadelphia together, united in their grief—and in their
determination. But Alex didn't think to call a player meeting. Most of us
didn't see each other until we got into the locker room that night. . . .
Like Boston, we were grief-stricken. But we were confused, bewildered,
uncertain. It showed that night."[75] Indeed, the Celtics easily defeated
Philadelphia, 127–118, to take away their home court advantage.

Chamberlain and the 76ers battled back to win the next three games
to secure a seemingly insurmountable 3–1 advantage, but the Celtics refused to roll over, winning the next two games to tie the series and set up
another nail-biting seventh game in Philadelphia. Already plagued by
several injuries, including the losses of Luke Jackson and Billy Cunningham, Philadelphia fell to Boston in the closing moments, 100–96.
Chamberlain, who was reportedly playing with a torn calf muscle,
grabbed 34 rebounds for the game, but attempted only two field goals in
the second half. Ugly rumors began circulating after the playoff loss that
the 76ers had deliberately tanked the series. Indeed, the fact that Chamberlain took only two shots in the closing two quarters of play undoubt-
edly raised eyebrows.

Chamberlain was no stranger to such allegations. In the late 1960s he
was the focus of an FBI probe looking into whether he placed gambling
bets on and against his team. "It is a general opinion that Chamberlain
has shaded points in the professional games that he is a part of and
places bets on the shading situations through [redacted]," a 1967 FBI
memo claimed. On an earlier occasion, the FBI noted that it had received word from a source that a possible "fix" might be in the works for
a 1966 Boston-Philadelphia game. "Informant stated that favorite was
Philadelphia and 5 points and that on the evening of the game, game
was 'off the board' in Boston; however, Boston bookmakers 'in the

know' were keeping bets on the Celtics," the FBI reported.[76] While tantalizing and suggestive, the allegations against Chamberlain were never substantiated. In fact, longtime FBI director J. Edgar Hoover dismissed such charges out of hand, claiming that while some players "bet on a game or games in which they are involved," this did not "in itself constitute a violation of the Sports Bribery statute."[77] As for the rumors that a possible gambling fix was responsible for Philadelphia's humiliating 1967–68 playoff loss, there is no existing documentation to suggest that the FBI or any other law enforcement agency took them seriously, if at all. Chamberlain teammate and star forward Chet Walker termed such allegations as "ridiculous" in his thoughtful 1995 memoir *Long Time Coming*. "All our injuries had caught up with us, and the Celtics' great veteran team had risen to the occasion," he maintained.[78]

A reservoir of bitterness left over from the team's disheartening playoff collapse, however, compelled the 76er front office to make several personnel changes in the off-season. And topping off the list here was Chamberlain. Since 1967 he had made no secret of his desire to play in the warmer climes of Los Angeles. Mercurial Lakers owner Jack Kent Cooke was only too willing to grant his wish. When Philadelphia owner Irving Kosloff approached him at the end of the 1967–68 season and asked whether he would be interested in acquiring Chamberlain, Cooke jumped at the opportunity. A deal was quickly worked out. Los Angeles sent cash and warm bodies Archie Clark, Darrall Imhoff, and Jerry Chambers to Philadelphia in exchange for Chamberlain. In addition, the All-Star center was inked to a lucrative five-year deal worth an estimated $250,000 a year. To Cooke, who had a penchant for the dramatic, the deal was a no-brainer. Chamberlain was the premier box office attraction in the league, and his well-publicized skills on the basketball floor were expected to bring Los Angeles its first NBA title. "If Wilt wins a championship for me," Cooke said, "he will be worth what I paid him. Even if he does not, he may be worth it. I enjoy him."[79]

Lakers coach Bill "Butch" van Breda Kolff, however, had other ideas. A former Marine sergeant who had piloted Princeton to a Final Four berth in 1965, van Breda Kolff had a blunt, no-nonsense temperament. He expected his players to play the game "right," which to him meant diving for loose balls, playing tough defense, and being unselfish at all times. To be sure, this hoop philosophy hardly seemed compatible with the me-first reputation that Chamberlain carried with him to the Lakers.

Van Breda Kolff "was upset by the trade," longtime Los Angeles scout Bill Bertka later told writer Roland Lazenby. "Butch didn't have anything against Chamberlain or his effectiveness. But you had to have Chamberlain in the post, and that dictated a style of offense that Butch didn't particularly like. He'd rather have all five men moving, all five men interchangeable and sharing the ball."[80] By the same token, van Breda Kolff did not endear himself to Chamberlain when he told the brooding center that he needed to block more shots in the upcoming season. When Chamberlain replied he blocked more shots than anyone else in the league, van Breda Kolff responded, "But I want you to do it like *Russell*."[81] The not-so-subtle inference was clear. Van Breda Kolff wanted Chamberlain to selectively keep the ball in play to set up his teammates for easy transition baskets, instead of indiscriminately launching opponents' shots several rows into the stands as was his custom.

To add fuel to the fire, van Breda Kolff also desired Chamberlain to move away from his customary perch near the basket and play the high post, the idea being that this would allow him to set more picks for his teammates and create greater ball movement on offense. "Wilt's philosophy," he later said, "was that he should be playing where he could score the most points, which was therefore what was best for the team, instead of a philosophy of 'What can I do, and what would be best for other members of the team?' He might be hindering three other players, but that wasn't in his mind. You couldn't tell him anything."[82]

In point of fact, maximizing his own personal offensive totals was exactly what Chamberlain had in mind. "If a man can score the way I can, I don't see why anybody would want to change him," he fumed to *The Sporting News* early in the 1968–69 basketball campaign. "Suppose somebody in Boston wanted Bill Russell to suddenly put all his concentration on offense. People would say Russell was crazy to change because defense is the thing that made him. Am I any different because offense is the thing that made me? I don't think so."[83] Though it had been several seasons since he had averaged 50 points a game, Chamberlain insisted it was not beyond the realm of comprehension to think he could do it again. "If anything, with all the young and inexperienced centers we have in the league right now, it would be easier."[84] As to the suggestion that scoring so many points a game might be detrimental to club chemistry, in that it would discourage teammates from taking shots open to them in favor of feeding the big man inside, he took personal umbrage.

"Now that's a mistake," he said. "Anybody will tell you that. But you know something, Frank McGuire didn't let that happen the year he coached Philadelphia and I got my 50 every game. We had four players in double figures that year, including Paul Arizin, Tom Meschery, Al Attles, and Tom Gola. And Eddie Conlon didn't miss by much. I like to think I helped those guys a little by giving the ball to the free man every time I was double teamed. I could do the same with the Lakers."[85]

Such self-serving bluster failed to earn Chamberlain much respect or support from his new Los Angeles teammates, particularly perennial All-Star forward Elgin Baylor. Accustomed to being the team leader as much off the court as on, Baylor did not appreciate Chamberlain coming in and trying to take over the locker room with his larger-than-life persona. "Oh geez, he and Elg just jawed at each other all the time," Lakers trainer Frank O'Neill later recounted.[86] Indeed, the two superstars would argue over the most trifling of things.

Once before a practice in Boston, Baylor needled teammate and former Celtics backup center Mel Counts about how slow he and his college team, Oregon State, had been several years earlier. "That team must have run like a bunch of turtles with arthritis," Baylor joked to the delight of his fellow Lakers.

"Are you talking about people again?" Chamberlain inquired seriously.

"I'm not talking about people," Baylor answered.

"You always talk about people," Chamberlain replied.

"What do you mean?" Baylor asked.

"How do you think people feel when, you know, you call them turtles with arthritis?" Chamberlain said.

"I didn't say they *were* turtles with arthritis. I said they *run* like turtles with arthritis," Baylor responded.

According to basketball beat writer Frank Deford, who was on hand to record the incident, what had begun as jovial locker room interplay between teammates quickly descended into an unpleasant clash of egos, thanks largely to Chamberlain. "There was only the shifting of seats, the hurried tying of shoelaces, and the Lakers suddenly subdued, moved upstairs to practice," Deford wrote.[87]

Chamberlain's tendency to be an expert on all manner of subjects outside of basketball also did not go over very well. When Laker rookie Jay Carty complained one day about the amount of studying he was doing to earn a doctorate degree, Chamberlain could not resist commenting.

"I know exactly how you feel," proclaimed the Kansas dropout to the guffaws of teammates. "When I finished school, I couldn't open a book. I just forgot everything. School came easy to me. I did well in everything. Calculus I could do in my sleep. I was a *genius*."[88] Such boorish behavior encouraged Bill Russell to later observe that Chamberlain had no one to blame but himself for his largely negative public image. "He thinks he's a genius," Russell said. "He isn't." But then, charity to his fellow teammates and coaches was never a priority with Chamberlain. "I've never professed to win any popularity contests," he claimed in self-defense. "I know I talk too much. That is one of my problems. But all I ever meant to be is constructive."[89]

His tactlessness would provoke a firestorm of controversy years after his retirement, when he boasted in a 1991 best-selling autobiography *A View from Above* that he had slept with twenty thousand women during his lifetime. "Yes, that's correct, *twenty thousand ladies*," he wrote. "At my age, that equals out to having sex with 1.2 women a day, every day since I was 15 years old."[90] Public condemnation was swift and overwhelming, as to be expected in an age when the dreaded AIDS virus claimed thousands of lives annually. Respected figures such as tennis great Arthur Ashe also came forth to criticize Chamberlain for reinforcing a negative racial stereotype of African-American males as "sexual primitives."[91] Chastened by the response, Chamberlain attempted to salvage what he could of his shattered reputation. "We're all fascinated by the numbers, as we were about the 100 points," he sheepishly commented in one of his last interviews. " . . . So I thought of a number that was a round number that may be close and may be whatever, and I used that number. Now according to the average person, that number is so preposterous that I can understand them not believing it. But the point of using the number was to show that sex was a great part of my life as basketball was a great part of my life. That's the reason why I was single."[92]

As was the case with many of his on-court battles with Bill Russell over the years, Chamberlain could not avoid looking like a loser.

Sinking
in the
East

As November gave way to December and the coming New Year, the
country was still recovering from one of the bitterest presidential
campaigns in recent memory. After initially looking like he would win
by a landslide, Richard M. Nixon barely squeaked by Vice President
Hubert H. Humphrey in the popular vote to take the White House.
"Having lost a close one eight years ago and having won a close one this
year," he told his supporters, "I can say this—winning's a lot more fun.
A great philosophy is never one without defeat. It is always one without
fear. What is important is that a man or a woman engage in battle, be in
the arena." As for the divisive nature of the contest, Nixon tried to sound
a note of reconciliation. "I saw many signs in this campaign," he said.
"Some of them were not friendly and some were very friendly. But the
one that touched me the most was the one I saw in Deshler, Ohio, at the
end of a long day of whistle-stopping. . . . A teenager held up a sign,
'Bring Us Together.' And that will be the great objective of this administration at the outset, to bring the American people together."[1]

In sports, Marvin Miller, executive director of the Major League Baseball Player's Association, characterized the latest proposal by owners to
purportedly increase player pension benefits by $1 million as "fraudu-
lent, inadequate and outrageous." "It pretends," Miller told reporters,
"that they have made an offer which will permit a substantial increase in
the pension benefits for the players. The offer actually will permit no
increase in benefits to the players whatsoever. Major league expansion

plus the owners insisting on paying off the unfunded liability of the pension plan at a faster rate than ever before would reach the $5.1 million total they propose."[2]

Elsewhere, three Roman Catholic priests, all hailing from Massachusetts, were facing a potential 31-year prison sentence on charges stemming from their having stolen and burned draft board records in Milwaukee, Wisconsin, the previous year. "I don't like the idea of going to jail," said Father Robert Cunnane, one of the priests involved in the alleged crime, "but it is worth the price if people respond. I'll take the risk of jail if it prompts people to reexamine what it means to be human in our society."[3]

Questions of morality were also being raised about former First Lady Jacqueline Bouvier Kennedy. On October 20, she had married controversial Greek shipping tycoon Aristotle Onassis on the isle of Skorpios in the Ionian Sea. Onassis, a 62-year-old divorcé, had a well-deserved reputation for ruthlessness and was rumored to have done business with both sides during World War II. To many Americans, the nuptial seemed to mark "the end of Camelot," that heady period in the early 1960s when anything seemed possible under the leadership of the late president John F. Kennedy. Now only disillusionment remained. As French political commentator André Fontaine observed, "Jackie, whose staunch courage during John's funeral made such an impression, now chooses to shock by marrying a man who could be her father and whose career contradicts—rather strongly, to say the least—the liberal spirit that animated President Kennedy."[4]

Following the lopsided road loss to the Lakers in late November, the Celtics managed to regroup and win eight of their next ten games, including an exhilarating 117–114 overtime victory over the Royals in Cincinnati on Pearl Harbor Day. Trailing by as many as 15 points in the third quarter, the Celtics came roaring back behind the explosive offense of John Havlicek who netted a team-high 27 points. Bailey Howell and Don Nelson also came up big with 22 and 21 points respectively. Yet the real eye-catching performance belonged to newly acquired frontcourt man Jim "Bad News" Barnes, who was filling in for Russell in the pivot after the latter had been sidelined with the flu. All Barnes did was score 20 points and hold his own on defense against sharpshooting center Connie Dierking of the Royals. He also was credited with scoring a game-tying basket in overtime.

The Celtics had purchased the contract of the 6-foot-8-inch, 240-pound Barnes from the Chicago Bulls on December 1. To make room for him on the roster, the team placed veteran journeyman Bud Olsen on waivers. In acquiring Barnes, the Celtics were hoping to provide Russell with some much-needed backup help at center, in addition to having another scoring threat off the bench. "Barnes can go into a low post and take a smaller man into the pivot," an enthusiastic Bailey Howell told writers upon learning of the deal. "He's rugged in there and he's got the speed to get off the boards and run the break."[5]

Barnes had entered the NBA with considerable fanfare and expectation back in 1964, following a stellar collegiate career at Texas Western University in which he averaged 29.1 points a game his senior year. In fact, so highly touted was Barnes that the Knicks selected him over future Hall of Famer Willis Reed in that year's draft. "He had the quickness and strength and the game was becoming one of more speed every day," then Knicks scout Red Holzman explained. "We figured Bad News would give height away to Chamberlain and Russell and Thurmond but would make it up with quickness. There was no one in the league Barnes's size who had his speed."[6]

For a time, the choice seemed inspired. Barnes averaged 15.5 points a game in his first season with the Knicks and made the All-Rookie team. Then things proceeded to fall apart. For reasons that are still not entirely clear, Barnes began to live up to his nickname of "Bad News" by averaging 12.4 points his second season. Unfortunately, this mediocre showing could not be shrugged off as just another sophomore slump, as he could barely crack 6 points a game over the next two and half seasons. By this time, however, the Knicks had decided to cut their losses and traded him to the Bullets. From there he moved on to short playing stints with the Lakers and Bulls before the Celtics finally picked him up.

Alas, despite his performance in the Cincinnati game, Barnes was destined to be a disappointment for the Celtics as well. Just three weeks after joining the Celtics, Barnes was involved in a freak accident that almost cost him his life. While changing planes with his teammates at O'Hare Airport in Chicago on New Year's Day, Barnes received a serious head injury when he was knocked over by the recoil blast of a jet engine at takeoff. Aside from a concussion, Barnes also suffered from whiplash and a loss of hearing in his right ear. "The thing with me," he said, "is that I can hear, but everything comes through as if I'm wearing headphones.

I hear crackles and pops. It bothers me. It bothers me all the time."[7] As it turned out, he got into only a few more contests during the regular season, averaging a feeble 5.1 points per game. Even more telling, he would not log a single minute of playing time in the playoffs.

If Boston fans became disillusioned by Barnes's lack of production, they were positively upbeat over the pairing of former Celtics star Tom Heinsohn and Red Auerbach in the television booth to cover the team's games for Channel 56, a Boston station that specialized in old movie reruns and local sports programming. "It worked out pretty well," Heinsohn later said of the experience. "We had a lot of fun doing the broadcasts. Red was absolutely pro-Celtic. [The fans] may have thought I was pro-Celtic, but Red was definitely pro-Celtic. He would go after referees, what have you. I think Red brought a different look to the broadcast, a different sound and a different attitude. Johnny Most was doing the radio at the time and he had built up such a huge audience on radio because when the Celtics began winning all those titles that's who they listened to. It wasn't television. So he was the voice of the Celtics and we were trying to capture our own audience and at the time Channel 56 was still a UHF station. In order to get it, you had to buy a special antenna. We had a limited audience at the time and we tried to build an audience, [but people] had to go out of their way to tune in."[8]

For those fortunate enough to tune in, however, Auerbach and Heinsohn provided more than their fair share of entertaining moments, especially when the competition heated up on the floor. There was, for instance, the time when the duo were broadcasting a playoff game in Philadelphia. Auerbach, who had fallen into the habit of eating peanuts during telecasts, dropped a bag on the floor just as Philadelphia's Chet Walker was viciously fouled by Larry Siegfried going to the hoop. But Auerbach had missed this crucial part of the play. He was too busy retrieving his peanuts. "Everyone in the arena and watching television at home had seen the play except Red," Heinsohn later explained. "He had been involved in a more important matter. Walker was stretched out when Red finally looked to the court. 'What's he doing?' he screamed into his mike. 'Is he pulling that same old jazz about 20 seconds?'" Even when Heinsohn gently informed his old coach that Siegfried had knocked him down, Auerbach remained unconvinced.

"He was not in the play!" he insisted.

"Okay, Red," Heinsohn replied. "Have it your way. He was not in the play, but would you settle for this—he was in the movie?"[9]

As is the case with most innovative concepts, the idea of putting Auerbach alongside Heinsohn as a color man came about by sheer accident. During a road contest against the 76ers in the middle of the 1967–68 season, Auerbach was having difficulty finding an empty seat in the then-packed Philadelphia arena. Seeing that Heinsohn, who was broadcasting the game solo, had an opening next to him, the Celtics GM ambled on over to claim his prize. "And the next thing I knew," he said, "I was on the air."[10] Equally significant was the fact that Channel 56 officials liked what they saw in terms of the charismatic energy Auerbach brought to the proceedings. They soon signed up the opinionated Brooklyn native as their number two basketball man in the booth. This new arrangement sat well with Heinsohn because he had been lobbying station officials for some time to provide him with on-air relief during broadcasts. "I had to at least go to the men's room," Heinsohn later joked.[11]

Fortunately, providing television commentary was not something new for Auerbach. He had previously worked as a color man on a number of ECAC college basketball games. "But that was different," Auerbach said. "I could just sit there and tell the folks that one team was using a 3–2 defense and the other team was in a full-court press. Technical stuff like that. When I do the Celtics game, I'm emotionally involved."[12]

Indeed, Auerbach could become so personally wrapped up in a game that he never gave a thought to how unfair and biased his comments sometimes were. During one contest he telecast, for example, referee Earl Strom came down with a painful leg injury, thus temporarily putting a halt to the action on the floor. Instead of expressing sympathy, Auerbach seized the opportunity to settle an old personal score he had with Strom. "Shake it off!" he yelled into his mike. "I never thought a referee could get hurt. If he stands there nursing it everybody will get cold. Let's go! Doesn't he know there's a 20-second rule? He's only got 20 seconds to get back in there."[13]

Heinsohn prided himself on being the more professionally polished of the two, as he had been regularly doing the team's games since 1966. "Hey," Auerbach informed him over the summer break that year, "we're going to be televising road games this season in Channel 56. Are you interested in doing the play-by-play?" It didn't require much arm-twisting by Auerbach to bring Heinsohn on board, especially since the latter had been itching to get back into the game following his retirement as a player in 1965. But before taking over the telecasts, Heinsohn had to first serve a brief apprenticeship with veteran broadcaster Marty

Glickman, a longtime voice of the Knicks. "I acquired the feel of the microphone, the pace of the game, the commercials, and the entire mechanics," Heinsohn later wrote of this formative period. "I borrowed the Celtics' videotape equipment and practiced at home games. Fred Cusick, the sports director of Channel 56, would sit alongside and review my homework after the Boston Garden games."[14]

Satisfied with the progress he was making behind the mike, Heinsohn decided he was ready to fly solo for a contest against the Bullets in Baltimore. "I had no color man, nothing," he later recalled. "I did every commercial, every lead-in, and the halftime interview without a problem, which made me feel great—like the night I scored 47 points [as a player] in Seattle. Only this time, a star was born in Baltimore. I sweated frequently that first show but I drank enough Cokes to cool me off. That led to the discovery of an occupational hazard of TV announcers. It is called the relief stop by truck drivers and other patrons of the highways. It is called something more descriptive by ballplayers when they go to the dressing rooms at half time."[15]

Apart from this call of nature, Heinsohn made only one major gaff during the entire broadcast. That occurred when he read a promotional announcement for the movie *Yankee Doodle Dandy*. Heinsohn pronounced it "Yenkel Doodle Dendy." Thinking of a way to extricate himself from this embarrassing lapse, he quickly came up with an improbable yet amusing explanation. "Of course, that's a Jewish movie," he told viewers.[16]

As the years wore on, such mistakes grew less frequent as Heinsohn became increasingly more comfortable in front of the camera. He particularly enjoyed broadcasting games from historic arenas like the old Madison Square Garden of New York and Boston Garden. "You were in the first row of the balcony in the overhang [of these arenas], so you had the game close to you and you were hanging over the action," he said. "Subsequent to those buildings going down, all the other buildings that were built [after them] put you further up and out of the action or they put you actually on the floor where you were being blocked out by the coach standing up or the referees standing in front of you."[17]

While taking in this unique perspective of the game, Heinsohn also found himself mastering the nuts and bolts of television broadcasting. "I was learning to deal with different directors and producers because that's what they did on the road those days," he said. "They didn't travel everybody, just the broadcasters. So we always had a different producer or director."[18] One of the producers he collaborated with in New York in particular proved helpful. "I would give him verbal cues so he would have an indication this is where we needed to go in tight on this picture," he related. "From that we started to develop a different way to broadcast pro basketball—to catch the action, not just do hero shots."[19] By "hero shots," Heinsohn was referring to the unfortunate tendency of sports television producers of this era to allow cameras to linger on players after they made a basket, instead of following the rest of the action on the floor. He felt this hamstrung the efforts of conscientious game announcers like himself to give an accurate depiction of events as they occurred. Indeed, the fast-paced nature of professional basketball required a different broadcasting approach altogether. As he later explained, "You have a certain rhythm in football and baseball where there is a stoppage in action, times between plays to get across your thoughts. In basketball, there is extreme pressure to be succinct. You have only four or five seconds to tie all the pieces together."[20]

Heinsohn would later incorporate these novel ideas into his work as an analyst for NBA telecasts on CBS-TV in the early 1980s. His approach was straightforward and simple. He believed his main purpose was to educate the general public on the strategies and inner workings of the game. "Part of my preparation is to be the coach of each team," he said. "We meet with each coach before the game and I verify the thoughts I have. I script out a series of potential replays which will help in the early stages to give the story line. And the players on each team make the plot work." To be sure, this was a far cry from the way the sport was covered when he first started out in the business. "We've gone from televising the high-flyers, which made it seem like the game was so easy with no defense, to the highly sophisticated game. There has been an evolution in presenting a more sophisticated approach to pro basketball, a game which I feel has been maligned for years. The challenge is to make the broadcast so the first-time viewer doesn't have to be Albert Einstein to understand it."[21]

While no one ever accused Heinsohn of being an Einstein on the court, he nevertheless displayed enough mental toughness as a player to qualify as one of the premier big game performers of his era. This was certainly true during the deciding game of the 1957 NBA finals, when as a rookie he scored a team-high 37 points and grabbed 23 rebounds to lift the Celtics to a 125–123 victory over the St. Louis Hawks. "What a show Tommy put on," raved teammate Bill Sharman afterward. "I never saw anyone play like that under pressure, let alone a rookie."[22]

Despite such spectacular performances, many of Heinsohn's NBA contemporaries looked upon the former Holy Cross star as a selfish ball handler and shooter. Indeed, his own teammates jokingly referred to him as "Tommygun" and "Ack-Ack" for the high number of shots he took during games. "We used to kid him about it," Bob Cousy later confirmed. "He would from time to time take very low-percentage shots. But never at the expense of [a] teammate who had a better shot. He liked to shoot and I liked to see him shoot. As a playmaker, if I got the ball to a guy who didn't get the job done, he'd hear about it from me. But if you'd get the ball to Tommy, the SOB would get it in the hole. That's really the bottom line."[23]

To his credit, Heinsohn, who averaged 18.6 points a game during his nine-year Celtics career, never let such unfair criticism detract from his performance on the playing floor. "Some thought I was a selfish player, but I really didn't think I was," he said. "Shooting the ball was my job on the team. And you didn't get the ball on the Boston Celtics unless you were in a position to score. I was probably the best one-on-one player on the team. When the plays broke down and the clock was running out, more often than not they got the ball to me. They knew that no matter what the other guy was doing to me, I could get my shot off. Hey, I think I earned my points."[24]

If there was one legitimate criticism concerning Heinsohn's game, it had to do with his poor physical conditioning. Put another way, Heinsohn never met a meal or a cigarette he didn't like. As a result, he saw his overall stamina decline markedly as the seasons wore on. "Tommy should have been a much better rebounder than he was, and he never got into peak physical condition," Russell later wrote. "I believe Red should have run him up and down the floor like a Marine drill instructor till he dropped. Tommy was so gifted and so smart that if he'd gotten into top shape and made up his mind that he was going to play every night, the only forward who'd have been any competition for him was Elgin Baylor. Not even [Bob] Petit could have come close to him."[25]

While Auerbach may have come up short in terms of motivating Heinsohn to reach his full potential, it was not through any lack of effort. To be sure, Auerbach could be merciless in his verbal assaults on Heinsohn. "Because of the mix of personalities on the ballclub, I became

Red's whipping boy," Heinsohn said. "You couldn't yell at Cousy, because he was the team leader. Russell was the first real great black player. If you yelled at Ramsey, he'd believe you. Bill Sharman would get real mad. Red would pick on me because he figured I had the personality to let it roll off my back. It went on for years."[26] Sometimes, however, the criticism could reach absurd lengths. In one particular contest, Heinsohn had 20 points and 12 rebounds by halftime, but Auerbach still wouldn't let up on him during the intermission. "Red, what the hell have I done wrong tonight?" Heinsohn finally asked in exasperation. "Tommy, you warmed up lousy," Auerbach replied.[27]

Heinsohn had long since grown accustomed to such abuse, having been raised the only German kid in a tough Irish-Italian neighborhood in Union City, New Jersey, during World War II. "After going to the movies to see how John Wayne took care of the Nazis—which is what I was in the neighborhood—they used to beat me up," he said. "That's how I became competitive."[28] Fortunately, these competitive energies found a healthy outlet in sports, as Heinsohn went on to become an All-American schoolboy basketball player at St. Michael's High School. "We played so much that by the end of my senior season I had lost 25 pounds and looked like Kevin McHale, on top of which I had the flu and felt like a dog," he recalled. "But I also had scholarship offers from more than a hundred colleges."[29]

In the end, he chose Holy Cross College because he felt the small Jesuit college in central Massachusetts had been the most honest with him, especially when he expressed a desire to become a doctor. "Everybody else," he later wrote, "was promising me the sun, the moon, and the stars—'Yeah, we'll take your girlfriend! Sure, we'll put you through medical school . . . '—while the admissions people I met at the Cross were right up front in telling me it was extremely difficult for an athlete to complete their premed course."[30]

At the Cross, Heinsohn was nothing less than spectacular as he teamed up with Togo Palazzi to give the Crusaders 26 victories in 28 games during his sophomore year. When Palazzi departed the following year, neither Heinsohn nor the Crusaders missed a beat as the 6-foot-7-inch, 220-pound forward carried the team to 19–7 and 22–5 marks over the next two seasons. In his senior year, Heinsohn set a school record by averaging 27.4 points a game while garnering first team All-American honors. He felt he was ready for the pros, and Red Auerbach obliged his wishes by using Boston's territorial draft pick to select him behind Bill Russell in the first round of the 1956 NBA draft.

It didn't take long for Heinsohn to make a positive impression in his new digs as he tossed in 16.2 points a game to secure the league's Rookie of the Year award. Over the next eight seasons, Heinsohn would lead the team in scoring three times and average close to 10 boards a game. "Heinsohn can do everything Baylor can do," Bob Cousy said. "On top of that, he's the best offensive rebounder in the business."[31]

Despite the outstanding play, Heinsohn found his contributions increasingly overlooked as the seasons progressed. This was not surprising given the Hall of Fame–caliber talent he found himself surrounded with on the Celtics roster. "After a certain point in my career, I didn't care about All-Pro or Hall of Fame or best this, best that," Heinsohn said. "I just wanted to be on a winning ballclub. And I just wanted to be happy with myself. I came to that conclusion a long time ago. I had played a fantastic game against the Lakers. In truth, I was the whole game. Next morning, I came down to the hotel with my roommate, [backup center and major league baseball pitcher] Gene Conley, to read about myself in the newspapers. There were two pages on the game. It was Elgin Baylor did this, and Jerry West did that, and Bill Sharman and Bill Russell and Bob Cousy. The last paragraph said 'Tommy Heinsohn also scored 42 points with 27 rebounds.' I tossed the newspaper aside, looked at Conley and said 'Well, I guess I'm never going to be a star.'"[32]

Still, Heinsohn could take considerable comfort in the fact that he was a valuable performer on eight NBA championship teams. Other than Russell and Sam Jones, no other Celtic from this era can make such a claim. "I was very competitive," Heinsohn said. "I'd like to go out and win. And I felt very comfortable with my teammates because they had the same attitude."[33]

Heinsohn brought a similar kind of intensity with him into the broadcast booth. "It was like art to me," he later confessed. "We started out with the broad brush strokes, or the basic concepts of rebounding, of shooting, of defense, of a fast break. Then once those broad brush strokes were applied—things as basic as 'There are nine pounds of air in the ball'—we went to work on the finer details: 'Why isn't that fast break working? What's the defense going to do to stop it?'"[34] In the end, television viewers were able to find the answers to these vital basketball questions, thanks to Heinsohn.

Answers were what the Celtics were searching for as the month of December progressed. Following their uplifting December 7 victory over Cincinnati, the team embarked on an extended losing streak, dropping six of their next nine games. The losses conspired to put the Celtics in third place, a full four games behind Baltimore in the Eastern Division. Philadelphia settled in at second place, one game off the pace. "I'm concerned, but not losing any sleep over it," Russell said. "We've had losing streaks before—like a five-gamer last season, I believe. Our losing is a combination of little things which add up to about 20 points a game." Topping the list of "little things" was the health of sharpshooting guard Sam Jones, who had to miss nine games due to a painful groin injury. "Yes, Sam is back, but he didn't play well . . . and I think it'll take him awhile to return to his usual form," Russell said. "This pinch sets off a major chain reaction. Not only does it mean backcourt problems, but affects [us] up front too. For instance, John Havlicek is more effective in the corner against certain teams, yet we have to keep him in the backcourt [due to Jones's injury]. This shortage affects everybody. Like Larry Siegfried. He's tired. And when he's tired the first thing that suffers is his defense—and people start going around him. This doesn't mean he isn't giving 100 percent— just that he's tired and needs more rest. And so it goes—a chain reaction. No, Sam's return isn't necessarily the key to solving it."[35]

Fortunately, there was some good news to report in the midst of all the losing. In recognition for being named the 1968 Sportsman of the Year by *Sports Illustrated,* Russell was given a commemorative brown Grecian urn at the Boston Harvard Club on December 18. "This award means to me, 'You've been a man. We respect you,'" Russell remarked. "I know I was a great athlete a long time ago. A lot of people knew it. But not as many people know that I am a man. Not a tall man, or a black man. Not a basketball player. But a man. Being a man. That's what this is all about." For this reason, Russell revealed that this would be the first trophy he would ever discuss with his children. "I want to prepare my children to face the world and I'm working to make a world where they will succeed or fail on their own merits," he said. "But succeed or fail, I'll always love them. I'm really excited about this award. More than anything I've ever received. It's my kind of thing."[36]

After slogging through a disappointing December, the Celtics started the New Year off on the right foot by winning eight of their first nine games, including six of seven on the road. Fueling the team's resurgence was the return to form of Sam Jones, who was finally able to put aside his injury troubles. Indeed, in a morale boosting 88–82 win over the Lakers on January 11, Jones hit 10 of 16 shots from the floor, including four clutch baskets down the stretch, to derail a Lakers' comeback. "Sure it feels good," Jones told reporters afterward. "It's a good feeling any time you keep your team ahead, whether you make one basket or three."[37]

Ironically, Jones almost didn't suit up for the game after experiencing some initial discomfort in his leg while running. But Russell insisted on his playing and the results spoke for themselves. "The doctors and the X-rays say there's nothing wrong with him," Russell maintained. "Of course, nobody knows what Sam feels. Some people have a lower tolerance of pain than others. It's as simple as that. It doesn't mean they're less dedicated or anything like that. It just means they have a lower tolerance of pain. If he says he ran hard it means he ran as hard as he thought he could."[38]

As for the notion put forward by some members of the Boston media that Jones had become "psyched" by his injury, Russell was quick to dismiss the idea, claiming that Jones was "too smart" to be psyched. "I think I know what he's going through," he said. "At this point in my career I hate to take that clutch shot. You know why? Because people will always remember the last one. You might make it 10 times or 100 times. But if you miss the last one that's all they'll remember."[39]

Despite the string of early January victories, the Celtics still found themselves looking up at the Bullets and the 76ers in the overall standings. If there was any doubt whether they could overtake these two teams, however, the proud veteran squad was loathe to admit it. "We'll do it," Russell said. "We've got a tough schedule over the last half, but we'll finish first. I think it will be Baltimore second, New York third, Philly fourth."[40] Helping kindle this sense of optimism was the fine play of forward Don Nelson, who would finish the season with a solid 11.6 scoring average. A seven-year league veteran, Nelson had already established himself as a major contributor in the Celtics winning lineup over the previous three seasons. "Sure, I got more glamorous guys, guys that score more," Auerbach once commented. "But Don makes the most of his God-given talents—more than any athlete I've ever seen."[41]

Nelson learned to maximize his meager physical abilities while growing up on a farm near Rock Island, Illinois, in the 1950s. Money was always tight in his family, and young Don did more than his fair share of chores to keep the farm afloat financially. When he wasn't hard at work helping raise crops and tending to the livestock, Nelson went to a local one-room schoolhouse with nine grades where he received instruction from a single teacher along with five other students. "The big game there was ollie-ollie-over—throwing a ball back and forth over the school house roof," he said.[42]

Nelson wasn't introduced to basketball until his uncle Walt nailed a spokeless wagon wheel to a cob shed and encouraged him to toss corn cobs through the makeshift hoop. "Oh we got a ball after a while," he said. "It was tough dribbling the cobs."[43] Nelson didn't get the opportunity to play organized ball until he attended Rock Island High, by which time he had sprouted to an imposing 6 feet 4 inches. There he learned some basic lessons about competition that he would carry with him the rest of his life. "Our coach thought we were dogging it," he once explained, "and one day he just locked us in the gym and had us beat the hell out of each other. I don't know if that was it, but I think we started to win more ballgames after that."[44] After high school, Nelson went to the University of Iowa on a basketball scholarship and immediately made a name for himself in big-time college hoops. Now 6 feet 6 inches, he shattered all of the school's scoring records while averaging 23 points a contest in his junior and senior years. "It's an overused phrase, but the tougher the game got, the tougher Don played," Iowa coach Sharm Scheuerman later said. "He always had a lot of savvy. Don did some things you just can't coach. Some players have the body, but aren't mentally tough. Others are mentally tough, but don't have the body. Don had both."[45]

Indeed, Scheuerman recounted a game when Nelson received "a wicked blow to the head" and had to be pulled bleeding from the floor for immediate medical attention. After enough bandages were applied to his head to staunch the blood flow, Nelson stoically returned to the contest looking as if he was wearing a turban. "I thought I was playing a maharishi," Scheuerman joked.[46]

This combination of toughness and offensive prowess eventually earned him an NBA roster spot with the Chicago Zephyrs in 1962. He averaged only 6.8 points and 4.5 rebounds a game in limited duty, but the heady experience of playing pro ball for the first time was one he would never forget. "Boy, things have changed since then," he later told writer Bud Collins. "I think the NBA's gotten a lot more sophisticated. There are more good players. It's better for blacks. When I came in the

Celtic veterans (left to right): Bailey Howell, Don Nelson, Larry Siegfried
Copyright 1969 Globe Newspaper Company, Inc. Republished with permission of the
Globe Newspaper Company, Inc.

league you had black stars of course, but blacks were the first to go if
there was a question of cutting a black or white. You didn't see blacks
at the bottom of a team. Now you do. The game isn't as rough now.
When the league was smaller and you played teams more often, played
against the same guys a lot, grudges developed. You used to expect a
fight a week. Now one a season is a lot. A guy could make a career out of
being an enforcer, like Charlie Tyra and Jim Loscutoff. Not today. Tom
Hoover of the Knicks was the toughest guy I played against. Once when
I was back with LA, Jim Krebs got in a hassle with Bill McGill of the
Knicks, I grabbed McGill, Gene Wiley of our team grabbed me. Hoover
swung a roundhouse on me and knocked all three of us down."[47]

Plane travel could also become a dicey affair. "We traveled in this
DC-8," he remembered. "Took nine hours to get from Chicago to
Boston. Chicago bought the plane from the Lakers, and got a good deal
because it had crash landed the year before. It was all pretty informal.
We had a non-stop crap game in the aisle, and the pilots would come
back and play, alternating between themselves. One flight I looked over
and saw a pilot rolling the dice and thought nothing of it until I noticed

the other pilot's in the game, too. Who the hell's flying this plane? We looked up in the cockpit, and it's the stewardess!"[48]

Having failed to distinguish himself with the Zephyrs, Nelson moved on to the Los Angeles Lakers for the 1963–64 and 1964–65 seasons. But once again, a lack of playing time doomed his overall effectiveness. He averaged a mediocre 5 points a game in spot duty, as he saw his minutes drop from 1,400 his first year to 238 in his second. So determined was he to earn a regular spot in the lineup that not even a serious back injury deterred him from taking the floor. "I remember somebody was out injured," he said. "I think it was Rudy LaRusso with a bad back, and I was suddenly a starter for the final game [of a playoff series] against St. Louis. Well, during practice the day of the game, I fell. I went back to my room, and when I was taking a shower, I went to pick up the soap, and bang, that was it. I went into immediate spasms. I couldn't move or breathe. I tried warming up with the team before the game, but it was obvious that I wouldn't be able to play the way I was. So they gave me all those [pain-killing] injections because they weren't sure where in my back the problem was. I was able to play, but I played a terrible 20–25 minutes."[49]

As for the advisability of taking pain-killing drugs that could potentially cause long-term harm to his personal health, Nelson shrugged it off. "In the old days," he explained, "everyone did it. Anything they could've done to allow me to play I wanted them to do. If you needed some injections to get your body out to play, then you took them without questioning it." Sometimes he would even resort to taking "greenies," dangerous stimulant pills that contained Dexedrine, to artificially enhance his performance on the court. Nor was he the only one taking them. The use of greenies became so widespread around the league in the 1960s that Nelson claimed they were usually located next to the salt tablets in most team locker rooms. "You took as many as you wanted," he said, "and they were taken for granted."[50]

Still, not even greenies could prevent Nelson from being cut and placed on waivers by the Lakers in the fall of 1965. "That hurt," he later said. "It's hard to catch on with another team at the beginning of a season, because the rosters are already set."[51] With no other playing options available, he returned home to Moline, Illinois, hoping against all hope he would get another shot at the pros. "There was no place to go," he later said. "Nobody even contacted me from the Eastern League. I didn't want to call the Lakers, because I was too embarrassed. So I just sat around."[52]

He wouldn't sit for long. For one person who was paying close attention to his situation was Celtics GM Red Auerbach. "When I found Nelson was available, I was tempted to rush out and claim him," Auerbach said. "We needed something exactly like him—a good defensive player who didn't make many mistakes. But even if we were the first club in the league to get our money up, any rival team with a poor won-lost record could still step in and grab him. I figured if I made my intentions known, someone else in the NBA might have claimed him just to keep him away from the Celtics. So I waited until 48 hours were up and then called L.A. We made the deal for $1,000." At least one Laker was greatly displeased by this move. "I never could understand why we let Don go," star forward Elgin Baylor said. "We used to play a lot of one-on-one basketball in practice and Nelson always gave me as much trouble as anybody. I know this: he never had a full opportunity with the Lakers. There were always two or three forwards ahead of him with more experience."[53]

By his own admission, Nelson said he was "down and out" when he received the phone call from Auerbach notifying him the Celtics had picked him up. "He told me to go to the Lenox Hotel and wait for the team to come off the road," he later told writer Joe Fitzgerald. "I sat there, scared to death, not knowing where to work out. It was a tough time for me. Finally the team comes home and Red gives them a few days off. Except for Ronnie Watts. He's the one I had to beat out, so Red had the two of us going one-on-one at the Cambridge Y. That was Auerbach's way; he'd at least give Ronnie a chance to fight for his job. It was awkward. The rest of the players were pretty cool to me; Ronnie had been with them since the start of camp and I was the outsider. Red was the only one who encouraged me because he wanted to bring out my best. Then he announced his decision. I'll never forget it. K.C. [Jones] walked across the room, stuck out his hand and said, 'Welcome to the Celtics.' That was it. They all began explaining the system, educating me, showing how things worked. I was part of their organization now and that made everything different."[54] Retired onlooker Tom Heinsohn, who would go on to coach Nelson on two Celtic championship squads in the mid-1970s, also became a big booster. "Nelson's shot was an economy of motion," Heinsohn said. "Don had the ability to intuitively gauge a shot over an opponent. It wasn't a high arc, but it didn't get blocked either."[55]

Getting used to the unselfish style of play of his new teammates was another matter, however. Having spent his first three pro seasons on teams that revolved their whole offense around one or two players, Nelson found the Celtic way of doing things at first disconcerting. "I couldn't believe how the Celtic players worked for each other when I first came to Boston," Nelson said. "I'd have the ball and I'd be looking to pass off and Russell or Sam Jones or one of the guys on the bench would be yelling at me to shoot. When I played with the Lakers, the only two guys who were ever allowed to control the game were Baylor and West. But I found if you got open with the Celtics, you got the ball."[56] Indeed, Nelson grew so comfortable in his new playing environment that he posted then career-best numbers in scoring (10.2 points per game) and rebounding (5.4) en route to helping the Celtics win their ninth NBA title.

And he did so despite suffering through a frustrating midseason scoring drought. "I was just in a slump," Nelson said. "I began missing and it started gnawing away at my confidence. So I started pressing, and matters got worse. It seemed a long time between double figures. What hurt was that we were playing practically every day. So there was no chance to practice. And I needed practice to get back in the groove. Finally, Red and I had a talk in Los Angeles over the weekend. He called in each player, and when it was my turn he said I seemed to be losing concentration. It's a long season and this happens, I guess. You don't realize it until somebody points it out."[57]

If anyone could diagnose what was ailing his game it was Auerbach, who had earlier announced that he would be leaving the bench at the end of the season. "Playing a year under Red as coach was something I wouldn't have wanted to miss," Nelson said. "I don't know if he was a genius or not, but he was a coach with great intelligence who played all the angles. Leadership qualities were his forte. He'd always say the right thing and keep you in his corner. We have a lot more scouting now than in Red's day. But back then, Red did it all himself, and he did it by just handling men the right way."[58]

Yet everything was not all wine and roses with the Celtics coach–general manager. "I came to the Celtics as a free agent and Red made me pay the price for that," Nelson later told writer Joe Fitzgerald. "He cut my salary down to the league minimum. I had to accept it because I had nowhere else to go. Really, he could have signed me for just about any amount and I'd have taken it. It would have been okay with me, because I wanted to play. And I don't hold any grudges against Red today for that. I understand it. That's just business."[59]

As for Auerbach, he had nothing but praise for the man, who would go on to help the Celtics win five NBA championships. "Nelson was one of my best pickups," he said. "Most guys you take off a waiver list are in their thirties and invariably past their peak. But Don was only 25 and still learning. He had a chance for a future. We got him mostly for his tough defense. The scoring part didn't come until later."[60]

Just as Nelson had earned Auerbach's deepest respect for his gritty brand of play, other Celtics were equally effusive in their praise. "Before he joined us," K.C. Jones said, "nobody was hitting the offensive boards. We have to have the rebounding because it figures Bill Russell is going to be screened out a lot offensively. Nelson promptly gave it to us. And it became contagious. Everybody started rebounding." John Havlicek struck a similar chord of approval. "I'd hate to have seen where we'd finish if we hadn't acquired Don," he said. "The job he's done has been invaluable—especially when Tom Sanders and Willie Naulls were hurt. . . . Don's role with the Lakers was primarily defensive. With us he plays the good defense, but is a key part of the offense, too—an offense that calls for a lot of running and cutting. It's a big adjustment that will tire a man—especially one like Don, not the fastest man in the world."[61]

As to this latter point, that Nelson did not possess a great deal of natural athletic ability, Havlicek would have gotten no argument from his teammate. "I know I'm not going to score a lot of points, so I have to do other things to help out—things that don't show in the box score," Nelson once commented. "It doesn't make any difference who I substitute for, the man I'm replacing is always better than I am. That's why I give it everything I've got while I'm on the floor. I can't afford any less or I'd be hurting the ball club."[62] This hustling attitude would eventually see him ring up 9,968 points after 11 productive seasons with the Celtics.

In addition, he would earn everlasting basketball immortality when his familiar number 19 was raised to the Boston Garden rafters during a retirement ceremony in 1977. Through it all, this former NBA castoff tried to make sense of all the things that had happened to him during his topsy-turvy career. "Sometimes I'd wonder why Red picked me," he later said. "He could have picked say, Jackie Mooreland, a guy who had better stats. But he picked me, and I'd like to think it's because he saw something there, maybe the same thing he saw in a Wayne Embry, a Bailey Howell, a Paul Silas. What do you see when you look at them? You see a winner. I'd like to think he saw a winner in me."[63]

Winning, however, became more difficult for Nelson and the Celtics as the month of January progressed. Indeed, after a promising 7–1 start, the team split its next ten games. The slide started with a 114–110 loss to the Bucks in Milwaukee on January 12. Paced by the offense of Flynn Robinson, who scored a game-high 26 points, the Bucks surged to a 16-point lead in the third quarter, only to see the Celtics cut the margin down to a single point with a minute and a half to play. John Havlicek and Emmette Bryant did most of the damage here, combining for 38 points in the contest. But Boston's comeback was cut short when Robinson and All-Star Jon McGlocklin made a pair of clutch baskets for Milwaukee in the closing moments.

Like the rest of the league, the Celtics had the next three days off due to the nineteenth annual NBA All-Star game being held in Baltimore on January 14. Boston's two lone representatives in that contest, Russell and Havlicek, performed ably, if unspectacularly, during the East's 123–112 upending of the West. In 28 minutes of action, Bill Russell managed a workmanlike 3 points and 6 rebounds, while John Havlicek connected for 14 points and 7 rebounds in 31 minutes. But not even the presence of two certifiable All-Stars on the Celtics roster could prevent the team from playing .500 ball for the rest of the month.

For while the Celtics were able to pick up a pair of wins against San Francisco and Seattle following the break, they completely hit the skids in successive games against Baltimore, Chicago, and Philadelphia, dropping all three in painful fashion. In the Baltimore contest, the Celtics were bested in almost every aspect of the game as the young Bullets outhustled and outmuscled them to the tune of a 122–109 score. Sam Jones was one of the lone bright spots for Boston as he netted 35 points. Swingman John Havlicek, who was sharing backcourt duties with Jones in the wake of a painful forefinger injury to Larry Siegfried, also contributed with 26 points. Baltimore's Kevin Loughery took home the game's top scoring honors with 38 points. The loss, the third in as many meetings with the Bullets, dropped the Celtics a full four games behind Baltimore in the loss column.

As demoralizing as the Baltimore defeat was, things grew even uglier for the team two nights later when they squared off against the Bulls in Chicago. The Bulls, a sub-.500 ball club that would finish 33–49 on the season, utterly shocked their visitors by putting on an offensive surge in the fourth quarter and pulling out a 95–94 victory. The Celtics led by as many as 15 points in the first half but blew the lead thanks to various defensive breakdowns and the hot shooting of Chicago freshman center Tom Boerwinkle, who finished with 21 points. As in the previous game, Sam Jones led the Boston offense with 24 points, while Bailey Howell and John Havlicek added 22 and 18 respectively. "Everything seemed to be coming into place," Havlicek told reporters after the flight home to Boston. "But that loss to Chicago, that really sets you back. You just can't figure out why everyone played so poorly." Russell expressed a similar feeling of amazement. "I thought our team was all right," he said. "But after that game in Chicago, I don't know. Maybe we need a resident psychiatrist around here."[64]

Things continued to go downhill in a 120–111 home loss to Philadelphia two nights later, as the Celtics had no defensive answer to Billy Cunningham, who had a game-high 27 points and 16 rebounds before fouling out with 6:33 remaining in the contest. 76er forward Chet Walker also made things difficult for Boston by scoring 20 points, 12 of them coming in the final quarter. "Every time we needed a basket, we made one," said Philadelphia coach Jack Ramsey. "Chet Walker made great offensive plays in the final quarter, but we had to work hard all the way and always put on the spurt we needed to slow down Boston."[65] As for the Celtics, there were no excuses, only frustration at having dropped another crucial game to a contender. Indeed, they had now fallen 4½ games behind Baltimore in the tight Eastern Division race with Philadelphia just above them in the standings at 2½ games out and the upstart Knicks breathing down their necks in fourth place at 5½ games out. "We couldn't put it together," Russell said of the Philadelphia loss. "Four times we had a chance to go ahead, but each time we missed the basket try. I thought we were going to do it at the end of the third period. We were down by one and they go up by three on Wally Jones free throws."[66]

Lost in all the doom and gloom over the Philadelphia loss was the continued strong play of Tom Sanders, who quietly was putting up the best offensive numbers of his career, averaging better than 14 points for most of the season. Like Russell, however, personal statistics had never been his primary focus; winning championships was. And since joining the Celtics in 1960, Sanders had been a vital contributor on no fewer than seven title squads. "It was a much bigger claim to say I was part of the world champion Celtics than to say I averaged 35 points for an also-ran," he once

"Satch" Sanders rebounds in a half-empty Boston Garden
Courtesy of the Boston Public Library

said. "I had what a lot of All-Stars wanted but couldn't have—championships. And cashing the checks that go with them covers a lot, too."[67]

Interestingly, basketball had never been Sanders's primary sport while growing up in Harlem in the 1950s. Baseball was, and he spent many an hour trying to perfect his skills on the diamond. "I was tall, thin and long-armed, and people thought I looked like [former Negro Leagues hurler] Satchell Paige," he later told writer Tony Kornheiser. Indeed, his resemblance to the baseball Hall of Famer was so uncanny that he earned the nickname "Satch" when he took up pitching. "But I didn't stay a pitcher long," he said, "because I treasured my teeth too much. I developed a bad habit of catching the ball with my mouth, and it got to be a painful experience every time I went to the mound." It also didn't help that he was deathly afraid of the ball. "It was too hard," he said. "Anything that came close would chase me out of the box. Especially those curveballs. Oh, how I hated those curveballs. I was always afraid they wouldn't break. Finally, I decided to take up another game."[68]

That game turned out to be basketball, as it was extremely popular among his peers in Harlem. But the sport did not come naturally to him. "Satch was the tallest, most uncoordinated kid in junior high," remembered Cal Ramsey, a hoop standout who grew up in the same neighborhood as Sanders. "He had to work at basketball. What he got, he earned. When we were both [in school], he lifted weights to toughen himself for the college game. He started walking erect to make the most of his height, to the point where we called him, 'Mr. Posture.'"[69] Aside from conditioning, Sanders also learned the importance of teamwork and ball movement. "I had the feeling that there were other guys out there and if I shot too much they were going to be kind of left out of the game," he said. "I looked at shooting as a reward for playing. If everybody didn't get their reward, they might let down in other areas and the team would get hurt."[70]

Sanders took this unselfish attitude with him when he accepted an academic scholarship to attend New York University. While overshadowed by the All-American play of teammate Cal Ramsey, Sanders was an outstanding performer in his own right at NYU. He set six school records and led the Violets to a 22–5 mark his senior year. Yet he was not without his own detractors, among them Hall of Fame basketball coach Jack Ramsey, who was then holding the clipboard for rival St. Joseph's College. "I remember thinking that the boy had no future at all," Ramsey said. "I used a tall, skinny boy against him, a boy who was nothing special, and he kept Sanders tied up all night. I couldn't imagine Satch ever playing pro ball."[71]

Neither could Sanders as he prepared for a business career with the Tuck Paper Company of New York. "I had always wanted to be in business," he later said. "I majored in marketing, minored in management while I was at NYU. Basketball was a game I enjoyed and I appreciated what it meant. I hoped it would help me go to college and help me get a free education, but that was the end of my scheme with basketball. I had no plans to turn pro. I figured I'd go to college, then go out into the world of business." Not even being selected the first-round draft choice of the defending world champion Celtics convinced him to alter his career path. That is, until he sat down and chatted with the ever-persuasive Red Auerbach. "He told me I should be flattered about being drafted Number One, and he pointed out some obvious advantages to playing ball," Sanders later recalled. "The team had won two or three titles. But I remember Red's exact words; let's see: 'A job, everyone has to get; but an opportunity to play professional ball comes along once in a lifetime.'"[72]

Sanders stayed with basketball and in doing so embarked on a course that would see him earn fame and fortune as one of the premier defensive forwards of his era. "He's the best, no question about it," Philadelphia's Chet Walker said. "A lot of guys are down at that end of the court just killing time. But defense is bread and butter to Satch, and he never forgets it for a second. I have a real hard time getting free from him to get the ball. One reason is because he plays me with his hands. His hands are always on me, feeling so he knows where I am. At the same time, his eyes are on the ball."[73]

To Sanders, this aggressive style was predicated on good positioning. "The big thing," he said, "is to try and keep some body between [the offensive player] and the ball. And once your man does get the ball, you had better get between him and the basket—quick. And then, good luck. All you can do is resort to the fact he's got a weak side and a strong side, and overplay the strong side. You try to remember what his moves are and what you think he's going to do. But he's thinking, too. He knows that last night you blocked his shot coming across the pivot when he went straight up. So this time he might give you a fake. . . . The big trouble is that the defense is always a step behind. I can't dictate offense. If you study hard and pay attention, you might be able to anticipate some moves, but then you've got to be willing to take chances. All of them can score one on one. That's why they're there. Unless you have a bit of luck, and anticipate a certain move, they're either going to get their shot off or you're going to foul them. The best thing to do is to foul them to death."[74]

And Sanders was not deficient in this category as he consistently led the team in personal fouls. Yet how many fouls he committed was irrelevant if he could not judiciously employ them during the key moments of a contest. As in life, timing was everything. "Suppose it's near the end of the game and [Elgin] Baylor has 36 points," he later told writer Joe Fitzgerald. "His team needs a basket and he's the obvious man to go to. If I get into his jockstrap for two minutes, and force a guy like [Rudy] LaRusso or [Johnny] Krebs to take the shot instead, then I've done my job. Just a good defensive effort in those 2 minutes lets me know in my own mind that I've done what was expected of me. I had the satisfaction of walking back to our bench where Red and the guys knew I had done my job well."[75]

While Auerbach and Sanders's teammates may have appreciated his defensive contributions, the same could not be said for the rest of the league as he was perennially left off the All-Star team. Nevertheless, Sanders was always willing to take on the toughest defensive assignments even if that meant matching up against a scoring machine like Elgin Baylor. "Satch once held Elgin to 63 points in a playoff game in Boston," recalled former teammate Bob Cousy. "I remember sincerely telling Satch after the game that he'd done a helluva job against Baylor. It sounds stupid considering 63 points, but I felt that Satch made Elgin work as hard for every one of those points as anyone could have. Satch was in his face on each shot. . . . As a player, Satch got all the dirty jobs; he never complained, he just went out and did what he had to do."[76] John Havlicek agreed. Sanders is "everything people say he is," he said. "To me, he's a Celtic. He's had to sacrifice personal glory throughout his career while having the toughest role on the team. . . . I think Satch could have been a 15–18 point a game man with another club. But here, plays were never called for him. All his points came filling the lane on the break or on hustle baskets."[77]

Yet behind this team-first mind-set lurked a gnawing fear. Sanders always believed he was expendable and that his job was on the line. "I can't come to [training] camp saying I've got it made," he once said.

"There are seniors graduating from college every year that want to play pro ball. I remember how I was then, so how can I relax now? Every year, the fellow comes in, a real nice fellow, from college someplace, and he has come for my job. It's kind of brutal, cruel because you come face to face with the fellow. It's not like a whole bunch of people sitting in a room somewhere and taking an exam and the ones who score highest get the job. This is the law of the jungle. I always feel I can hold the job but feeling and doing is two different things. . . . So you play your best, knowing that if it's good enough the job will be yours and if not you can go home."[78]

Away from the basketball court, however, overcoming adversity was not so easily achieved, especially when issues of societal racism and prejudice were involved. "I'll never forget what happened to Satch [at the beginning of his career]," Tom Heinsohn once recounted. "We visited a so-called All-American city in Indiana, and they rolled out the carpet for the Celtics. They gave us the keys to the city. Then came the bad part. We went to the only restaurant still open at night, and they refused to serve meals to our black players, including Sanders, Bill Russell and Sam Jones. So you know what they did. . . . They marched in a group to the mayor's home, rang the doorbell, and flung the keys at him. 'You know what you can do with these keys,' they yelled in anger. The next day we arrived in Lexington, [Kentucky]. The black players went into a coffee shop and were refused service. You know what Satch did? He cried. I was so hurt and angry for him, I could have punched someone in the nose. Imagine that happening to a nice guy like Satch? How could I not feel something special for a guy like Satch."[79]

Through it all, Sanders persevered and grew stronger both as a player and as a person. But these sobering experiences did not preclude him from having a lighter side. For Sanders was known as being something of a cutup around the Celtics. An expert mimic, he would frequently amuse his teammates by exaggerating how Russell brooded around the clubhouse. "I'd find him hunched over in the locker room with his fist in his chin, like Rodin's 'Thinker,' scowling ridiculously," a clearly delighted Russell wrote. On other occasions, the humor was less intentional. In January of 1963, Sanders and most of his teammates journeyed to the White House for a scheduled 20-minute conversation with then-president John F. Kennedy. "It lasted the 20 minutes," Heinsohn later recalled. "We all introduced ourselves, told what school we went to, what position we played. . . . He said he watched basketball on television once in a while, and had seen the West Virginia team the other day. Of course, he knew Red Auerbach. They chatted for a while. But we all had something to say to the man. Then it came time for us to go. The President shook hands with us. Wished us all good luck. Then he came to Tom Sanders.

"He said, 'Good luck' to Satch.

"Satch looked at him and said, 'Take it easy, baby.'"[80]

Neither the leader of the free world nor the rest of the Celtics could contain themselves. They all broke out in spontaneous laughter.

This charming eccentricity was also on display whenever Sanders traveled on the road with the team. A private man, he would go to extreme lengths to bar anyone from entering his room without his knowledge. As longtime roommate John Havlicek related, "Every night we were on the road, Satch would go through his routine. He would insert a door jam, for one thing. Then, he'd fill a wastebasket with ash trays and prop that up against the door. He would take empty cans of Coke or beer and dangle them from the ceiling with tape for a chimed effect. And sometimes he would complete the job by hanging hangers from the chain portion of the door lock. When people walked by our room . . . they would just shake their head. They couldn't believe it."[81]

For his part, Sanders never viewed such whimsical forays as being in any way out of the ordinary. He was just following his instincts while trying to get by in one of the most competitive professions in the world. "To me, what I'm doing right now is normal," he told a writer in 1967, "I guess because I've been doing it for so long. Sure, I realize that this is only a brief interlude, that the greater part of my adult life will be spent doing something else, but this is not something I worry about. When the time comes to do something else, I'll be ready to do it. Until then, I'll work as hard as I can at basketball. And I'll keep it up as long as I can. They'll have to drag the uniform off me."[82]

To prepare for that inevitable eventuality, however, the former marketing major made a point of keeping abreast of then-current business trends and investing in the stock market. In fact, one of his early investment partners was former Celtics trainer Buddy LeRoux, who would go on to be a part owner of the Red Sox in the late 1970s. "We'd been seeing each other every day since during the training period [of 1964]," LeRoux recalled. "Used to eat together and the talk was small. You know that 'what-else-is-new?' stuff. So this day we decided to talk about making money, our future, etc., and we hit on the stock market, and we decided then and there that we'd put our minds to work hard on it, and we have. I'd say that Tom and I put in at least two hours a day in our homes working on the market. I start around 6:30 in the morning. Tom finds his time during the day."[83]

As in professional athletics, however, chance often went a long way in determining one's success. "We get more warnings than encouragement," LeRoux admitted. "But we make our own decision, most of the time. We're lucky. You've got to be lucky. The first stock we bought was General Telephone at 23. It's 48 now. We know it takes money to make money. But we do pretty well with what we have." Indeed, they usually had more winners than losers. "We're both optimistic people," LeRoux explained. "If we were pessimistic we'd second guess ourselves and fail. We both keep all kinds of records."[84]

But despite how much money he made in the market, Sanders never forgot the poor Harlem background he came from. To this end he made himself active in local community affairs, becoming one of the founders of Athletes for a Better Urban Society and serving on the Roxbury Boys' Club board of directors. He also played a pivotal role as a businessman in securing a $1 million grant from the Federal Housing Administration for rehabilitating 83 units of housing for Boston's disadvantaged inner city population.

This strong social conscience stemmed in part from Sanders's recognition that there was more to life than putting a round rubber ball through a metal hoop. "Every kid wants to be a professional basketball player," he later said. "Okay, don't try to tell him that he can't make it. But try to get across to him the idea that he should be prepared for something else. Set up a list of priorities. All right, so basketball is number one. But what's next? Don't get stuck in a situation where you have to face the grim reality that you have no future in basketball and have nothing else to fall back on. Believe me, I saw that happen to some of my teammates on the Celtics. And it wasn't a very happy thing to see."[85]

Equally displeasing to the eye were the three straight losses the Celtics suffered at the hands of Baltimore, Chicago, and Philadelphia near the end of January. So dispiriting were these defeats that Russell called a special off-day team meeting on January 25 to clear the air. "We talked about the things we're doing that we shouldn't be doing and about the things we aren't doing that we should do," Bailey Howell told reporters afterward. "It was a bad day off. This losing puts a damper on everything."[86] Russell did not disagree. "Baltimore is playing well and the big thing is they don't make too many mistakes," he said. "Against Philly when we got behind, we got anxious—overanxious—and each guy was trying to do it by himself, and you can't do that."[87]

The Celtics managed to pull out of their collective funk the following evening by registering a clutch 124–86 victory over the Bullets before a capacity crowd of 14,000 at the Garden. "There isn't too much for me to say," said Baltimore coach Gene Shue. "We were walloped. The stats tell everything. We had a .277 shooting percentage, had 30 turnovers. Boston worked hard on our guards after we lost Earl Monroe."[88] Indeed, following the Bullets backcourt star's departure in the opening minutes due to a nagging foot injury, Russell adjusted his team's game plan accordingly. "As soon as he went out," the Celtics player-coach said, "we decided to put all the pressure on [Kevin] Loughery. We could afford to make him work a lot harder with Monroe out of there."[89] This strategy worked perfectly as Sam Jones and Don Nelson were able to torch the Bullets for a combined 54 points on offense.

Defensively, the Celtics also didn't let up as they neutralized Baltimore's top scoring threats, Wes Unseld and Gus Johnson, with a tenacious full court press. "We hadn't been playing our game," Larry Siegfried said. "We had a meeting and decided the Celtics have to press and scramble on defense to be the Celtics. That's what we did today."[90] Of greater import, the win was Boston's first in four tries against the Bullets on the season and allowed the team to pull to within three games of the divisional leaders.

Yet there were no wild celebrations or effusive victory pronouncements in the veteran Celtics locker room afterward. "With 36 games to go, there's nothing yet to celebrate," explained a coolly introspective Russell. "The time to celebrate is at the end, and we may do it then, although four teams are still in it—Baltimore, Philadelphia, ourselves and New York. It will almost depend on injuries who wins it."[91]

Russell was closer to the truth than he might have liked.

Limping into the Playoffs

As February began, President Richard M. Nixon and his administration shocked many conservative supporters with the announcement that federal funds would henceforward be denied to school districts failing to provide "acceptable" desegregation plans. The new policy appeared to fly in the face of earlier statements Nixon had made during his fall presidential campaign. Then, he had professed "to look with great concern whenever I see federal agencies, or whenever I see the courts, attempting to become, in effect, local school boards." Now, with less than a full month in office, Nixon had experienced a change of heart. With his apparent approval, the Department of Health, Education, and Welfare "cut off" aid to five southern school districts who persisted in clinging to the old segregationist ways. They were told they could get the money back, on a retroactive basis, provided they desegregated within 60 days.[1]

An ultimatum of a different sort was delivered by the Vietcong to the United States government. Condemning American peace efforts in Southeast Asia as "perfidious," the Vietcong vowed to "push forward" with a "general offensive" and "widespread uprisings" in South Vietnam. The United States "still maintains its obdurate stand of aggression," the guerrilla rebel group charged in a propaganda radio broadcast. "Meanwhile, in South Vietnam, it feverishly steps up the war and keeps piling up barbarous crimes against the people. The above facts prove that the United States imperialists are the die-hard aggressor in South Vietnam." Ironically, these uncompromising words came just a few days after top

U.S. envoy Henry Cabot Lodge called for a "mutual withdrawal" of American and North Vietnamese troops from South Vietnam as "a first step toward peace." "We can review endlessly the events of the past and why they occurred and we would be probably as far apart at the end as at the beginning," Lodge told North Vietnamese and Vietcong delegates at the second session of the Paris Peace Talks. "Let us, instead, turn our attention to the future, what must be done to bring an end to the fighting and to bring peace to the people of Vietnam."[2]

The prospect for brokering a political peace between antismoking forces and supporters of the tobacco industry in the U.S. Congress was proving equally illusive. The main sticking point concerned a 1965 law prohibiting any federal, state, or local government agencies from requiring the inclusion of health warnings in cigarette advertising. The law was due to expire in five months and industry lobbyists were gearing up for an "all-out effort" to see it extended. In anticipation of this move, antismoking activists, led by Democratic senator Frank E. Moss of Utah, pledged opposition to any antismoking legislation that came to the floor "because it might serve as a vehicle for an amendment extending the prohibition of a warning on advertising." Even the use of a disruptive filibuster was not ruled out. "When it comes to a matter involving the lives and health of millions of Americans," Moss said, "I shall not hesitate to take full advantage of the existing rules and to enlist the support of my many colleagues of like mind in the Senate—and there are many—to stop passage of disabling legislation."[3]

Health also became a major concern for the Celtics after the team suffered through a 95–94 loss to the Knicks at Boston Garden on February 2. With twelve seconds remaining in the contest, Bill Russell collided with Knicks center Willis Reed and collapsed in a heap under the home team backboard, severely injuring his right knee in the process. "He made a noise like whommmp," Reed told reporters afterward. "He had just gone up for [a] shot, lost his balance and couldn't regain it. I let him shoot. I thought he was going to miss, because he had missed some easier ones earlier. . . . That noise, I thought, you could hear that noise above the crowd."[4]

On just five hours of sleep, Russell was playing his third game in 42 hours, and the sheer exhaustion of it all now clearly showed on his contorted face and pain-wracked body. In obvious discomfort after the collision, Russell tried valiantly to get up, only to fall backward once again.

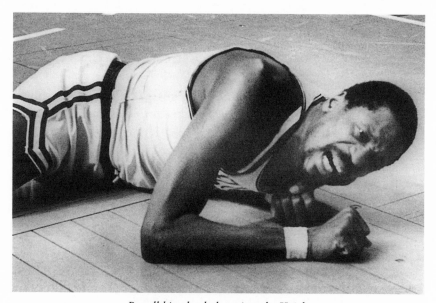

Russell hits the deck against the Knicks
Copyright 1969 Globe Newspaper Company, Inc.
Republished with permission of the Globe Newspaper Company, Inc.

He then lay helplessly sprawled on the parquet floor with his hands stretched out beside him as play resumed. "Bill was in a state of shock for about 15 minutes," Celtics trainer Joe DeLauri related. "He was given medication to calm him down. He just asked to be left alone. That was his only request. He wasn't in a mood to discuss the injury."[5] His teammates were, however, at least about the potential consequences stemming from the mishap. "Losing him," John Havlicek assessed, "if we do, for any length of time, makes this game look like nothing. You'd rather lose one game than have him out . . . five games." Sam Jones tried to put the best possible spin on the unexpected turn of events. "If he's out, we've got to dig down and go," he said. "We've got to play a different kind of defense and everybody's got to hit the boards. We can't depend on him. He's a great rebounder, one of the greatest in the world. But that man is 34 years old. He needs a little help."[6]

Russell had to be moved off the court on a stretcher and taken to the trainer's room before being transported to nearby University Hospital. "I've never seen him in pain like that," DeLauri said, "and he has a high tolerance for pain. I've seen him just stand there while I pushed a dislocated finger back in."[7] Although not as dire as first thought, the medical prognosis on Russell's injury was serious enough. "This was a very major injury," Dr. Thomas Silva, the Celtics' team physician, commented the following day. "And a painful one. But he is a superbly conditioned athlete and a keen competitor. His spirits improved greatly overnight. I said to him that he's back to his normal moody self and he concurred."[8] Russell had acutely strained the ligaments in his right knee and was "emotionally and physically exhausted" according to Silva.[9] Several days of complete rest were prescribed for the ailing Celtics center, meaning neither coaching nor playing duties were permissible. This did not exactly sit well with the fidgety Russell, who began making immediate noises about being up and about against doctor's orders.

Red Auerbach, for one, was impressed with this show of tenacity. "I don't care what else people think of the guy," the unabashedly admiring Celtics GM said. "They can say what they want about his disposition and his ideas on certain subjects and the business of not signing autographs. But they've got to admire his heart. They've got to admit he's 100 percent heart out there. Three games in three days. The guy literally played himself into the floor but he still wouldn't quit until they had to carry him out on a stretcher. And already he's talking of coming back."[10]

In Russell's absence, Auerbach announced that he would temporarily take over the coaching reins while little-used backup center Jim "Bad News" Barnes would assume the vacated starting pivot spot. "All I can say now," Auerbach told the *Boston Herald-Traveler,* "is that we won't play scared. We'll go out there figuring to win every game. . . . I really don't know what else we'll do. Maybe we'll press more, run more. We'll decide as we go along."[11] Unfortunately for Auerbach, his return to the coaching ranks went anything but smoothly his first game back.

Playing before an enthusiastic throng of 41,163 at Houston's Astrodome, the largest crowd ever to witness an NBA game up to this point, the Celtics bowed to the lowly San Diego Rockets, 135–126. Behind the offensive contributions of John Havlicek (24 points) and Bailey Howell (20), the Celtics had led by as many as 10 points in the second quarter, but San Diego reeled off a 14–4 scoring run at the start of the second half and never let up. As Russell's fill-in, Barnes recorded an unimpressive 7 points before fouling out in the fourth quarter. The defeat was particularly grating for the Celtics as they had defeated the Rockets, an expansion team the year before, nine straight times going into the game.

To make matters worse, the team lost the services of high scoring forward Howell, who aggravated an ankle injury. "The crowd was enthused . . . ," Auerbach said in his somber postgame remarks. "I only wish these people had an opportunity to see Bill Russell play. These fans had been looking forward to this occasion for some time. Now it's on to Baltimore for us to play the first place Bullets who had the night off."[12]

As events unfolded, the woefully undermanned Celtics had no better luck against the Bullets. Playing like a team that was mired in fourth place for the first time since 1954, the Celtics had no answers to Baltimore's stellar backcourt ace Earl "the Pearl" Monroe and outstanding rookie center Wes Unseld. Combined, the two torched the Celtics for 50 points while controlling the offensive tempo of the game in a 124–112 upending of the defending world champs. The Celtics hung tough throughout most of the contest and had even cut a once-commanding Baltimore lead down to 3 points with 4 minutes left to play. But then the silky smooth Monroe, the original "Magic Man" of the NBA, scored two "clutch" baskets in a row and the Bullets put the defensive clamps on the Celtics, limiting the green team to 3 points for the remainder of the game. The loss dropped the Celtics to 6½ games behind Baltimore, a margin that now seemed too insurmountable to overcome, given Boston's inconsistent play on the season and assorted injury problems.

Typically, Auerbach was unwilling to throw in the towel. The next day he put his charges through a grueling Garden workout that proved, according to one reporter, "that two years behind a desk has done nothing to the biting Auerbach tongue—except perhaps to add a few words such as 'motivate' and 'agenda' to his vocabulary." "The next guy who loses the ball is going to do 300 laps around the floor," he bellowed with his famous cigar protruding from his mouth. "Don't lose the ball even in practice." When asked during the workout if he would continue coaching the squad for an upcoming four-game road trip while Russell continued to recuperate, Auerbach gave a frank assessment. "I hope not!" he exclaimed. "At least I don't want to. I've got a lot of scouting I've got to catch up with. I thought this was one year when I'd be able to do all the scouting I felt we needed to do. But it hasn't worked out that way." Upon making this statement, Auerbach jumped to his feet and cajoled his squad to even greater effort on the practice floor. "All right you guys, you been scrimmaging for 10 minutes. Now I want you to start scrimmaging for real. Let's show me some running out there." When jokingly informed by an onlooker that the players would be happy to see Russell come back after being subjected to so rigorous a workout, Auerbach replied, "You know, [s]o will I."[13]

Auerbach got his wish sooner than expected. Just two days after the team dropped another tough decision, a 109–107 heartbreaker to the Atlanta Hawks on February 7, Russell triumphantly returned to the playing fold for a rousing 122–117 overtime victory over the Philadelphia 76ers in the Garden. Fittingly, Russell made two key plays down the stretch that snatched victory out of the jaws of defeat for the Celtics. With 15 seconds left on the regulation game clock and Boston trailing 108–106, Russell blocked a shot by Philadelphia's Archie Clark and started a fast break that resulted in a game-tying basket for the home team. "All we had to do," explained Philadelphia coach Jack Ramsey, "was not shoot and we had the game. But Archie did shoot and it turned out to be a bad mistake." The 76ers were not done, however. Billy Cunningham nailed a long-range jumper with 3 seconds remaining that forced the Celtics into a time-out situation. When play resumed, John Havlicek set up Russell for a picture-perfect alley-oop pass near the basket that the latter promptly stuffed as time nearly expired. "I threw the ball at the right corner of the square on the backboard," Havlicek said. "That's over the basket. Russell grabbed it over the heads of the others and dunked it."[14]

While some Philadelphia writers argued that offensive goaltending should have been called on the play, an impatient Auerbach, who sat on the Boston bench to assist Russell, dismissed such assertions as sour grapes. "Nuts," the fiery Celtics GM said. "That was a perfect pass to Russell. Definitely a legal play. They were shocked. They didn't expect it." In the overtime period, Russell hauled down 4 rebounds to add to the 19 he already had for the game and contributed a key steal to seal the 76ers' fate. "I was hoping that I could sit out the game and just go in when [Jim] Barnes needed a rest," said Russell, who did not start the game. "But when he ran into early foul trouble I had to go." All together, a visibly limping Russell played a gritty 45 minutes on the day, despite his right knee being encased in a cumbersome brace that limited his mobility. "It felt a little weak," he allowed. "And the brace bothered me a bit. I'd never worn one before and it felt funny. But the more I played, the better I felt."[15]

Of equal importance, the victory snapped a five-game losing streak for the Celtics. Not since 1949, when the team set a franchise record with 10 consecutive losses, had the Celtics lost more than four games in a row. "If we lost today, it was Russell's fault," joked a relieved Auerbach after the game. "We won so I'll take some credit."[16] For the Celtics GM's contributions, however, the club was assessed a $100 fine by NBA commissioner J. Walter Kennedy. The cause for the levy had to do with league rules that specified only the coach, players and trainer were allowed to sit on the team bench during games. With Russell's reactivation, Auerbach's status as a fill-in coach had been technically negated, making his presence on the bench a direct violation of league protocol. "Next year before the season starts," Auerbach snarled, "I'm gonna appoint myself assistant coach for the year. On the face of it this fine is wrong, yes and no. By that I mean I certainly notified the press. When Russell was hurt I said I'd put myself on the bench. I didn't know how long he would last Sunday. Suppose he gets hurt again. Who would handle the game? I didn't think it was necessary to reestablish my intentions. Besides, I didn't know until game time about Russ, so how could I notify Kennedy? I plead ignorance of the rule, which is a minute rule which has never been broken before. I'll send [Kennedy] the $100 and I'll sign the letter, 'Kindest personal regards.'"[17]

While the matter of the fine was being settled, the Celtics received a badly needed lift when Bailey Howell followed Russell in coming off the injury list. In his nearly three seasons with the team, Howell had played an important part in sustaining the Celtics' winning tradition. Not only did he average 20 points and 9 rebounds a game, he exhibited a fierce competitive attitude that endeared him to his veteran teammates. As Russell remarked, "We knew Howell was a good player. He had an average of better than 20 points for seven seasons in the NBA. And he played in most of the All-Star games since he's been in the league. Yet, sometimes you don't realize a player's true value until he's on your side for a while. After all, we would see Howell for 9 or 10 times a year at the most. From what he's shown me, I have to say he's a great player. He's got the good offensive drive. He's a real holler-guy on the bench, too. Bailey likes team basketball. Joining the Celtics made him a happy player. He doesn't care how much he scores. He just wants to win."[18]

This singular desire to succeed also caught the attention of Red Auerbach, who considered himself something of an expert on the subject of winning. "Howell is a real, real pro," praised Auerbach. "There is no such thing as this guy having to be motivated—he comes to play every night. I've always liked him, not just as a player, but for his attitude."[19] Many times this "attitude" could take the form of extreme aggressiveness. "Bailey would step on your foot, elbow you in the throat," former Cincinnati Royals center Wayne Embry told author Terry Pluto in his book *Tall Tales*. "He was a great offensive rebounder, but he'd kick you to get the ball."[20] Nonetheless, as competitive as Howell was on the basketball court, he was the soul of propriety away from it. A religious family man who neither smoked nor drank, Howell shunned the sybaritic lifestyle practiced by many celebrity athletes in the "Swinging Sixties." "I feel that a man has to live what he believes," he explained. "To my mind, life must be lived in accordance with God's word. It is not enough to have faith but just go along in life any old way. I would never impress my way of life on anyone else, but I live a certain way and will do everything I can to maintain it."[21]

To this end, Howell could not disguise the private anguish he felt over having to leave his family for long stretches of time during club road trips. In fact, he would book the first available flight to Boston after a game to be with his wife and two young daughters, rather than stick around and board the team charter the following day. "He felt his family was growing up and he didn't like to spend much time on the road," Havlicek later wrote.[22] Still, playing pro basketball, especially for the Celtics, offered its own special rewards. "We were a group of guys from different backgrounds," Howell said. "I think we were an example of how people of different backgrounds, different races or whatever played together, worked together and developed a love and respect for each other. Like I say, it's the epitome of what humans can accomplish when you get rid of all those petty things, the vices that you have, the prejudices that you have. . . . Everybody pulled together. It was a great situation to be in."[23]

His teammates were likewise appreciative of his contributions, especially less talented players like John Jones who had a brief stint with the Celtics during the 1967–68 season. Howell went out of his way to help Jones when the latter was having difficulty with his offensive rebounding. "Listening to Bails talk about getting the ball off the boards was an education," Jones related. "My but that man has a lot of tricks. He could have gone through the motions with me, you know. But he didn't. He'd go over things twice and three times with me if he had to."[24] This meticulousness spilled over to Howell's daily eating habits, which included having a cup of tea with his pinky finger extended outward. "Everything had to be cooked to perfection," John Havlicek later wrote in his autobiography. "In ordering toast, he would say, 'I like buttered toast, but I don't want you bringing me out here any cold toast with a lump of butter on it. As for steak, he could be equally choosy: "I would like that medium. Now, I don't want that on the medium-well side, or the medium-rare side. I just want it real nice and medium and pink in there.'"[25] These personal peculiarities aside, Havlicek considered Howell a paragon of hard-nosed professionalism. "He might be sitting in the locker room brewing a pot of tea, but when the game started he was a terror," he related. "A couple of years before he joined the team, he was playing such a rough game against us one night in Providence that our broadcaster, Johnny Most, bellowed, 'Bailey Howell's got twelve elbows!' He was the pushingest, shovingest guy I have ever seen. If someone got mad at him for that, he'd just laugh at him. He was a physical player who wouldn't back down from anything, but I never saw him in a fight."[26]

Howell gravitated to the game at a young age while growing up in the small-town atmosphere of Middleton, Tennessee, in the late 1940s. In truth, he had little choice, as basketball was the only sport available for children to play in this rural community of 500. "Basketball was a year-round sport back home," said Howell, who went on to average 31.2 points a game in high school and set an all-time Tennessee prep scoring record with 1,187 points.[27] His brilliance on the court led to several college scholarship offers before he eventually settled on Mississippi State University in Starkville, Mississippi, in 1955. A two-time All-American with the Bulldogs, Howell became a dominant force in the highly competitive Southeastern Conference, averaging 27.1 points and 17 rebounds a contest in three varsity seasons. In his senior year, the 6-foot-7-inch, 205-pound pivotman directed the Maroons to a conference championship with a 24–1 mark. But hopes of a national title were dashed when authorities at the historically segregated school removed the team from the NCAA tournament due to their objections over the "presence" of African-American athletes. It was a crushing disappointment to Howell, who maintained he was free of any racial prejudice. As he commented in 1969, "I had always been taught we're all the same, and if I believe what the Bible says, then it's true."[28] Unfortunately, this opinion was not shared by the racist all-white administration of Mississippi State.

Shrugging off this setback, Howell entered the NBA in 1959 after being selected in the first round by the Detroit Pistons. While he posted some outstanding numbers with his rookie campaign, a 17.8 point scoring average to go along with 790 rebounds, he had the misfortune of coming up the same season as the "phenomenal" Wilt Chamberlain of the Philadelphia Warriors. Otherwise, he might have been the prohibitive shoo-in for Rookie of the Year honors. Even then, however, he was not devoid of support for the award. "There can be no disputing Chamberlain's greatness," maintained Bob Latshaw of the *Detroit Free Press,* "but Bailey Howell of the Pistons gets my vote as the best 'first-year pro' in the National Basketball Association."[29] Howell earned this acclaim while making perhaps the most difficult transition of his basketball career: moving from center to forward. "It's a lot different, facing the goal from the corner instead of having my back to it, as I did in the pivot during the college years," he said. "Then, too, you are guarded face-to-face instead of back-to-face. I'd say another adjustment every guy must make is getting used to bigger, tougher opponents under the boards, where contact is allowed."[30]

Over his next four seasons with the Pistons, Howell continued to distinguish himself by becoming a consistent 20-point scorer and hauling down 10 rebounds a game. Veteran teammate Earl Lloyd counted himself among the many who were impressed by Howell's skill in the latter category. "He does the one thing well in this league that's important when you play corner," he told Jack Zanger of *Sport* in 1962. "He goes up for rebounds. You watch him, he's always there."[31] Yet for all of Howell's All-Star-caliber statistics, he could not avoid being traded to the Baltimore Bullets in 1964 along with two other minor players. The deal was called "a house-cleaning move" by the media as the Pistons had finished a lowly fifth in the league's Western Division the previous season and were looking to rebuild with new players. But the pain of rejection gnawed at Howell.

Despite two more productive seasons with the Bullets in which he averaged 18 points and 10 boards a game, Howell was unceremoniously put on the trading block once again when he asked for a "token" salary increase before the start of the 1966–67 season. "I played hard and I figured I deserved something," he told *The Sporting News.* "For a while, I didn't seem to be getting anywhere. Then Buddy Jeannette, the Baltimore Bullets' general manager, called me at my home, September 1, and told me I was going to get the money I asked for. 'Only it won't be coming from us,' Buddy said. 'It will be coming from Boston.' That's how I found out the Bullets traded me."[32]

Howell claimed he wasn't surprised by the deal, which sent Celtics backup center Mel Counts to Baltimore in exchange for himself in a straight player deal. The Bullets had a surplus of veteran forwards on their roster, and there was not enough playing time to accommodate all of them. In addition, Howell had experienced a nasty personality conflict with Bullets head coach Paul Seymour, which adversely affected his status with the club. "Paul and I never did agree on a lot of things when he coached Baltimore, including the way he played me—40 minutes one night and 14 the next," he said. "The Bullets' management is inexperienced and I think Seymour convinced them I was over the hill. I know he suggested they cut me 25 percent [in salary]."[33]

Always alert for opportunities to strengthen his team, Red Auerbach was more than delighted to take Howell off Baltimore's hands for the relatively modest price of Counts, who averaged 6.6 points and 5.7 rebounds in two seasons with the Celtics. "We were very high on Counts and hated to lose him because of his potential," Auerbach said. "But in Howell we have something we were lacking—strength in the corner."[34]

For his part, Howell became ecstatic over the news. "Never in my wildest dreams," he said, "did I ever imagine I'd be playing for Boston some day."[35] Indeed, the difference between playing for the Celtics as opposed to the lackluster Pistons and Bullets squads he had labored seven long seasons for became apparent right away. "For one thing, when you play with the Celtics, you always know that the other team is up and ready for you," he said. "But the big difference is that on this club, everybody is always looking for the open man. If you're open on the Celtics, you have to be looking for the ball because you're going to get it. If somebody else is open, you get the ball to him. On other teams, play is a little different. You know with a losing club that the man with the ball is probably going to take the shot because he's got his job to worry about."[36]

Howell had never let such base concerns interfere with his own game, as it was predicated on unselfishness and putting in a second effort on every play. "Hustle made me a pro," he said proudly. "I know that I do not have the natural skills of many ballplayers, but I can compensate for any lack with hustle and it has paid off."[37] Russell could testify firsthand to the success of this approach, as he had been on the receiving end of

Howell's bruising physicality for several seasons. "When Bailey played with Detroit and Baltimore, he used to run up and down my back on the offensive board," he recalled. "The guy really bugged me. And if that wasn't bad enough, he was also from Mississippi and had a Southern accent. But secretly I've always admired the way Howell plays. He never takes anything from anybody. He's been a Celtic-type player for a long time."[38]

At no time was this more evident than in Game 6 of the 1968 NBA finals against the Los Angeles Lakers. With the Celtics needing just one more victory to clinch their tenth league championship in 12 years, Howell rose to the occasion by scoring 30 points, tearing down 11 boards, and dishing out 3 assists in a 124–109 Boston triumph. "It certainly was my happiest moment in basketball when that final gong sounded," Howell said. "I had spent so many years trying to help clubs stay in the playoffs, like Detroit and Baltimore, and last year we lost out to Philly. This has to be my greatest thrill."[39]

Greater still was the fine defensive effort he put in against high-scoring Laker forward Elgin Baylor in holding him to under 30 points. "I played Elg close to prevent him from shooting outside, as he does not drive as much as he used to," Howell said. "I'd also play him on the right side so he couldn't drive to the middle. He's not so strong going to his left. If he went to the baseline Russ would be there to help out, although we know Baylor is great passing off to a free man. . . . In three games he scored 4, 7, and 11 during the first halves, but then he went to town over the second 24 minutes. I did get tired, but he's such a great shooter you can just do so much against him."[40] Interestingly enough, Howell had specifically requested the difficult assignment of covering Baylor after the Celtics had eliminated the Philadelphia 76ers in the previous playoff round. But then, aggressively taking on such challenges had always been a distinguishing trait of Howell's career. "Howell is real, real pro," Auerbach said. "There is no such thing as this guy having to be motivated— he comes to play every night. I've always liked him, not just as a player, but for his attitude. He's such a nice kid, I can't understand how anybody could trade him twice. He's the kind of kid who, if I get him from the start, I keep."[41]

With Howell back on board and Russell making a remarkable recovery from a painful knee injury, the Celtics were able to finish out the month of February on a somewhat upbeat note, winning six of ten games. But four of the victories came at the expense of sub-.500, non–playoff contending teams like Detroit and Phoenix, whom the Celtics had the schedule maker's good fortune of playing three times. Their other victories were against Los Angeles and Atlanta, the top two teams of the Western Division. Yet on closer inspection, even these wins were not as impressive as they first appeared. The Lakers, who were blown out at home, 124–102, were without the services of All-Star guard Jerry West, the team's leading scorer. As for the Hawks, they were victims of a sluggish second quarter and the clutch shooting of Sam Jones, who drained the game winner with 6 seconds remaining in a 122–120 Boston triumph.

Something was still definitely wrong with the Celtics as they found themselves nine games out of first place with fourteen to go, albeit with a comfortable seven-game lead over Cincinnati for the fourth and final playoff spot in the East. Bill Russell, never one to shy away from hard truths, did his best to confront the situation head-on by acting in a firm and decisive manner.

Following a 115–96 loss to the Knicks in New York on March 1, Russell shook up the Celtics lineup by having John Havlicek and Emmette Bryant start over regulars Tom Sanders and Larry Siegfried at forward and guard respectively. "I thought it was time for a change," Russell said. "Havlicek has been a starter for us on many occasions. And Emmette has been playing exceptionally well for a month and a half." While dramatic and swift, the moves did not catch Siegfried and Sanders entirely by surprise. "Every guy wants to be a starter," Siegfried confessed, "but I was playing terribly. The important thing to me is whether or not we win, not how much I play. I would figure there was something wrong if I was relegated to the bench and played only 3 minutes." Sanders, who was suffering through a particularly bad playing stretch himself, also offered no excuses. "Something had to be done," he said.[42]

The changes appeared to pay off in the team's next game against Chicago at the Garden. Fighting back the fatigue that inevitably came with playing their third game in less than 48 hours, the Celtics mustered up enough energy to down the Bulls, 99–92, before a Garden audience of 10,045. Sam Jones was the team's offensive leader with 20 points, while Don Nelson scored all 13 of his points in the fourth quarter to quash any hopes for a Chicago comeback. As for Havlicek and Bryant, they got off on the right foot in their new starting roles by combining for 30 points and 12 rebounds.

While John Havlicek had proven in championship seasons past that he was capable of such clutch production, the same could not be said of Emmette Bryant. Entering his fifth pro season in 1968–69, Bryant seemed to be well on his way to having an undistinguished career. He had never averaged more than 9 points and 4 assists a game, and for a guard his size (he was 6 feet, 1 inch), he didn't possess a consistent outside shot. His field goal percentage usually hovered in the low 40 percent range. Still, his speed and ball-hawking skills were undeniable assets to a team that embraced the running game like the Celtics. "He digs it out," Red Auerbach said. "Every club can use a digger."[43] Added Havlicek, "I hated playing against him. . . . He's so quick. Em runs us a little faster. I like running with him."[44]

Bryant did not voice disagreement on any of these essential points. "I had pretty good ball-handling abilities," he said. "And then playing pressure defense, I was quick. So by the time they got me upcourt, there wasn't time to post me up. Oscar [Robertson] used to post me up a little. . . . He was such a great ball handler and you'd think you were doing such a great job against him and then at the end of the game you'd look at the stat sheet and say damn. He'd have his 30 points, 12–13 rebounds and 11 assists."[45] Yet such was the quality of Bryant's defense against the Cincinnati superstar that Robertson paid him the ultimate compliment when he said, Emmette "plays me as tough as anyone in the league."[46]

Bryant could also take special pride in his rebounding prowess as he had averaged as many as 4 boards a game in 1966–67. "It was something I always did," he explained. "I always tried to rebound. In fact, I was averaging 10 rebounds a game my senior year [in college]. . . . My highest is 16 in a game against Chicago. I would just beat them to the ball basically. I'd watch where the shot was going up, because I very seldom got out when a shot was taken. . . . I always went back to get the ball or I got it foul line extended. I just jumped out on the boards."[47] Sometimes, however, this unfettered exuberance on the court could claim the better of him. "The only thing I had to caution Bryant about was his lack of appreciation for the basketball," Auerbach said. "In his eagerness to get us on the scoreboard early in the season, he was just gambling too much with his playmaking. He was trying to force things too much on offense. He was trying to pass the ball into openings for passes which didn't exist. The result was we were losing the ball too many times without getting a shot. But the minute I explained the situation to him, he cut it out."[48]

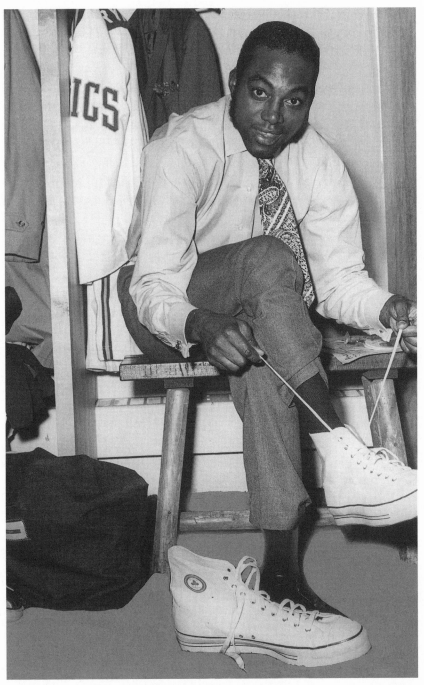

Emmette Bryant laces 'em up
Courtesy of the *Boston Herald*

A native of Chicago, Illinois, Bryant didn't think he had much of a future in the game until he served with the U.S. Air Force in Panama in the late 1950s. "I played a lot of basketball in the Air Force," he said. "It was very pivotal. I was very young at the time. I was playing with guys who were college graduates. . . . They said, 'You play better than a lot of guys we played with in school and they're playing in college.'"[49] Taking their words of encouragement to heart, Bryant went on to accept a basketball scholarship from Chicago's DePaul University in 1960. Despite four injury-plagued years there, he established himself as one of the top point guards in the country and helped lead the Blue Demons to a 23–3 record his senior year. "When I played, we won," he said proudly.[50] Yet because of a serious leg injury he had incurred in his final college season, the pros were leery of taking him high in the NBA draft. "His legs were doubtful," New York Knicks coach Red Holzman later confirmed. "Everyone knew that."[51] Bryant instead fell all the way to the seventh round, where the Knicks finally grabbed him.

Over the next four seasons, Bryant showed glimpses of great potential, but he could never put together a period of sustained excellence on the floor to merit a permanent starting berth. As a result, the Knicks left him unprotected in the NBA expansion draft at the conclusion of the 1967–68 season. "I was disappointed, but I understood the numbers game," he said. "Walt [Frazier] was coming into his own [in the backcourt]. He was in his second year. We had [All-Star] Dick Barnett. [Swingman] Cazzie [Russell] played some big guard . . . so I understood that."[52] The Phoenix Suns wasted little time in claiming Bryant for their roster, but the DePaul graduate was less than enthusiastic about playing for a first-year franchise that he called the "Siberia" of professional basketball. There "was just no way the Suns were going to sign me," he said. "It would have been too much like starting over. I figured I had some good business contacts outside basketball and now was the time to pursue them. I made it very clear to Phoenix that I planned to retire."[53]

Getting wind of this, Red Auerbach made arrangements to see Bryant play at a summer basketball tournament in upstate New York. Liking what he saw, he candidly approached the diminutive guard with a proposition. "First he asked me if he made a deal for me would I come," Bryant later recalled. "I told him 'Yeah, I would consider that and get a chance to stay on the east coast.' And he said since [guard] K.C. Jones had retired, he needed somebody to play defense, distribute the ball and just play hard every night. So I told him that was fine. He said, 'Okay, that's fine but there's one thing. You have to cut that beard off.' I had a full beard [at the time]. So I said, 'Okay.' So what I did was shave it down to where I had mutton chops and a Van Dyke [beard]. I started that mutton chop craze [in the 1970s]. I was the first one to have long sideburns. Although [Walt Frazier] became famous for them in New York, I was the first one to have them in the league. Red said, 'Okay, that's fine.'"[54]

The deal was made. The Celtics gave up a second round choice to Phoenix in exchange for the contractual rights to Bryant. "That's a pretty steep price, although it's turned out to be a good deal," Auerbach said.[55] For his part, Bryant had little doubt in his mind that his skills and talents were a perfect match for the Celtics. "I had played against those guys for four years in New York and we had limited success against them," he recounted. "But I had several good games against them where we actually beat them once in awhile. They liked to run and I loved to run. They played great defense and I loved playing defense. I thought I'd fit right in."[56] He did, but the period of adjustment took far longer than he expected. Utilized mainly for spot defensive duty at the start of the season, Bryant spent most of his time sitting on the bench. "I only played against Phoenix for some reason," Bryant laughed. "I did a good job on Gail Goodrich and I scored in double figures. It got so I only looked forward to playing against Phoenix."[57] Only gradually did Russell gain enough confidence in Bryant to increase his minutes over the last quarter of the season. "Frankly, I didn't know he could be this good or I'd have started him sooner," Russell said. "Early in the season, I used him mostly to go in and foul. I hated to do it. He's been around for five years and I was asking him to do something that most guys wouldn't consider important. But he did it. And he did it without complaining, and I liked that."[58] Bryant showed Russell he could play by running the floor well, not turning the ball over, and consistently hitting his shots. He also exhibited a penchant for getting his uniform dirty. As *The Sporting News* reported, "He hustles as much when Boston is 10 points ahead as when the Celtics are 10 behind. And he comes up with a great many loose balls, mostly because he's willing to dive on the floor for them."[59]

In securing the Celtics' starting backcourt job, Bryant had to beat out not only veteran Larry Siegfried but also rookie Don Chaney and second-year man Mal Graham as well. A native of Baton Rouge, Louisiana,

Chaney became the Celtics' first-round draft pick in 1968 after having starred with the University of Houston Cougars the previous three seasons. Although he played in the shadow of Elvin Hayes, one of the all-time scoring greats in collegiate history, Chaney's quickness and superior skills as a defender earned him considerable praise. "Chaney had long arms and great anticipation for a pass," University of Houston head coach Guy Lewis later remembered. "We didn't keep steals in those days, and there's no telling how many he had. But it would have been some kind of record."[60]

The 6-foot-5-inch, 210-pound guard, better known as "Duck" to his teammates, was not deficient in the scoring department either, as he tossed in 12.6 points a game during his varsity career. But the majority of his offense was derived from fast breaks and uncontested layups after steals. He was considerably less accurate from the outside. According to basketball writer Bob Ryan, if he hit a jump shot, "serious thought was given to declaring the rest of the day a holiday in the state of Texas."[61] This aside, his on-court leadership abilities were such that in his senior year he helped guide the Cougars to a stunning upset over John Wooden's defending NCAA champion UCLA Bruins and a number one ranking overall. "Chaney was a super leader, a quiet leader but a super one all the same," Lewis maintained. "He knew the game of basketball in and out."[62]

Regrettably, Chaney did not get much of an opportunity to demonstrate these qualities for the Celtics during the 1968–69 season. Due to a prior commitment he had with the Army Reserves, he missed all of training camp and the first four months of the regular season. When Chaney finally joined the club in February, he discovered he was not in the best of basketball shape nor as mentally prepared for the rigors of the NBA as he would have liked. "This had to be one of the worst times in my life," he later said. "I wasn't ready to play basketball, although it took me a while to realize it. From the standpoint of endurance I was in good physical condition. I could run all day. But the muscles you use in the army aren't the same ones you use to play basketball. I didn't have any coordination or timing. I didn't know my teammates and they didn't know me. Frankly, I pressed a lot. Bill Russell . . . used to pick spots for me where it looked as though I could help on defense. But even then I could feel myself getting tight. In some games I was real bad. And because I didn't drive much, I had trouble putting the ball in the basket.

Rival players would drop off me and give me the outside shot and I'd be afraid to take it."[63]

Seeing this weakness, Celtics GM Red Auerbach attempted to rectify the situation by taking Chaney aside for a shooting session with Sam Jones. "Watch Sam now, Don," Auerbach instructed. "See how he uses the fingers on the ball, after first adjusting it in his hands with the seams felt. That gives you grip. You do that immediately upon receiving the ball before you're about to shoot. Then, get up high and, most of all, mentally try to reach out and grab the rim of the basket when you follow through. It helps your direction, distance and rhythm."[64] While appreciative of the hands-on instruction, Chaney still struggled offensively in the 20 games he played that season. He connected on only 31 percent of his shots and led the team in air balls.

Nevertheless, there were certain aspects of his game that prompted many grizzled hardwood veterans to sit up and take notice. "I really liked him from the start," wrote John Havlicek in *Hondo*. "I liked his defense and his rebounding, and right away I could envision a role for him as sort of a successor to K.C. Jones. Physically, he was ideal. He was 6-foot-5-inches with very long arms. He had great strength for a guard and decent quickness. The only guard built remotely like him was Oscar Robertson. The only thing you ever heard about Chaney was that he couldn't shoot. People said he'd never make it because of his offense, but the Celtics have always been able to make room for specialists."[65]

In the years ahead, Chaney rewarded Havlicek's faith in him by becoming a five-time NBA All-Defensive selection and a reliable floor general who directed the Celtics to their first championship without Russell in 1974. He also developed a serviceable outside shot that allowed him to average double figures in scoring during the prime of his 12-year pro career. Yet despite all these accomplishments, Chaney could be self-effacing to a fault. As the *Christian Science Monitor* reported, "Chaney is quieter than a hospital zone. [Fidel] Castro's profile says more on a postage stamp. Harpo Marx was a chatterbox by comparison. The only time Don opens his mouth is to put food in it."[66] Thankfully, this personality tick did not prevent him from becoming a highly respected member of the NBA head coaching fraternity after his retirement as a player in 1980. He served stints with the Los Angeles Clippers, Detroit Pistons, and New York Knicks and earned NBA Coach of the Year honors with the Houston Rockets in 1991.

Significantly, he credited his time with the Celtics in helping prepare him for these new responsibilities. "I think it started years ago with Red Auerbach and his selection of players and the process the Celtics went through in training and conditioning," he told writer Dennis D'Agostino. "In my rookie year [1969], they really made sure that you gained knowledge of the game, you didn't just sit there on the bench. Often, they placed you with a veteran player who would tell you what you were doing wrong. You learned and absorbed a lot about the game. The other thing was that you had player contributions while the game was going on, guys making suggestions along the way, so you had to have a feel for the game while it was going on."[67]

A "feel for the game" was also something Mal Graham was thought to possess when he first joined the Celtics as a highly touted first-round draft choice from New York University in 1967. "Graham is the best backcourt man I ever coached," said NYU coach Lou Rossini at the time of his selection. "He should do very well with the Celtics. Boston can use a playmaker and Mal should fit in well with Sam Jones, John Havlicek and Larry Siegfried. He is very effective. He's strong, tough and still improving."[68] Indeed, so proficient was Graham at offense that he became the third leading scorer in the country his senior year with a 28.7 average. In addition, the soft-spoken, 6-foot-1-inch, 185-pound guard from White Plains, New York, "shattered" every existing NYU scoring record, which was "no mean feat" given the impressive pro talent that had passed through the school over the years, including Boston's own Tom "Satch" Sanders. Small wonder then that Graham was the only NYU athlete to be chosen Athlete of the Year for two consecutive seasons in 1965–66 and 1966–67.

Graham, who earned a degree in marketing with a minor in psychology, found playing for the Celtics a far more challenging enterprise. "They move the ball a lot," he said. "It really gives you an opportunity to show what you can do. I like basketball. It's a microcosm of life. There is a challenge and a response. You have your ups and your downs and—that's all life is."[69] Though he started in several games his rookie year after Larry Siegfried had come down with an injury, he seldom showed any of the old offensive sparkle that had made him such an outstanding player in college. He recorded just 290 points in 48 games for a 6.0 average, to go along with 94 rebounds and 61 assists. Defensively, however, he demonstrated a high degree of promise as he made the most of his "speed and ball-hawking ability" to out-hustle bigger and more powerful opponents.

Yet any hope of carving out a long NBA career for himself as a defensive specialist vanished at the start of the 1968–69 season. "I think it began in the preseason of my second year," he later told Leigh Montville of the *Boston Globe*. "In the first half of the games, I'd be running around, stealing the ball, overplaying the man, playing the game as well as I ever did. Then, in the second half I'd just feel draggy. Tired." The fatigue only grew worse the deeper he went into the season. "It was progressive," he said. "I'd be able to play the first quarter fine, but now in the second quarter I'd be draggy. Then it got to be that I'd play one or two minutes and I'd be tired. Then I was just tired all the time."[70] He also developed skin lesions and a swelling of certain glands.

Alarmed at his condition, Celtics team physician Dr. Thomas Silva had Graham hospitalized for tests. What was discovered radically changed the direction of Graham's life. He was diagnosed with sarcoid, a glandular disease that has the tendency to sap the physical vitality from its victims. Rest was prescribed, and Graham dutifully sat on the bench for six weeks in the middle of the season to contemplate his options. Though he would feel well enough to get into a handful of games down the stretch, his basketball career was effectively over. "It's just the wrong game for this disease," he explained in 1982. "I've read since that [major league baseball's] Cecil Cooper of the Milwaukee Brewers has it. But every case is different. And what does he have to do? He's an athlete whose job is to stand at first base. I was a basketball player."[71]

Graham continued on with the Celtics for a couple more seasons as head of scouting, a position that Red Auerbach had created especially for him. But the field of law began to appeal to him as a profession. With Auerbach's blessing, he entered Boston College Law School and emerged with a diploma in 1974. He practiced general law for almost a decade before being tapped to serve as a judge for the Roxbury District Court by Massachusetts governor Edward King in 1982. Four years later he was appointed to the bench of the Massachusetts Superior Court, where he has remained ever since. Through it all, he never forgot the support Auerbach and the Celtics gave him at his darkest hour. "What was important to me was the understanding of Red Auerbach," he said. "Any other organization in basketball, as soon as it found out I couldn't play, the message would have been 'see you later, pal.' With Red, it was 'what are you going to do?' He was ready to help. The two years of transition on that scouting job helped me break away gradually, to handle everything. I was about to say that even though that magic bubble had burst, my future was in my own hands. I could decide what I wanted to do with it."[72]

The Celtics were similarly in a position to control their own destiny after dispatching the Bulls on March 2. With 12 games remaining on the regular schedule, the team desperately needed to put together a string of victories not only to better position themselves for the upcoming playoffs, but also to let the rest of the league know they were still viable contenders for the championship. But try as they might, the Celtics could not immediately extricate themselves from the funk they had played in all season. They dropped their next three contests on the road and looked to be additional fodder for visiting San Francisco on March 9, due to the fact the Warriors had bested the Celtics in three of their previous five meetings. Luckily for the Celtics, however, their collision with the Warriors coincided with a hometown tribute to one of the greatest players ever to don a Boston uniform. For no self-respecting Celtic could be expected to perform below their optimal best in a game honoring the retiring Sam Jones. And none did.

Storming out to a 27-point lead at halftime, the Celtics never let their foot off the accelerator and buried the Warriors, 138–89, behind the smoking offense of Larry Siegfried (a game-high 26 points) and John Havlicek (22 points). "They made it easy for Sam Jones to enjoy his day," Jack Clary of the *Boston Herald-Traveler* wrote.[73] The Celtics also benefited from the inspired play of Bill Russell, who grabbed 13 rebounds and exhibited an "unusual zest on offense" with 14 points. "You always like to win, especially on these days," Russell said, "and we've had some terrible games [against] them."[74] For Jones the victory and the warm reception he received from Boston fans during an emotional send-off ceremony at halftime marked a special moment in his illustrious basketball career. "Twelve years has been a long time," he told the crowd. "When I first reported to the Boston Celtics I thought it would be for just a few days. I had no idea I would be playing for the greatest team that ever put on basketball uniforms. . . . This is a day that [my family] will always remember. It's been a pleasure playing for you and I thank you for having me these last 12 years."[75]

Ironically, it was only by sheer chance that Jones ever ended up playing for the Celtics. An unheralded star from North Carolina Central

Sam Jones Day

College, the 6-foot-4-inch, 198-pound guard had elicited scant interest from the pros, apart from the Minneapolis Lakers. "I was sure I was going to Minneapolis," Jones later said. "I got to know Bob Leonard of the Lakers while I was in the Army. He asked me if I had any plans to play pro ball. I told him that I was interested but that I had another year in school. He must have told the Lakers about me because they drafted me in 1956. I wrote to them that I was going back to school to get my degree. My name went back in the pot."[76] Having been given assurances by Lakers management they would draft him again, Jones was understandably surprised when the Celtics grabbed him in the first round the following year. Unbeknownst to Jones, Red Auerbach had been tipped off about his talent by Horace "Bones" McKinney, a former Celtic who was coaching at Wake Forest University. "I saw a boy named Sam Jones play in a game here in Winston-Salem this winter," McKinney reportedly told Auerbach. "He's a great shot and the fastest man I've ever watched on a basketball court. If I were you, I'd grab him."[77] His curiosity piqued, Auerbach decided to roll the dice. "Sam was an unknown boy from an unknown school," he said. "But we had last draft choice, and I figured, Why not? There's nobody left."[78]

Jones was hardly overjoyed by the news. "I wasn't too happy when [I] learned that I had been drafted by the Celtics," he remembered. "After all, they had just won a world championship, and as a rule you don't break up a team that is the greatest. Because of this, I had doubts as to whether I could make the squad and turned toward teaching."[79] Indeed, Jones had an offer to teach at the Second Ward High School in Charlotte, North Carolina, already on the table. Due to the low starting pay scale, however, Jones decided to request an additional $500 from the school. When no extra money ensued, Jones's mind was made up for him. "I finally decided to take the chance," he said. "They had 12 men back from the last year. Maybe I could beat out one of them. They also had 10 other draftees who were real good ball players. But I had one advantage over most of them. I had already been in the army."[80]

Just the same, all the military training in the world could not prepare him for the physical challenges that awaited him at his first Celtics preseason camp in the late summer of 1957. "Red [Auerbach] was tough," Jones said. "I never saw so many conditioning exercises in my life. You know, it was Red who started me wearing loafers. I'd get so tight in my legs and stomach from his exercises that I couldn't bend over to tie my shoes. Red struck me at first as being a very mean man. Oh, everyone respected him. I guess it was the way he talked, the way he put you through the exercises as if he didn't care about you as long as you got in shape for him."[81] While maintaining this outwardly rigid attitude, the Celtics coach privately was delighted by what he saw in Jones. "When he first came to the club he wasn't the shooter that he is now," Auerbach told the *Boston Globe* in 1963. "Actually, there were three other kids that year who were almost just like Sam. The difference was, the other three just thought about shooting. But Sam, after a couple of days, starte[d] to hand out some nice passes, and blocking so other guys could shoot."[82] Most importantly, Jones displayed an ability to absorb constructive criticism and act accordingly. "He was then, and still is a very coachable guy," Auerbach continued. "With most fellas, you try to teach them something, or make a correction that might help them, and they'll try it once. After that, they'll forget it."[83]

Unable to crack the All-Star starting backcourt of Bob Cousy and Bill Sharman in his first three seasons, Jones had to content himself with being a substitute who never averaged more than 12 points and 18 minutes a game. "Watch the other guys," Auerbach instructed him before each contest. "Learn their habits. Know what to expect from them."[84] As always, there were no complaints. He soaked up as much information as he could about the game from his teammates and quietly bided his time. During this long apprenticeship period, Jones teamed up with defensive guard K.C. Jones to give the Celtics a dynamic substitute backcourt popularly known as the "Jones Boys." "Around the second quarter or so," Cousy told *Sports Illustrated* in 1961, "I actually plan on being taken out of the game, and I pace myself accordingly. That's when Sam and K.C. come in. They not only sustain a lead, they add to it. And on defense, they hound the opposition guards so much that any man's all softened up for me when I come back in."[85]

Following Sharman's departure in 1961, Jones was elevated to the starting shooting guard position. He did not disappoint in his new role. Over the next seven seasons, he averaged 20 points a game with a scoring arsenal that included an impossible to defend bank shot. "I developed the bank shot in high school because I couldn't make a layup," Jones later said. "I used to spend hours by myself aiming at the strips on the backboard. After I did it enough times, it became instinctive. And something you don't have to think about, you usually do well." Indeed, with each passing year, Jones only grew more comfortable in his offense. "As a man gets old, I think he probably gets smarter," Jones once told *The Sporting News.* "He knows what things work for him, so he relies primarily on them. Take me, for example. I shoot exactly the same against Los Angeles as I do against the rest of the teams in the league. If I change my style against Wilt Chamberlain, then I'm giving up something I do best for something I don't do as well. Look, I know Chamberlain is going to block some shots on me. But I also know he isn't going to do it enough times a game to make any real difference. If I can get to the spot I like on the floor before the man who is guarding me, I'm going to score."[86]

Like any virtuoso, Jones was not without his idiosyncrasies. The owner of a quirky personality, Jones often said and did things that caused his coaches and teammates to shake their heads in collective disbelief. Once, Red Auerbach grew exasperated with Jones for passing up a number of open shots in a contest. When asked to explain himself, Jones responded, "I can't shoot the ball when my feet are cold."[87] On another occasion, Celtics swingman Frank Ramsey innocently inquired as to the reason why Jones appeared to be in obvious physical pain on the floor. "Oh, my mortgage," Jones said matter-of-factly. Asked to clarify his statement, Jones answered, "My knee hurts and I just bought a new house. Who's gonna pay the mortgage?"[88] Such bizarre explanations became par for the course with Jones, who also demonstrated a strong reluctance to take on a major team leadership role, despite his status as a highly respected veteran. For example, when Russell took over as coach, he specifically asked Jones to call the plays when the Celtics offense came down the court. Jones, however, flatly refused.

"What do you mean?" a puzzled Russell asked.

"I don't have the authority to call the plays," replied Jones.

"Sam," an exasperated Russell explained, "I'm the coach and I just *gave* you the authority!"

"Oh, no," Jones corrected. "You're the coach, but I still don't have the authority, so I can't call the plays."

Realizing the futility of pursuing the matter any further, Russell uncharacteristically conceded defeat. "You're right, Sam," he sighed. "You can't call the plays."[89]

A notorious trash talker on the court, Jones liked to throw his opponents off balance by offering such time-honored insults as "You can't guard me" or "Where's your shot?"[90] When playing against Wilt Chamberlain, Jones would yell, "Too late, Wilt," while depositing yet another jumper over the befuddled superstar's head.[91] Such brazenness inevitably infuriated Chamberlain, and in Game 5 of the 1962 Eastern Division finals between Boston and the Philadelphia Warriors, the big center sought his revenge. Late in the contest, Jones drove toward the basket, only to be intercepted by Chamberlain. "Don't you drive on me," said Chamberlain, drawing to his full 7-foot-1-inch height. "Don't you drive on me," he repeated.[92] Properly forewarned, Jones remained silent until he picked up Chamberlain on a switch play down the opposite end of the court. With his back to the Philadelphia behemoth, Jones "jostled"

Chamberlain, but as he did so, he felt the full force of the latter's arm make contact with his chin. An ugly exchange followed with Jones picking up a photographer's stool to ward off any additional Chamberlain attacks. "He wanted to break my arm," Jones claimed. "If I'm going to fight him, I'm not going to fight fair. So I grabbed the stool."[93] Chamberlain had a slightly different version of events. "Big show Sam wanted to put on before the home fans," he said.[94] Fortunately for Jones, Chamberlain cooled down, but the same could not be said of the Celtics guard's offense. He poured in 23 points for the game, to lead Boston to a 119–104 victory over the Warriors.

Typical of contests of this magnitude, Jones performed at a level far above his peers. For no one outside of Bill Russell played better when championships and winning playoff shares were on the line. "Sam is the greatest clutch shooter I have ever seen," Wilt Chamberlain said. "He murdered us."[95] On this point, Russell wholeheartedly concurred. "Sam Jones has a champion's heart," Russell later wrote. "On the court he always had something in reserve. You could think he'd been squeezed of his last drop of strength and cunning, but if you looked closely, you'd see him coming up with something else he'd tucked away out of sight. . . . Under pressure, we had hidden on our team a class superstar of the highest caliber. In Los Angeles, Jerry West was called 'Mr. Clutch,' and he was, but in the seventh game of a championship series I'll take Sam over any player who's ever walked on a court."[96] As was customary for the mild-mannered North Carolinian, Jones consistently sought to downplay his contributions, however extraordinary they were. "Individual records mean nothing to me," he once said. "All that is important is victory. And for that reason I have really loved playing for the Celts. We have been winners and champions."[97]

Jones's unselfishness also extended off the court. Throughout his long tenure with the Celtics, he frequently made himself available for a number of youth basketball clinics in and around Boston. At one such gathering, he witnessed firsthand the exceptional ability of Jimmy Walker, an impoverished laundry worker's son from Roxbury. "I first saw Jimmy on a playground at Norwalk House Center," Jones said. "He was going to Boston Trade. I asked him if he was interested in going to college. He said he was. I told him he couldn't get ready for college by going to trade school."[98] Convinced that Walker had a bright hoop future ahead of him, Jones dipped into his own wallet to pay for Walker's tuition to

Laurinburg Institute, the same all-black prep school near Fayetteville, North Carolina, that Jones had once attended. Walker blossomed at Laurinburg and from there was able to earn a basketball scholarship to Providence College and eventually a six-figure contract from the Detroit Pistons. Feeling deeply indebted, Walker attempted to pay back Jones for all his generous financial support over the years. "But I wouldn't take the money because it wasn't a loan, it was a gift," Jones said. "The mere fact that Jimmy chose my number [24] to wear on his uniform was good enough for me. But I did tell him once that if he ever found a boy playing basketball with the potential of a Jimmy Walker, and the kid didn't have the money, I hoped he'd help him."[99]

For a proven winner like Jones, anything less would be unimaginable. But then, Jones always had an unerring sense for doing the right thing. As Bailey Howell later said, "I remember [Jones] as someone who had a magic touch with whatever he did, whether it was playing cards or basketball or whatever. Just a winner. A great competitor and a great athlete. The total package."[100]

Unfortunately the Celtics lacked a similar "magic touch," as they could not parlay the good karma generated by Sam Jones Day into a winning streak. Although they clinched their nineteenth consecutive trip to the playoffs by virtue of a Baltimore win over Cincinnati on March 14, the Celtics dropped three of their next four games, including a humiliating 108–73 loss to the Lakers in Los Angeles before a national television audience. Plagued by anemic shooting throughout, the Celtics converted on only 28 of 109 shots, including a miserable 5 of 30 showing in the second quarter. Lakers center Wilt Chamberlain reaffirmed his status as Boston's nemesis, by hauling down 21 rebounds and blocking six shots to lead a "tenacious" Los Angeles defense that stymied the Celtics from the opening buzzer. Indeed, the Celtics were unable to record their first basket until 3:25 had already elapsed in the contest.

In response to the defeat, a visibly upset Russell closed the Celtics dressing room for 20 minutes after the game. He then proceeded to deliver a "verbal whipping" of his team that by his own admission got "very personal." "We had a nice friendly discussion," he told reporters afterward while unwinding in the club whirlpool. "I won't tell you what I said and you couldn't print it anyway. This game was bad but it was not so much the one game by itself. We can't go into the playoffs the way we're playing. One game like this in the playoffs and you're so far behind you never catch up. . . . We had no hustle and we had no teamwork. When you play like that, you expect to get the hell kicked out of you."[101] Nor did he rule out the possibility of levying future fines on individuals not providing the maximum effort on the floor. "There will be no fines this time," he said, "but if there is a repetition . . . then it could be very expensive."[102]

When pressed further on the subject, Russell indicated he was not seeking scapegoats for his team's poor performance, only a way to emphasize the importance of teamwork. "This is a nice, sweet, lovely bunch of guys," he said. "But sometimes they relax and you have to jolt them back to the facts of life—that we live in a hard, cold commercial society. This is a team, and it may sound trite, who will live or die together. We're the best there is when playing together. But we die separately. We're not strong enough to go it one-on-one."[103] Red Auerbach did not hesitate to back up his bearded player-coach, saying he had no problem as general manager in approving of a team fine. "In all my years I've never made a general fine," he said. "But this time is different. And I'm sure if Russell fines, he won't fine 11 guys and not himself." Auerbach went on to lament the club's inconsistent play all season long in the supposedly friendly confines of Boston Garden. "I know we can have bad days but it's a funny thing that 90 percent of our bad games have been in Boston," he said. "We've lost 12 or 13 games at home and that's an unheard of thing. You just can't come home and relax, not in this league. The most important thing is motivation. Russell wants all the players to go all out in the last four games. He wants 100 percent momentum for the playoffs. People say 'Rest your club, you're in fourth place.' But it doesn't work that way."[104]

The dressing-down had the desired effect. In the team's next scheduled contest against the Chicago Bulls, the Celtics shrugged off some "sloppy play" and "ice-cold shooting" at the start of the fourth quarter to go on a 14–2 run that salted away a 104–92 victory. Bailey Howell, showing no ill side effects from his earlier ankle injury, was in top form with a game-leading 27 points, while four other Celtics contributed with 10 or more points. "The victory was far from an artistic success, but then almost anything would be better than that flopperoo against the Lakers," wrote Jack Clary of the *Boston Herald-Traveler.* "The Celtics made some glaring errors, but they never stopped trying. They dogged the Bulls into submission and perhaps started to generate the momentum Coach

Bill Russell has demanded for their trip into the playoffs."[105] Notwithstanding, there were few Celtics satisfied by the final result. "We've still got to run, run, run," commented team captain John Havlicek, who logged in with 13 points in 35 minutes. "We're too busy setting up plays and not running enough. It takes more than a play to win a ball game. It takes movement, lots of movement and we're still not getting enough."[106] He received no argument from Bill Russell, who saw plenty of room for improvement. "The only thing that pleased me was that we played good defense," Russell said. "We didn't play good offense. We scrambled too much."[107]

Russell's opinion of his squad's offensive capabilities improved over the final three games of the regular schedule as the Celtics swept the Royals, Bullets, and Rockets in quick succession. The team topped 110 points in all three contests and demonstrated they could still run with the "old vigor" that had been the hallmark of the great Boston clubs of the 1950s and early 1960s. "We're at the same point this year as we were a year ago," Russell said. "We have no serious injuries and we're in a good groove."[108] This "groove" was particularly evident in a 145–119 pounding the Celtics gave Cincinnati on March 21, in which six Boston players reached double figures in scoring, courtesy of an up-tempo transition game. Paced by the slick shooting of Sam Jones (23 points) and John Havlicek (22 points), the Celtics broke open the contest in the third quarter when they enlarged what had been a single-digit lead at halftime to 17 points after Emmette Bryant netted two straight baskets at the 5:06 mark. As Clif Keane of the *Boston Globe* observed, "These guys just want to run the opposition into the lumber. They have done well reverting to their old ways."[109] Indeed, well enough to close out the regular season with four straight wins and to burnish their fourth place finish in the East with a respectable 48–34 record, fifth best in the league.

But as to the team's chances in the upcoming playoffs, this was an entirely different matter altogether. For no major local or national publication was willing to climb out on a limb and pick the Celtics to go all the way. As Boston sports columnist Tim Horgan put it, "The Celtics have finally reached the point where they're only one key injury, one bad game away from the end. Of course, anything can happen in the playoffs. My point is that it'll have to happen if the Celts hope to make it all the way to their 11th title in 13 years."[110] Basketball columnist Phil

Elderkin of *The Sporting News,* although not as dismissive of Boston's playoff chances, nevertheless felt the situation was ripe for another team to step forward and dethrone the defending champs. "The NBA has changed—grown up," he argued. "Boston's dynasty has aged and cracked. If time has made a cliché of Dr. Naismith's words 'that any NBA team can beat any other NBA on a given night,' it also has made his statement a fact."[111]

As the rest of the league would soon discover, however, something more than the passage of time would be required to dislodge Bill Russell and the Celtics from their customary perch atop the pro basketball world.

CHAPTER
7

A Philly Rout
and a
Big Apple Upset

The opening round of the 1969 NBA playoffs coincided with the sad news that Dwight D. Eisenhower, the thirty-fourth president of the United States and supreme commander of Allied forces in Europe during World War II, had passed away from a heart attack at Walter Reed Hospital in Washington, D.C. "He was a product of America's soil, and of its ideals, driven by a compulsion to do right and to do well, a man of deep faith who believed in God and trusted in his will, a man who truly loved his country and for whom words like freedom and democracy were not clichés—but they were living truths," eulogized President Richard M. Nixon, Ike's former vice president, to a throng of mourners gathered in the Capitol Rotunda.[1] One hundred eighty-five heads of state and dignitaries from 75 nations attended the state funeral, including 78-year-old French president Charles de Gaulle, who Winston Churchill had once told Eisenhower resembled "a female llama who has just been surprised in her bath."[2] Dressed in a tan military outfit, white shirt, and black tie, de Gaulle stoically bid farewell to his old wartime comrade-in-arms with a salute.

On a less somber note, seven University of Massachusetts students, mockingly dressed in the white sheets and hoods traditionally worn by the Ku Klux Klan, disrupted a speech being given on their campus by arch-conservative senator Strom Thurmond of South Carolina. "Strom Thurmond loves burning yellow babies and starving black babies," read one of the placards being carried by the protesters. Apparently unperturbed by the uproar, Thurmond staunchly defended U.S. military efforts in South Vietnam. "We'll have to fight elsewhere if we don't win here," he said.[3] Controversial remarks pertaining to the war in Southeast Asia were also roiling the waters on network television. A taped dedication to a song performed by folksinger Joan Baez on *The Smothers Brothers Comedy Show* was cut by nervous CBS censors when it was discovered that the prefatory comments supported her husband's decision to go to jail for resisting the military draft and opposing "militarism in general." "Anybody who lays it out like that . . . generally gets busted . . . especially if you organize . . . which he did," Baez said.[4] Baez's observations were in accord with the overall antiwar, antiestablishment bent of the show, which CBS soon saw fit to cancel despite high ratings. "It'd be groovy," headlining star Tom Smothers said, "to work in a country where television is free and they don't yank the rug from under you every time you do something that somebody might not like."[5]

The Celtics hoped to avoid a premature dismissal themselves as they made preparations for their opening round playoff opponent: the surprising Philadelphia 76ers, second place finishers in the Eastern Division and owners of an impressive 55–27 mark during the regular season. Recovering from the departure of superstar center Wilt Chamberlain who left via a blockbuster off-season trade to Los Angeles, the 76ers stunned the rest of the NBA by tying the Lakers for the second best record in the league. "After Wilt was traded, the best the papers could say was we'd be a more exciting team without him," high-scoring 76er forward Billy Cunningham told *Sports Illustrated.* "That's like somebody fixing you up with an ugly blind date and then trying to hide what a loser she is by saying she is a great dancer."[6] To complicate matters further, the 76ers lost the services of former Olympic gold medalist and NBA Rookie of the Year Luke Jackson, Chamberlain's designated replacement in the pivot. He suffered an Achilles tendon injury in December and was a scratch for the rest of the season. Despite these setbacks, the 76ers were able to persevere and thrive behind the capable veteran leadership of Cunningham, Hal Greer, Chet Walker, and Wally Jones. Cunningham, in particular, stood out by posting the third best scoring average in the league with 24.8 points and finishing among the top ten rebounders with 12.8 boards per game. "You can't really stop him," claimed one awed observer. "I don't think he can make 'em when you're not on him. He needs contact. He likes to go down the middle or across the middle, sort of like Elgin Baylor used to play—hanging up there and making shots under his arm and every which way."[7]

Yet as impressive as Cunningham's contributions were, they paled in comparison to the matchless consistency displayed by teammate Hal Greer. Entering his eleventh NBA season in 1968–69, Greer had already established himself as one of the deadliest middle-distance shooters in the league, averaging over 20 points a game and climbing to number six on the all-time scoring list with 15,244 points. In 1967–68, he had even managed to overtake the offensively explosive Wilt Chamberlain for the Philadelphia team lead in scoring with a gaudy 24.1 average. "He was one of the finest open-court shooters I ever saw, for he could race down court, stop on a dime twenty feet out on the dead run and bury the shot," teammate Chet Walker later admiringly wrote.[8]

Greer accomplished these feats despite having to endure an array of nagging injuries that might have sidelined a lesser player. "Harold would have his ankles taped," Billy Cunningham later remembered. "Then he'd have a knee brace on and a thigh pad and another pad on his elbow. He never got the attention he deserved, and maybe that was because he was a quiet man who wouldn't sit in the locker room and tell the press how he performed. He let his performance speak for itself." Part of the reason for Greer's reluctance to toot his own horn with the media was a natural reserve. "I never was good with words like some of the other players," he told Jack Kiser of *Basketball Digest* in 1980. "The writers came around, I tried to answer their questions, but I never said anything that made headlines. Nothing colorful."[9] Sometimes, however, his performance was so spectacular that even his unalluring personality could not diminish his on-court achievements. A case in point was the 1968 NBA All-Star Game when Greer went 8 for 8 from the field while scoring a record 19 points in the third quarter. He came away with Most Valuable Player honors along with the deep respect of his peers. "Hal needs a certain amount of recognition to show people that he's on a par with Robertson and West," All-Star teammate Wilt Chamberlain said afterward. "The MVP award will help prove he's one of the great guards in the game."[10]

Greer needed no convincing himself. He knew he was the equal of any elite guard in the league, and that included Sam Jones of the Celtics. "He's on a team where they work for him," Greer said. "Our team is balanced. We're a team all the way. We don't work for one guy. Sam doesn't really have to work for his shots. They work for him. He's strictly offense.

I'm offense plus I move the ball, too. I move the fast break."[11] Indeed, few of his contemporaries could find fault in his game. As former 76er Richie Iannerella remembered, "He was tenacious. The first year we won the division championship with [Philadelphia] . . . the last game of the year, we were in Baltimore and Hal was having a bad night. By the third quarter, we were down 16 but the guys had such faith in Hal. They told him to just keep shooting. He snapped out of his slump and we went on to score 24 unanswered points. I think it's still a league record."[12]

The general lack of appreciation for Greer's talents would haunt him well into retirement as he was inexplicably ignored for first ballot induction into the Basketball Hall of Fame (he eventually made it in 1982) and had to endure being passed over for several NBA coaching jobs. "I have the credentials to coach and make the Hall of Fame," he told a reporter a year before he was finally inducted in Springfield, Massachusetts. "What else do you need? That's why I've reached a point where I have to take things the way they come without putting a life or death attachment on them. Otherwise, I'd be banging my head against the wall."[13] Still, he could not disguise his bitterness when he was overlooked for a vacant assistant coaching job with the 76ers during the 1981–82 season. "There's been no communication between me and the 76ers," he said. "There almost never was."[14]

Always intense and demanding of himself as a player, Greer strove for nothing short of basketball perfection in every contest. "After a game," he once revealed, "I think about the mistakes I made on defense that night. Sometimes I stay up all night thinking about defense, like after I've been chasing Oscar [Robertson] all over the court. That's enough to keep any man awake."[15] Not that somnolence was ever a problem with Greer. He attacked the game with a grim determination that could be off-putting to players and fans alike. "When you go onto the court you should think of only one thing—the game," he later said. "I never had time to smile, to joke with the other guys. Maybe that is one of the things that hurt me. Maybe people never did understand. Maybe they saw me frowning and thought I was some badass."[16]

Greer developed this drive to excel while growing up with six brothers and two sisters in Huntington, West Virginia, in the late 1940s. The baby of the family, Greer was encouraged at an early age to play basketball by his father, William Garfield Greer, a worker for the Chesapeake & Ohio Railroad. His brothers, avid hoop enthusiasts themselves, also provided inspiration. They would engage Greer in frequent one-on-one contests that taught young Hal the value of competition. "We had baskets on the back of the doors in every bedroom in the house, including my father's bedroom," Greer later told writer Raymond Hill.[17]

An All-State performer in high school, Greer accepted an offer to attend Marshall University in Huntington in 1954, thereby smashing a long-standing racial barrier that had existed in West Virginia college sports. For no African-American prior to Greer had ever been afforded the opportunity to showcase their athletic talents at such an advanced level. Characteristically, he made the most of his chance. Setting a school record for career field goal percentage (54 percent), Greer averaged 19.4 points and 10.8 rebounds in 71 games while leading the "Thundering Herd" to the Mid-American Conference championship in 1957. "I expected some problems," he later said of his years at Marshall. "But, there never really were any. The others [black students] had some problems—socially. But as far as problems in the classroom, or on the campus, there weren't any."[18]

Upon graduation Greer was selected as an unheralded second round draft choice by the Syracuse Nationals to play in the NBA. Though he scored an eye-opening 39 points in one half against the Celtics on February 14, 1959, the strapping 6-foot-2-inch, 170-pound guard was relegated to pine duty most of his rookie season. "Hal had this great talent, this exceptional gift of speed, and he couldn't understand why he was sitting on the bench," superstar teammate Dolph Schayes later observed. "He just needed time to adjust to pro ball. But Hal said he had come to play not sit on the bench."[19] Greer need not have worried about the latter becoming a permanent condition.

By his third year, he had achieved starting status, averaging just under 20 points per game, in addition to earning the first of 10 consecutive NBA All-Star team selections. Not even a distracting franchise shift from Syracuse to Philadelphia during the 1963–64 season could diminish his burgeoning greatness as a pro. Indeed, Greer continued his offensive brilliance in the City of Brotherly Love by hiking his scoring average to over 23 points and being a key contributor to the 1967 championship squad. "We were glad to get out of Syracuse, it was not as big a metropolis as Philadelphia was," Greer confessed to writer Wayne Lynch in his book *Season of the 76ers: The Story of Wilt Chamberlain and the 1967 NBA Champion Philadelphia 76ers.* "And I always said when I started in the league if I was to be traded anywhere, it would always be Philadelphia. I just liked the people of Philadelphia, and I enjoyed every time we played there, so it was a good situation."[20]

Less ideal was the situation Greer and his 76er teammates found themselves in after Game 1 of their 1969 Eastern Division semifinal playoff series with the Celtics. Propelled by the hot shooting of John Havlicek (35 points) and Sam Jones (20), the visiting Celtics demolished the 76ers, 114–100, before a disappointing gathering of 8,151 fans at the Spectrum. "People here have just about given up their frustrated dreams of seeing Boston collapse in a heap of old bones and the defending champions' performance in the opener of the best-of-seven series shored up that belief all the more," Jack Clary wrote in his *Boston Herald-Traveler* game summary.[21]

To be sure, the 76ers didn't help their cause by connecting on only 38 of 108 shots, including an embarrassing 3 for 23 effort by Greer, by far the worst shooting performance of his career. "The team played real good defense, and did it as a team," enthused Bill Russell in a special column feature he was writing for the *Boston Globe* during the playoffs. "We picked them at full court at the start of the game. . . . What we tried to do is keep ourselves in position enough to help each other out. This is what we call our scramble defense—we have to double team some guy at times, and we try to make them drop in. Sometimes it's not so successful because it's very hard work." It was successful enough on this particular night, despite the fact the 76ers took 17 more shots than the Celtics and decisively outrebounded them, 75–51. "When you play as steadily as we did, then you have some luck usually," noted Bailey Howell, who chipped in with 16 points.[22]

The 76ers, trailing by only 11 points at halftime, did try to narrow the deficit in the third quarter behind the torrid shooting of Billy Cunningham, who reeled off 11 straight points. But thanks to some intimidating shot-blocking defense by Russell, who had 12 stops for the game, the Celtics easily weathered this challenge and another Philadelphia mounted in the fourth quarter to derail the 76ers' hopes. As Clif Keane of the *Boston Globe* wrote, "It got so sorrowful for the 76ers [in the last period] that at one time the Celtics moved the ball down court without an answer as Cunningham [and his teammates] stood with their hands on their hips trying to figure out just how many hands Russell had."[23] To teammate and reserve guard Larry Siegfried, this turn of events was not surprising given the pressure-packed playoff atmosphere the Celtics found themselves in. "You can see the difference in Russ," he said. "It's like he is extra deep into his bag. He gives you that extra effort that wins championships. It brings out the best in all of the guys."[24]

The latter was certainly in evidence in Game 2 as six Celtics tallied 15 points or better to "crush" the 76ers, 134–103, to go up a commanding 2–0 in the series. Bailey Howell led all scorers with 29 points while Havlicek, Siegfried, and Don Nelson each came through with 20-point efforts. Remarkably, the victory was achieved without the usual Hall of Fame contributions of Sam Jones and Russell. Jones was automatically ejected 3:37 into the contest when referee Jack Madden assessed the Celtics guard with a pair of technical fouls for arguing two calls. Jones had to be physically restrained by a teammate from going after Madden as general manager Red Auerbach rushed down from his box seat to join the heated discussion along with team publicity man Howie McHugh. "All I did was to put my hand on my forehead disgustedly while he [Madden] was looking at me," said McHugh, who was also chased. "He told me to get out of here and I told him to put me out. That's all there was to it." Jones was equally perplexed by his expulsion. "All I did was complain about the traveling call at the other end of the floor," he said. "I told [Madden] I was being pushed from behind. The next thing I know he called a technical."[25] In the end, both ejections stood and the Celtics were minus one of their best shooters. Russell, meanwhile, uncharacteristically ran into foul trouble that limited his playing time to only eight minutes for the contest. "We should have been able to take advantage of the situation," 76er coach Jack Ramsey said. "We didn't."[26]

Instead, unheralded Celtic bench players like Tom "Satch" Sanders rose to the occasion with 18 points and 12 rebounds in 23 minutes of meaningful action. With the Celtic lead only 1 point entering the second half, Sanders took control of the game by scoring 7 points, grabbing 6 rebounds, and making 2 steals. His superb play helped stake the Celtics to a 13-point lead by the end of the third quarter, a margin they would improve upon in the final frame. "It's always tough for a man my age to come off the bench," Sanders joked afterward. "But tonight we were moving the ball and it was just one of those evening[s] when everything went right."[27]

Good fortune smiled again on the Celtics in Game 3 as they withstood a desperate 76er rally in the closing minutes to escape with a 125–118 road victory. Don Nelson played the hero's role as he scored 12 of his 18 points in the final period. "He worked to get his shots," praised Russell in his *Globe* column. "He took them when he had them, made them, and kept us right in the ball game. . . . He kept scoring, was rebounding well and did a pretty good job on defense." Russell was equally adept on the defensive end as he came up with a huge stop against Billy Cunningham in the final moments to help ice away the victory. The 76er sharpshooter, who led all scorers with 33 points, faced off against Russell in the back of the key. Feinting to his right, Cunningham reversed direction toward the hoop, confident that he had successfully shaken off Russell. But Russell, who had 18 rebounds and 9 points, was not so easily fooled. He patiently stayed a step behind Cunningham before finally lowering the boom and swatting away his shot attempt. "Sometimes," Russell said, "you have to let a man get a step. It's all according to the angle. You have to try to estimate where he'll shoot from and put yourself between the two points—the ball and the basket."[28]

In a wild contest that saw 21 ties in the first three quarters, the Celtics appeared to be in the driver's seat with 5:14 remaining as they built a 112–101 lead on the superlative marksmanship of Nelson, who was knocking down one clutch shot after another. However, the 76ers pulled to within a basket with 1:42 to go, thanks to the meteoric offense of Darrall Imhoff and Archie Clark, who scored 24 and 20 points respectively. Unfortunately for the 76ers, their comeback fell short as the Celtics turned up the defensive pressure and Sam Jones and John Havlicek each sank a pair of critical free throws down the stretch. "I think we're playing the best ball of the year," said Russell in his postgame comments. Still, he was taking nothing for granted now that his team enjoyed a seemingly insurmountable 3–0 playoff series edge over the 76ers. "I can't be confident until we win four games," he cautioned.[29]

Russell's reluctance to issue a victory statement was well-advised. For the 76ers, a proud and defiant team, demonstrated they still had plenty of fight left in them in Game 4. Sparked by the red-hot shooting of Archie Clark and Hal Greer, who combined for 53 points, the 76ers staved off elimination with an electrifying 119–116 come-from-behind win at the Garden. Clark capped off the comeback, which saw the 76ers overcome a five-point deficit late in the fourth quarter, by hitting a game-winning jumper with 19 seconds to go. "I've never really counted us out," exclaimed a jubilant Clark, who was told after the game that his wife had delivered a healthy seven-pound boy at Einstein Hospital in Philadelphia. "I realize they've won the three games and there still is no tomorrow. But anytime we go out there we can play the game. We just have to let it all hang out."[30]

For Greer, who collected 24 points to break out of the nightmarish shooting slump he had found himself in the entire series, the victory was extra sweet. "I had good shots [in the first game], but didn't make them," he said. "In the next two games I didn't have the shots so I tried to hit the open man. Tonight I had the shots and made them. I didn't do anything different. I just kept throwing them up there." 76ers coach Jack Ramsey reassured reporters that he had never lost confidence in his star backcourt man despite the scoring drought. "After all," he said, "[Greer's] the reason we're here. He's a great competitor, the team captain and a real leader. He lifted the team with a couple of clutch baskets in that final period."[31]

The Celtics could have used a similar lift in their offense as they shot an abysmal 40.7 percent from the field and missed 17 foul shots. One of the few bright spots was John Havlicek, who once again took home team scoring honors with 28 points in a losing cause. "It wasn't just a bad shooting game for us, it was more than that," Russell said. "We deviated from our game. For one thing, we started taking those guys into the hole. When we do that, one guy is working and four are standing around. When four guys are standing around there is no movement, and no offensive rebounding. Also, the transition from offense to defense becomes very difficult. But give the 76ers the credit. They played a good game. I just hope we got a bad game out of our system."[32]

Russell did not have to wait very long for an answer. Three days after being embarrassed in their own building, the Celtics charged back with a "hard-earned" 93–90 road victory over the 76ers to take the semifinal playoff series, four games to one. It wasn't easy, however. Seeing a 10-point, fourth quarter lead evaporate to one point with 80 seconds remaining, the Celtics got clutch foul shots from Emmette Bryant and John Havlicek to secure the win. Bryant hit his with 49 seconds to go after tearing away a rebound from Billy Cunningham and getting fouled. That gave the Celtics a 92–90 lead, but the 76ers were far from done. Cunningham received the ball in the left corner and let loose a jump shot that hit the rim and fell into the waiting hands of Bryant. The Celtics immediately called a time-out with 18 seconds left, and when play resumed Havlicek received the pass-in at the half court line. Inexplicably, 11 crucial seconds ticked away before any 76er saw fit to foul him, setting up the first penalty situation of the quarter. "I was sort of surprised that they didn't foul me right away," said Havlicek, who overcame a 0 for 9 shooting dry spell in the first half to finish with 22 points, 9 rebounds, and 5 assists.[33] He missed the first foul shot but nailed the bonus one with 7 seconds remaining to give the Celtics a 3-point lead. Grasping at last straws, the 76ers tried to engineer one final desperation shot attempt, but Russell foiled these plans by intercepting an ill-conceived Matt Goukas pass from midcourt to effectively end Philadelphia's season.

"It was a very tense situation and they didn't want to be eliminated and we knew that if they won again last night that we'd really be in for it," noted a relieved Russell in his *Globe* column the following day. "Consequently both teams were a bit nervous and threw the ball away, but the guys played hard, hustled hard and I was very pleased with their performance." Singled out for special praise here was the play of guard Emmette Bryant, who notched 14 points and five assists in 37 minutes. "He made a clutch free throw, one clutch rebound in the last few minutes and stole the ball once as [Billy] Cunningham was coming down with a rebound," lauded Russell. "I think these plays were crucial, to say the least."[34]

While the Celtics had easily disposed of the 76ers, their next round opponent loomed as a far greater challenge. For the New York Knicks of Willis Reed, Walt Frazier, Bill Bradley, Dave DeBusschere, and Dick Barnett were coming off a four-game playoff sweep of the Baltimore Bullets, the same Bullets who had rung up a league-best 57 victories on the regular season. The Knicks rolled over them with a swarming and bruising team defense that left the high-scoring Bullets' offense in a state of disarray. "New York's defense is the texture of barbed wire," wrote Phil Elderkin of the *Christian Science Monitor* at the conclusion of the Baltimore series. "The Knicks clutch-and-hold tactics were particularly impressive in the first three games of the Baltimore series. They held the Bullets to an average of 102.7 points, 13.7 under their regular season figure."[35] Offensively, the Knicks were no shrinking violets either. Four members of their starting five had averaged 15 points or better during the regular season, with Reed leading the pack at 21 points a game.

"The year before we got off to a bad start but then got to know each other," point guard Walt "Clyde" Frazier told *Sports Illustrated.* "This season we came back and were like strangers again. You'd have one guy working and four guys looking at him. We had numerous meetings to figure out what was wrong and we'd still go out and lose. Then we got confidence and after the trade we really got going."[36] The trade Frazier referred to was the December 19 deal that sent starting center Walt Bellamy and guard Howard Komives to Detroit for 6-foot-6-inch power forward Dave DeBusschere. Aside from giving the Knicks another reliable scoring threat inside and a dependable rebounder, the trade also allowed Reed to move over to center, his natural position. "It wasn't that I was happy to see Bellamy go; you never like to see a teammate get traded," Reed later reflected in his autobiography. "But I was happy with the trade because it meant I would again be playing center, the position in which I was more comfortable, more confident and, I believe, more capable."[37] The Knicks were a mediocre 18–17 when the trade was made, but went on a blistering 36–11 tear thereafter. "The most important factors concerning New York are their momentum and their attitude," apprised one rival coach in the middle of the streak. "Take [forward Bill] Bradley, for instance. A few days ago he was so sick he was throwing up all over the place, but he stayed in the game. When you're losing, the first little bump and everybody wants to get out, to rest, to save himself for something else. The Knicks have not only some fine talent, they've got a great attitude."[38]

Gone were the days when the Knicks were the perennial pushovers of the NBA. "New York used to be pro basketball's version of *Swan Lake*," Phil Elderkin wrote. "They had the best court manners in the league. Emily Post could have written books about them. They always had everything in the right place except the ball. They'd rather lose than mess up the basket. Now the Knicks are acting as though they just escaped from Transylvania. If Count Dracula can't find one of his toys, this is to let him know that it is alive and well in New York."[39] Entering the Eastern Division finals, the Knicks were clearly a team hitting their collective stride, while the battered and bruised Celtics resembled an aging prizefighter on the downward slope of a once brilliant career. Having bested the Celtics in six of their previous seven regular season meetings, the Knicks looked to continue their dominance in the playoffs. And the one individual most likely to ensure such a victory was center Willis Reed.

Proud, muscular, combative, and extremely intelligent, Reed was to the Knicks what baseball slugger Reggie Jackson was to the powerhouse

New York Yankees of the late 1970s: the proverbial straw that stirred the drink. "He was the captain, and he was in charge," wrote teammate Walt Frazier in his book, *One Magic Season and a Basketball Life*. "He liked to take charge. He exuded authority, even the way he carried himself. That was the way he played, too. Willis was an overachiever. He was not an exceptional jumper, and he wasn't that fast. But no one ever outhustled him—at practice, or during a game, or even at a kids' clinic. He had a great shot, particularly for a big man, and he was strong, and very quick, and smart, but what did it for him was desire. No one ever had a bigger heart than Willis Reed. As a player and a man, he was always on fire."[40]

Knicks coach Red Holzman enthusiastically shared this sentiment. "To me, Reed is a superstar," he told a writer after the Baltimore series. "I'm not surprised at anything he does. As far as me telling him when to put out, it's not necessary. You don't have to tell Willis."[41] Even opponents tipped their caps to the opportunistic aggressiveness he showed on the floor. "In the first two games of our series I had him going to my strength, away from the basket," said Bullets' defender Ray Scott. "I held him to 35 points. But Reed must have done his homework because he bombed me for 35 and 43 points the next time we met. Willis wasn't staying outside in those series. He was going inside. He is so strong that when he gets ideas like that the only way to stop him is to foul him."[42]

To be sure, Reed was not shy about taking advantage of his brawny 6-foot-10-inch, 240-pound frame and mixing it up under the boards. He averaged 14.6 rebounds during the 1968–69 regular season and provided consistent leadership on the defensive end. His talents did not escape the appreciative gaze of Bill Russell, Reed's boyhood idol. Curious to know more about this rising young talent, Russell once took Reed out to dinner before an All-Star game and nonchalantly asked him how he played every center in the league. Reed's response "confirmed" Russell's "hunch" that the Knicks star "knew what he was talking about." "He didn't play his opponents the same way I did, because he was a great big ox who loved to remind people how strong he was, but he was shrewd in his analysis," Russell later recalled in his second autobiography.[43]

This hoop savvy had been acquired through years of personal struggle both on and off the court. The only child of a truck driver and a domestic, Reed spent the formative years of his youth in rural Hico, Louisiana, or "Nowhere Louisiana" as he liked to call it.[44] Money was always tight at home, so young Willis went to work picking cotton, tending flower beds, and hauling hay. "I never regretted working," he later wrote. "I enjoyed it. It was the only way I could make money to buy things, like a bicycle and a basketball and hoop. I cut grass and saved up enough money to buy a lawn mower to increase my business."[45] When he wasn't working, Reed spent a considerable amount of his time getting into trouble. "When I was a kid, if anything would happen at all, I would fight it out," he said. "I got to enjoy fighting. I had a fight the first day of school. From the first grade through the third grade, I was fighting all the time. The trouble was, after a while, my father would whip me if I had a fight. So getting into a fight and winning didn't do me any good. Finally it sank in. I figured it was better not to fight at all."[46]

Reed found a release for his competitive energies in sports. Depending on the season, he played them all: football, basketball, and baseball. Basketball ultimately became his favorite athletic pursuit as his height made him a natural for the game. Indeed, he stood an imposing 6 feet 5 inches by the time he was in the ninth grade. Unfortunately, his size did not translate into immediate success on the court because his rapidly growing body made him a less than graceful athlete. "I could be walking down the street and I'd stumble over my own feet I was so clumsy," he later joked. If there was one area of the game where he did excel, however, it was dunking a basketball. "Dunking," Reed said, "was considered phenomenal then. One day a couple of guys were practicing on an outdoor court, trying to dunk, when I came along. They couldn't do it. They asked me to show them how. First I said, 'No, no.' But they kept after me. Finally I said, 'Okay.' I dunked the ball. Just then the high school coach walked over. He stood there, staring at me, disgusted. 'Look at him,' the coach said. 'There he is, the big clumsy kid, dunking, when he can't even catch a ball.' He bawled me out, right in the open. He called me a showoff. He was right."[47]

Through hard work and a near fanatical devotion to practice, Reed was eventually able to transform himself into an All-State basketball player and capture the attention of major college hoop programs around the country. In a surprise move, however, Reed decided to attend Grambling College in northern Louisiana upon his high school graduation. A chance meeting with Grambling basketball coach Fred Hobdy at a bus depot during his sophomore year had initially steered him in the direction of this all-black school. "I saw this tall kid on the street corner," Hobdy later remembered. "If you're in my business, you make it a point to get to know a kid like that, so I walked up to him and introduced myself. He said he was only in the tenth grade, but I promised to keep an eye on him and told him even if I never saw him again, he had a scholarship to Grambling when he graduated."[48]

Reed took up Hobdy's generous offer and proceeded to lead Grambling to three Southwestern Conference titles and one NAIA (National Association of Intercollegiate Athletics) championship over the course of his four varsity seasons at the school. Individually, he scored 2,335 points and was named to three college All-American squads. He later attributed his success to the superior level of competition he experienced in college. "In high school, I rarely faced anyone my size; now every team we played had at least one player as tall as me or taller," he wrote. "Even in practice, I played against big guys. It meant I had to consistently put out to do well."[49]

Having scaled new basketball heights in college, Reed eagerly looked forward to a career in the pro ranks. But his dreams of future stardom suffered a severe blow when no team bothered to draft him in the first round, an ominous sign the ruling basketball powers-that-be had doubts about his ability to succeed in the rugged NBA. Indeed, the Knicks waited until the second round to select Reed, having opted to use their first pick on the forgettable Jim "Bad News" Barnes. "I think the reason I was overlooked was that I played for a black school," Reed later surmised. "I'm saying the reason I was overlooked was not because I am black, but merely because I played for a black school and all-black schools did not then get the attention from the scouts and the press that they get today."[50] This realization failed to dampen the bitter disappointment he felt at the time, however. "All I could think of was, there goes $3,000, at least," Reed said. "I figured that was the difference between being drafted No. 1 and being drafted No. 2. It wasn't only the money. My pride was hurt. I expected to be picked on the first round, which would have meant that somebody considered me the best player in the country. I couldn't blame the Knicks. Taking Barnes was a good move. I guess I kind of expected that. But I couldn't believe there were eight players in the country better than me."[51]

Determined to prove that he belonged among pro basketball's elite, Reed made himself a force to be reckoned with "right from the start." He averaged 19.5 points and 14.7 rebounds a game his first season, numbers that earned him 1965 Rookie of the Year honors. More importantly, he demonstrated that in a league where Russell and Chamberlain "dominated" the center position, he could more than hold his own against these giants. As Russell later wrote, "Players like Willis Reed came along and had me pinching and scraping for any little edge I could get."[52] Still, Reed was forced to move over to forward the following season when the Knicks acquired All-Star center Walt Bellamy in a trade. "Center has probably always been Reed's best position," Red Holzman said. "Willis was asked to switch positions only because Walter couldn't do enough things well to play the corner."[53]

Though Bellamy would put up good numbers for the team over the next three and a half seasons, he lacked the emotional intensity and court leadership that Reed possessed. Consequently, there were not many tears shed in the Knicks locker room when Bellamy was shipped to Detroit for Dave DeBusschere in the middle of the 1968–69 season. Euphoria would be a more accurate term to describe Reed's reaction to the news. He knew the move meant he would be returning to center on a full-time basis, and he could barely contain his enthusiasm. "It's like being in a foreign country for a long, long time and then coming back to your old home town," he said.[54] His teammates shared in his happiness and good fortune, for Reed had already established himself as one of the most popular figures to ever don a Knicks uniform. "Everyone on the team liked Willis, and we all respected him," Frazier wrote. "There was nothing he wouldn't do for his teammates. I wouldn't loan any of those guys my car. My things were personal to me. But Willis never thought twice about loaning his car, even the convertible, to anybody."[55] As an indication of the high regard in which he was held, Reed was named team captain, a role he took very seriously. Indeed, he made a special point of leading by example, even on occasions when he was not feeling up to par physically. "Some nights I wouldn't even feel like suiting up," he said. "I'd be hurt and feeling low, and I'd wish I could just relax for a while. But if I didn't keep myself going, what could I expect the other guys to do? They respect me. I can't let them down."[56]

As the Knicks prepared to meet the Celtics in the 1968–69 Eastern Division finals, Reed hoped to maintain this faith his teammates had placed in him and lead his ballclub to victory. Unfortunately for the future Hall of Famer, Bill Russell would also have a say in the matter. Just prior to their playoff showdown, Russell had taken home statistics from the Celtics' previous encounters with the Knicks on the year and studied them. "I was aware that the Knicks had done a great job of closing us down, and I wanted to see if anything in the numbers would give me a clue," Russell later wrote in his 2001 bestseller *Russell Rules: 11 Lessons on Leadership from the Twentieth Century's Greatest Winner*. What he discovered was eye-opening. "I noticed that in each of the regular-season games against them, I had taken no more than five or six shots," he said. "Now the guy guarding me and the backbone of the Knicks defense was Willis Reed. Because I hadn't been shooting much, Reed had been free to help out on defense. He had been able to leave me safe in the assumption that I wasn't likely to get the ball and shoot." This allowed the Knicks to double-team the Celtics' best shooters, thus causing the Boston offense to stall. To break the defense, Russell concluded, he needed to shoot the ball more. "It was as simple as that," he said.[57]

Russell put his theory to the test when the Celtics traveled down to Madison Square Garden to open their best of seven playoff series with the Knicks on Palm Sunday, April 6. Nearly doubling his normal shot output against New York, Russell scored 10 points and grabbed 16 rebounds in directing the Celtics to a stunning 108–100 triumph over the heavily favored Knicks. Thus active on the offensive end, Russell forced Reed to pay closer attention to him on defense, which in turn opened things up for Celtics shooters John Havlicek (25 points), Bailey Howell (21 points), and Sam Jones (18 points). As Robert Lipsyte of the *New York Times* observed, "Like a great bird, wings flapping, head leading the body, Russell moves down court, coming to rest only briefly, and then warily, striking off again to rise, majestically, and pluck the ball out of the air."[58] Russell was seemingly everywhere, whether it was out-muscling Reed in the paint, setting up his teammates for transition baskets, or just generally making a nuisance of himself on defense. "What can a 35-year old do?" he was asked afterward. "Anything he wants to," Russell replied.[59] His teammates found no reason to dispute this logic. "Wasn't he a rebounder today?" enthused Havlicek. "At least three times he was in the pivot and he saw the loose man and dumped the ball off to him for baskets. And he made us run. He was quicker today getting the ball off the boards and clearing it out to me and Em [Bryant] on the break. He hasn't been that quick in a long time. Our game is a running game and he ignited it. He also kept the ball alive on the offensive board. He's so valuable, it's unbelievable."[60]

The game had started out an all-Knicks affair. Building a 9-point lead at 23–17 with under 4 minutes to play in the first quarter, the Knicks looked to be firmly in control of the contest. It was then that the Celtics offense kicked into high gear, narrowing the New York lead to 3 points at quarter's end and going ahead to stay on a Havlicek basket 1:57 into the next period. By the beginning of the second half, the Celtics had built a comfortable 15-point cushion that they used to coast on the rest of the way. "We ran with them today and maybe we outran them too," Howell said. "While our fast break may have been nothing to write home about at times, we kept it going, something we didn't do before against them."[61] Defensively, the Celtics weren't too shabby either as they relentlessly pressured the Knicks into making "bad or hurried passes, poor shots and costly turnovers." "They kicked the shit out of us, is what happened," Knicks backup center Bill Hoskett concluded.[62]

"Boston's team defense was one of the best I've ever seen this year, but Emmette [Bryant] was the key to the game," said Reed, who was an off-season fishing buddy of the 6-foot Celtic guard. "The next time I go fishing I'm going to use him as bait."[63] Indeed, Bryant came up with several clutch plays against his old New York teammates as he fell just shy of a triple double with 13 points, 8 assists, and 11 rebounds. "He killed us with some big baskets," Knicks coach Red Holzman lamented.[64] In postgame remarks, Bryant seemed to credit his fine performance to the green uniform jersey he now wore. "There is a difference playing with the Celtics," he said. "It's something you feel when you walk into an arena. People just expect you to win. When you lose, people are surprised and they make a big deal out of it."[65] Put another way, Celtic Pride was alive and well in the playoffs despite a lackluster regular season record.

Game 2 saw the host Celtics manhandle the Knicks once again as they posted a lopsided 112–97 win over the now thoroughly demoralized New Yorkers. "I'm a human being and I'm embarrassed," said Knick power forward Dave DeBusschere, who shot a dismal 0 for 9 on the day. "It's embarrassing to go out there and play the way I played tonight. It's not the end of the world, though. You can't let it bother you. I played too many games this year to end up like this and I'm not going to run away and hide."[66] Running away and hiding was precisely what the fast-breaking Celtics did in the first half as they soared to a 22-point advantage. Bailey Howell led the way here as he scored 13 of his team-high 27 points during this stretch. "You know," commented Russell in his special *Globe* column, "[Howell's] been so consistent for us that there is a tendency to overlook it. Like a calendar, he's there every day. He always makes a tremendous contribution. If I were to single out any one guy it'd be Bailey for the overall performance."[67]

Modesty, however, prohibited Russell from mentioning his own prodigious contributions to the winning effort. He grabbed 29 rebounds, scored 14 points, and flat out intimidated the opposition with his hawk-like shot-blocking skills. "The game had hardly started when this happened," explained Willis Reed who submitted a 28-point performance. "As it turned out we were intimidated by Bill. . . . It was one of Russell's best. And their whole team did well. It was probably the best running I've seen this team of theirs do in a long time. Whish! They were around me. Whish! They were over me. And Whish! They were all over the place. And then it got so every time Bill wanted to he seemed to be tied to the ball blocking our shots."[68]

As in Game 1, the Celtics turned up the defensive heat on the Knicks when it mattered, including a crucial 5-minute stretch at the start of the second quarter in which New York was held scoreless. The Knicks never seriously threatened after that. "We had them talking to themselves, 'should I or shouldn't I shoot,'" boasted Sam Jones.[69] Indeed, the Knicks put on their worst shooting exhibition of the season by going only 33 of 96 from the field for an average of 34 percent. "I can't recall us ever being colder than we were in the first half," said Knicks coach Red Holzman. "People keep asking how we could beat Boston six out of seven games during the regular season, and fall behind like this in the playoffs. The reason is the Celtics are a very good team. Our regular season record against them could as easily have been 4–3 or 3–4 or 6–1. The games were that close."[70]

Down 2–0 and facing the ignominy of a sweep, the Knicks climbed back into the series the next day with a 101–91 thumping of the Celtics before a capacity Madison Square Garden crowd of 19,500. "We had to come out swinging," said Knicks guard Walt Frazier who finished with a game-high 26 points. "Maybe [yesterday's] loss was what we needed to get motivated. We were embarrassed. If our guys have any pride, they had to go out there and get them. I know I couldn't wait for this game."[71] Neither apparently could teammates Dick Barnett (20 points), Bill Bradley (18 points), Dave DeBusschere (13 points), and Willis Reed (14 points), who joined Frazier in rejuvenating a heretofore moribund New York offense.

"I wanted to redeem myself," said DeBusschere, the victim of a scoreless performance the previous game. "At least I made a contribution."[72] A jubilant Red Holzman was at a loss for words to describe his team's victory. "I don't know how you explain a turnaround like this," he said. "But when you walk out there the way we did and make it look like we didn't fear those guys, then something happens."[73] To be sure, the Knicks "came out fighting" by sprinting out to an 11-point lead late in the first quarter and never letting up. The Celtics did manage to make a minor run midway through the fourth quarter and draw within four points on a Russell left-handed layup, but successive 3-point plays by Frazier and Bradley and a stifling New York defense put the game out of reach. "We took our shots and we made them," said Willis Reed. "Last night we had shots and missed them but tonight we made them, that was the difference."[74]

For the Celtics, Emmette Bryant continued his string of excellent playoff performances by scoring 16 points on an assortment of "outside pops" and "a driving length-of-court layup." Unfortunately Bryant got little assistance from his teammates, as the Celtics converted only 39 percent of their shots. So upset did Russell become by this poor showing that he locked the door to the team dressing room for 20 minutes after the game to review what happened. "No, I wasn't chewing anyone out," he said. "We were just going over what we did right and wrong in the game, our errors of omission and commission."[75]

High on Russell's list of sinners must have been John Havlicek, who managed just 2 points in the first half and a measly 8 for the game. A usually reliable 20-point scorer, Havlicek was shadowed the entire contest by Knicks forward Bill Bradley whose clutch and grab defensive technique took the Celtic captain out of his regular scoring rhythm. "Havlicek is fast and keeps moving the ball, and I just had to hound him as long as I could," said Bradley, who paced the Knicks offense in the second half by connecting on six of seven shots. "Bradley was all right," commented Havlicek, "I was just a little stale." But Bradley had been more than just "all right." In holding one of the game's top scorers to under 10 points and playing a significant role on team offense, Bradley was at last living up to the soaring potential he had displayed as a Princeton All-American.[76]

The future had always seemed bright for Bill Bradley. The only child of a midwestern bank president and a Sunday School teacher, Bradley was "groomed" by his Presbyterian parents to be "a Christian upright citizen." To this end, he was encouraged to take piano and dance lessons, learn the French language, and take up such genteel recreational pursuits as golf and tennis. But it was basketball that consumed him. "What attracted me was the sound of the swish, the sound of the dribble, the feeling of going up in the air," Bradley told author John McPhee in the 1965 best-seller, *A Sense of Where You Are: A Profile of Bill Bradley at Princeton.* "You don't need eight others, like in baseball. You don't need any brothers or sisters. Just you. I wonder what the guys are doing back home. I'd like to be there, but it's as much fun here, because I'm playing. It's getting dark. I have to go back for dinner. I'll shoot a couple more. Feels good. A couple more."[77]

This single-minded approach served him well as he developed into a certifiable high school phenom, attracting the attention of major college basketball programs nationwide. Yet in the first of many surprising moves in his accomplishment-laden life, Bradley opted to spend his undergraduate years at Princeton, an Ivy League school with no athletic scholarships and little basketball tradition. In doing so, Bradley served notice that he was more interested in receiving a first-rate education than becoming just another pro player in waiting at a big-time "basketball factory." Ironically, it would be his subsequent outstanding play at Princeton that persuaded many NBA teams to covet his services upon graduation. For Bradley became the premier college basketball player in the country, averaging 30.2 points and 12.2 boards in 83 varsity games over a 3-year period. His dead-eye marksmanship, take-charge floor leadership, strong passing skills, and model work ethic inspired his Princeton teammates to a Final Four finish at the 1965 NCAA Tournament, a competition that saw Bradley score a tourney record 58 points in his final game. A few months earlier, he had also distinguished himself by captaining the U.S. Olympic basketball team to a gold medal in Tokyo, Japan. "He is a Christian the best way he can be, through the rigors of Calvinism," a college friend said of the religiously devout Bradley. "Bill is always going to come back. Do you know just how hard it is to defeat a 16th-century Puritan?"[78]

Yet wins and losses on the basketball court weren't everything, as Bradley let the wider world know after picking up his Princeton diploma in the spring of 1965. Instead of turning pro as many were expecting, Bradley decided to accept a Rhodes scholarship to study two years in

Oxford, England. "I had been to Europe the summer after high school," he later recalled. "I enjoyed it immensely and I was really awed by England. I guess that's when I first thought about studying abroad. I also thought it would be beneficial to leave the States for a while. I had some personal questioning to do, I wanted to view this country from a different perspective, and I wanted to meet people with different viewpoints."[79] While studying at Oxford, Bradley did not abandon basketball entirely. In his spare time, he managed to hook up with a professional team in Milan, Italy, which he proceeded to lead to a European club title. "I met all kinds of people," he said. "But I got the impression that back in the States they thought I was some kind of vagabond basketball player. That was not so. The games mostly came on weekends or holidays. I missed very little time from Oxford."[80]

All the same, the 6-foot-5-inch hoop star constantly wrestled with the idea of playing in the NBA. While competing at such a high athletic level had obvious financial advantages, he wasn't sure it would necessarily bring him either personal fulfillment or happiness. "I know men in pro basketball who are on the go 20 hours a day during the few months they're not playing," he said, "taking care of businesses or other interests. The game doesn't leave much time for other things in life. Can the money make it worthwhile? I don't know."[81] Eventually, the tug of competition and the promise of a huge financial payday proved too great. He decided to sign a record four-year, $500,000 rookie contract with the New York Knicks, the team that had earlier selected him as their number one draft choice in 1965. "I could have gone full time to law school," he informed an assemblage of New York media at the press conference announcing his signing. "Or study another year at Oxford, or accept one of several opportunities in government work. And it isn't possible for me to give one simple answer and say, this isn't the reason for my decision. The main factor, though, was this: I found, what I had sort of suspected all along, that I really love the game of basketball and that I want to test myself against the best. It sounds trite, perhaps, but that's the truth."[82]

His professional debut before a sellout Madison Square Garden crowd on December 10, 1967, became one of the most hyped and eagerly anticipated sporting events of the year. However, two years away from top flight competition had sadly taken a toll. Put simply, he appeared rusty and out of shape, scoring only 8 points in 20 minutes of lackluster play. "It's not a one-game challenge," Bradley told a reporter afterward. "The enthusiasm from the [home] crowd was great and I was sorry I couldn't respond with skill."[83] Columnist Arthur Daley of the *New York Times* was noticeably less sanguine in his postgame analysis. "The Princeton alumnus and Rhodes scholar at Oxford is an extraordinary young man," he wrote. "It has been said of him that his talents are so varied and so enormous nothing is beyond his reach, even the Presidency of the United States. Be that as it may, it still doesn't equip him for the task of performing immediate miracles with the basketball team that's paying him a half million dollars over a four year term."[84]

Bradley's erratic play prompted further concern three nights later when he single-handedly threw away a sure Knicks victory against the St. Louis Hawks. "There were 15 seconds left to play, so all I had to do was hold the ball or wait until I was fouled or pass it off and run out the clock," Bradley later recounted to sportswriter Phil Pepe. "Instead, I dribbled toward the basket and went into the air, figuring I could shoot or dump it off to Willis [Reed]. Willis was covered, so I shot and as soon as I shot I knew that was wrong. I guess I hesitated because somebody got a hand on the ball, Bill Bridges I think it was, and [St. Louis guard Len] Wilkens got the ball with 4 seconds left and they took a time out. They scored the basket to tie the game and the momentum shifted and we lost the game in overtime. I can still recall the expression on Dick Barnett's face when I took that shot. It was one of disbelief."[85]

The play typified the kind of season Bradley had as a rookie. Though he possessed an obvious flair for the game, the future U.S. senator and Democratic presidential candidate could not translate this natural aptitude into consistent performance terms. Indeed, he averaged only 8 points per game that first year. "Bill had a preconceived idea when he came to the Knicks," said Los Angeles Lakers coach Bill van Breda Kolff, Bradley's old college coach. "He was going to be their leader, the quarterback, the catalyst, all that garbage. He had the subconscious idea he had to play that way. He's still not shooting like he can. He hasn't been shooting with authority. He thinks because it's the pros he has to get it off quicker. He should stop thinking and just *go*. Just *go* and *play*."[86] Adding to Bradley's problems was the fact that he was penciled in at guard, a position he was ill-suited to play given his lack of speed. "It is much more difficult for a guard to break into the pros than a forward," said Lakers GM Fred Schaus. "A cornerman has the baseline to go to and he can also look for help from the man in the middle. But more is asked of a guard defensively. He is on his own a lot, and out in the open he can get burned pretty easily in the pros. He's either got to be able to score a lot or make plays to contribute."[87] Bradley, of course, did neither his rookie year, but this was hardly grounds to write him off as a player, according to Red Auerbach. "Bradley may be playing the wrong position," he said. "The Knicks couldn't afford to experiment with him too much because they had to win and make the playoffs. But if I had him I'd want to look at him for a while as a forward."[88]

Interestingly enough, it was at the forward position that Bradley eventually blossomed midway through the 1968–69 season, but only after a broken ankle had sidelined starter Cazzie Russell for several games. Knicks coach Red Holzman immediately liked what he saw in his new cornerman. "Although he came out of the Ivy League and a cushier background than a lot of the players in the NBA, Bill was as tough as they come," Holzman later told biographer Harvey Frommer in his 1987 book *Red on Red.* "On defense he was an irritating player. He'd push a little, stick his hands all over a guy he was guarding, do anything he could to throw an opponent off his stride. Sometimes Bill came back to the bench after a skirmish, with his body looking like it had been flicked with a razor—there were cuts all over him."[89]

This displayed toughness helped win over many teammates who had initially been skeptical of Bradley's publicity buildup and big contract. But his move to starting forward was not without complications. As a "great white hope" of the NBA, Bradley had to contend with ugly speculation that he hadn't earned his promotion and had been put in the Knicks' predominantly black starting lineup merely as a sop to white fans. Whether he paid serious heed to this criticism or not, the fact remains Bradley stepped up his game for the remainder of the 1968–69 regular season, finishing fifth on the team in scoring and fourth in rebounding. By any reasonable standard, Bradley had proven he belonged as a Knicks starter. His standout performance against the Celtics in Game 3 of the Eastern Division playoffs only confirmed this fact.

However, one good game does not a series make. Bradley bitterly learned this lesson back in Boston midway through the third quarter of Game 4. "Sanders was guarding me," he later told *Sport.* "I scored three quick ones on Tom, which is fairly unusual. I don't do it that much. One of them was on the left side of the basket, as I remember. Sanders was beside me. Russell was beside him and as I hit it, Russell didn't say a word

to me. He looked at Satch. 'You got him, Satch?' he asked in a very meaningful way. He was talking to Tom, but he was saying it more for my ben-
efit. I went back up the court putting my own interpretation to his
words. In effect, he was saying to Sanders: 'You shouldn't have any trouble here. What's the matter?'"[90] Thus unnerved, Bradley proceeded to be
a relative nonfactor for the rest of the game, scoring only 4 points. Bill
Russell had gotten into the head of another opponent and in the process
helped pave the way for an emotionally intense 97–96 Celtics victory that
left Garden patrons "limp" and the Knicks on the "brink of elimination."

"I don't like this type of game," Russell said. "When it comes to ul-
cers, I prefer to be a carrier, not a sufferer." He was more the former than
the latter on this particular occasion as he somehow willed his battered
35-year-old body to play the full 48 minutes, scoring 21 points and
grabbing 23 rebounds. "I never thought I'd see the day when I'd lead this
team in scoring," Russell joked. "I think this is the first time this season
I've done it."[91]

Despite Russell's offensive heroics, the Celtics could manage only a
95–94 advantage entering the final 25 seconds of the contest. To make
matters worse, the Knicks had possession of the ball at midcourt with a
full 15 seconds left on the 24-second clock. Unwilling to rush a shot, the
Knicks prudently called a time-out to set up a play. In the New York huddle, it was decided the "slick-shooting" Walt Frazier would receive the
ball and take advantage of his superior one-on-one skills to create a scoring opportunity. The same thought, however, crossed the minds of the
Celtics in their huddle. To counter the Knicks strategy, Russell assigned
John Havlicek, a tenacious defender who was uncharacteristically ham-
pered with five personal fouls on the day, to cover Frazier. "I had to be
extremely careful—shadowing him as aggressively as possible without
fouling him," Havlicek said. "Not only would a foul have disqualified me
with my sixth personal, but more important, two free throws would
probably have given New York the lead and maybe the game."[92]

Fortunately for Havlicek, this worst-case scenario never developed.
When play resumed, Frazier received the ball as expected, but he could
not shake the determined Havlicek, who made his presence felt by dig-
ging an elbow into the Knick guard's kidney. "He's tough," Frazier said.
"He tries to intimidate you. He bumps you and lets you know he's
there."[93] Unable to find an offensive opening near the baseline, Frazier
"flipped" a desperation pass to Willis Reed, who was positioned to the left

of the hoop. "I realized," Frazier said, "that if I had to take a shot it would have been a bad shot. Reed was the first one I saw."[94] With 8 seconds left, Reed launched a hurried shot that missed high and "bounded back" to the key, where a "tangle" of Knicks knocked it out of bounds. The Celtics regained possession and were immediately fouled, sending Emmette Bryant to the line. Bryant calmly sank two of his three free throws in the penalty situation to make it 97–94 with 6 seconds remaining. Still breathing, the Knicks worked the ball to guard Dick Barnett, who penetrated for an uncontested layup as four valuable seconds ticked away. But after a time-out, Havlicek, the second leading Celtic scorer with 19 points, passed off to Bailey Howell, who dribbled out the clock.

"You know," Russell wrote in his newspaper column afterward, "I get so nervous that it will take me at least until this time tomorrow before I wind down because I get so tied up in a game—a 1-point game—it's too close for comfort."[95] His concern was understandable. The game "seesawed" through three quarters until Don Nelson rattled off 8 "quick" points during an 11–4 Boston run to lift the team to a 9-point lead with 6:49 left. This advantage soon vanished, however, when Havlicek picked up his fifth personal foul and the Celtics got sloppy with the ball. The Knicks immediately capitalized by going on a 14–5 streak that tied the score at 91–91 with under three minutes to play. Two Larry Siegfried free throws and a Russell field goal put the Celtics' lead back up to 3, but free throws by Frazier and Reed made it a 1-point contest with a minute and a half to go. The score remained that way until Frazier came out on the losing end of his mano a mano encounter with Havlicek.

The win gave the Celtics a commanding 3–1 advantage in the series, but Red Holzman refused to issue any postmortems for his team. "What can I do?" the Knicks coach asked reporters. "I'm going to go home, have a few scotches, have dinner and think about the next game. I'm not going to bleed, for nothing. I'd go and knock my head against the wall, if I thought it would do any good. It won't—I tried it once. I had a headache for weeks."[96]

It would be the Knicks dispensing the headaches in Game 5 as they "humbled" the visiting Celtics, 112–104, before another capacity audience at Madison Square Garden. "The Knicks is not dead . . . it seems they are just comatose," wrote Joe O'Day of the *New York Daily News*.[97] Indeed, the Knicks staved off an early funeral by vaulting out to a 60–46 lead in the first half, courtesy of 17 Celtics turnovers and the clutch shooting of Walt Frazier (23 points) and Dick Barnett (19 points). "We needed no pep talk before the game," said Knicks reserve guard Mike Riordan. "You could sense that feeling that we had to win or there was no tomorrow as we dressed for the game."[98]

The Celtics attempted a comeback in the second half by making 25 of 42 shots to boost their field goal percentage to 52 percent for the game. But the Knicks continued to remain hot offensively, and the Celtics turned the ball over eight more times to all but assure defeat. "I'm not going to say what percentage it was their defense or how much resulted from our own carelessness," Russell said. "We'd get the open shots if we worked at it. The guy that makes the other guy do what he wants is the one who comes out ahead. We didn't make them do what we wanted them to do. We weren't forcing them to play the way we wanted them to. We have plays we should have run and every one of them has an option, only we didn't use the options. We did from the third quarter on, but it's over and I'm not going to be annoyed now."[99]

Having a particularly painful game offensively was Sam Jones. The perennial All-Star shooting guard made good on only one of eight shots while missing one of two free throws. "You just don't let it worry you," said Jones of his scoring slump. "You keep shooting. You don't do anything differently. Practice? I'll do the same things. You have to do the same things." Cognizant of these habits, the Knick defenders made sure he never fell into a comfortable scoring zone by dogging him every step of the way down the court. "Sam is old," said Walt Frazier. "We try and make him work. We want him to take that ball up as much as possible. We want to make him work." Ever the proud veteran, Jones denied age had anything to do with his poor performance and instead credited an aggressive Knicks defense with shutting him down. "They cover you good," he praised. "It's a switching defense. Everybody plays you. As soon as you cross, they switch. They don't care if you're a little man or a big man, they switch."[100]

The subject of age also came up in connection to Russell's performance. Asked if the physical strain of having to play back-to-back playoff games had anything to do with the general fatigue he and his aging teammates exhibited during the game, Russell minced no words. "You saw the way I played," said the Celtics superstar-coach, who finished with a personal playoff high of 25 points, 16 rebounds, and 6 assists. "Do you think it bothered me?"[101] Willis Reed also dismissed such speculation as unfounded. "He's a competitor," the Knicks center said. "He may be worn down but you would never know it on the floor. He gives every ounce he's got all the time. That's why I respect him so much."[102]

If there was any downside to the Knicks victory, which narrowed the Celtics' series lead to 3–2, it was the health of Walt Frazier. With a minute remaining in the contest, Frazier suffered a groin pull that immediately threw his playing status for Game 6 into doubt. "I'm very discouraged," he told a reporter during the scheduled three-day layoff between games. "Basically, we go with five men and this could really disrupt our attack. If I can go at all, I'll try to play."[103]

Frazier did manage to take the Boston Garden floor for Game 6, though he performed enough below his usual high standard of excellence to indicate the groin was seriously bothering him. "I took one look at Clyde [during warm-ups] and I knew we were out of it," Willis Reed later remembered.[104] Indeed, despite scoring 17 points, Frazier could barely run, thereby making himself a huge liability on defense. "I'd say that Frazier had only 65 to 75 percent of his effectiveness on offense," assessed New York general manager Eddie Donovan. "Defensively he just couldn't keep up with the quick guards [Sam] Jones and Em Bryant. They kept penetrating the middle."[105] Nevertheless, the Knicks did not make it easy for the Celtics, who squeaked by with a series-clinching 106–105 victory.

The game came down to the closing moments when John Havlicek, 28 points and 13 boards, uncorked a twisting desperation shot from the top of the key that found the net with 39 seconds to go and 8 seconds remaining on the shot clock. The basket gave the Celtics a 103–99 lead and some much-needed momentum heading toward the final buzzer. "Larry Siegfried turned to me on the bench when John hit that and said, 'Man, I don't believe it,'" said Sam Jones. "He had a point."[106] Refusing to roll over, the Knicks responded seconds later with a Willis Reed jumper that brought the Celtics lead back down to two points. But the supremely "cool" Havlicek was not finished operating on the Knicks defense. Dribbling toward the basket, the Celtics captain calmly broke down the available scoring options in his mind. "I knew I had that shot," Havlicek said. "But I'd rather use up a couple or more seconds. Maybe, if I go to the hoop I've got a chance for a three-point play. Or I could throw it back to Emmette [Bryant] for a 15-foot jumper."[107] He opted instead for a "little jumper" from the left baseline, which fell with 9 seconds left. The Knicks were still not finished, however. Mike Riordan came up with a clutch 15-footer that pulled New York to within 2 points, 105–103, with 3 seconds left. Following a time-out, the Celtics worked the ball to Sam Jones on the right side of the court, where he was fouled with a second remaining. "I wasn't nervous," Jones said. "According to the rules, the clock is supposed to start when the ball hits the rim if I miss the shot. So even if I did, the game should be over."[108] Not quite. After missing his first foul shot, Jones hit the second. But the Knicks managed to "loop" the ball downcourt to Reed, who was positioned underneath the New York goal. He got the final basket but no called foul as the Celtics patiently "stood around" with hands on their hips as time expired. "Whew, I'm glad that's over," exhaled Russell as he trotted his way into the dressing room.[109]

The win gave the Celtics not only their twelfth Eastern Division title in 13 years but also a sense of deep respect for their younger if nettlesome opponents. "It's hard to be proud in defeat," said Bailey Howell, "but they should be and they have nothing to be ashamed of."[110] To be sure, the Knicks had hung tough despite being decisively outscored for the first three quarters. Behind 94–85 with 6½ minutes left in the game, the Knicks' offense clicked into overdrive behind the unlikely leadership of Mike Riordan, who made three drives to the hoop during a 17–10 New York surge. Only the last-minute heroics of Havlicek and Jones staved off disaster for the Celtics.

"I would have been very surprised if we hadn't have won tonight," Russell remarked in the celebratory Celtic locker room afterward. "I was really confident we'd win. I knew we were ready. I was also pretty certain Sam Jones was going to have a big scoring night. I could see it in him. No, he wasn't angry or anything. It was just that glint of extra determination I spotted in practice. When you play alongside a man for so many years, you can tell these things. But actually I was a bit off in my feeling. I figured Sam would hit in the mid-30s. The piker only hit for 29."[111]

Jones piled up his points at the expense of the injured Walt Frazier, who had gone out of his way after their previous encounter to suggest the future Celtics Hall of Famer was all but washed up. "Now I know what Sam feels when he's lost a step," a chastened Frazier told reporters. "Tonight I was a step behind him the whole game."[112] Ever the gracious winner, Jones resisted the temptation to take a pot shot. "No, I wasn't mad out there," Jones said. "I was just playing my game. I just had a bad game before at New York. But that's all in the past now."[113] Regarding Frazier's impaired physical status, Jones expressed sympathy. "Generally,

The Celtics tradition rises to the cause
Courtesy of the *Boston Herald*

he [Frazier] is one of the best three defensive guards I've played against," he said. "Jerry West and Lenny Wilkens are the other two. When Walt is right, he's fabulous." But the Knicks defensive ace was far from top form on this occasion. "I saw him holding his groin," Jones said. "When I saw that, that was the key. I started to call my play. . . . We saw a weakness and we just took advantage of it."[114] Still, Frazier and his teammates tried not to dwell too much on what might have been. They were a young and talented squad who had just given the defending world champs all they could handle. Their time to shine in NBA playoff competition would come in the not so distant future. In the meantime, however, they could do nothing but tip their caps to the battle-proven Celtics. "You've got to give them credit," Frazier said. "They made some impossible shots at the end to win the game. That's why you've got to respect them. Every year they keep proving how good they are."[115]

Now it would be the Lakers' turn to find out.

CHAPTER
8

The Greatest
Team in
the World

The country was reeling from an outbreak of radical student protests when the 1969 NBA finals opened in late April. The most publicized had occurred at Harvard University, which sat along the twisting banks of the Charles River in Cambridge, Massachusetts. Amid cries of "Fight! Fight!" an estimated 300 students seized control of the school's administration building and issued demands calling for the "abolition" of ROTC (Reserve Officers' Training Corps). These students, most of whom belonged to the extremist Students for a Democratic Society (SDS), expressed particular outrage at the school's governing corporation. "These businessmen want Harvard to continue producing officers for the Viet Nam war or for use against black rebellions at home for political reasons," they contended.[1]

Harvard president Nathan M. Pusey, however, was having none of it. Contemptuously dismissing suggestions that he negotiate with the intruders, Pusey instead opted for a show of force. Local police were called in to retake University Hall, and the resulting "Battle of Harvard Yard" produced 45 injuries and 145 arrests. Almost immediately, charges of police brutality were raised. "Strictly as a military operation," reported one veteran journalist, "the police charge was beautiful. They accomplished their mission—to clear the building—in 20 minutes. But the way they did it reminded me of those Search and Destroy missions in Vietnam, where a 'successful' one often throws more people into the Vietcong camp."[2]

Conflict of a far worse sort threatened to engulf the entire Middle East region according to King Hussein of Jordan. While on an official state visit to the United States, Hussein warned that nothing short of Israel's withdrawal from the Arab lands it had won during 1967's Six-Day War would produce peace. "Time is running out because frustrations are building, and so are dangerous incidents in the area," he said. "I believe we have our last chance now to realize a settlement. But we cannot dally. Perhaps we still have a few months or a bit more time than that—but not much before it will be almost impossible to solve things peacefully." As to the pressing question whether he favored direct negotiations with Israel, he expressed strong opposition. "I am indeed familiar with their argument that the only way to achieve peace is to sit down with the Arabs at the conference table," he said. "But what is there to talk about? . . . No. I am afraid the Israelis are more interested in holding on to their occupied territories than they are in finding a solution. The Israeli demand for face-to-face talks seems to me to be a flimsy excuse not to confront the real opportunity for a solution."[3]

A solution was worked out between major league baseball and disgruntled slugging outfielder Ken "the Hawk" Harrelson, when the latter refused to report to the Cleveland Indians following a controversial six-player trade with the Boston Red Sox. Unhappy with going to a team that had no realistic chance of winning a pennant, the 27-year-old Harrelson had initially balked at leaving Boston and announced his decision to retire prematurely as a player. But with the careful prodding of baseball commissioner Bowie Kuhn and a fat new contract offer from the Indians, Harrelson quickly changed his mind and signed on with Cleveland. "I'm glad to be back in baseball," he said following his three-day retirement. "I have a strong personal feeling for Alvin Dark [Cleveland manager] and I feel that the Indians will turn around from their bad start and win the pennant."[4]

The opportunity of capturing their first world championship since moving to Los Angeles for the 1960–61 season was what the Lakers sought as they prepared to meet the Celtics in the 1969 NBA finals. "I'll tell you one thing," cautioned one Laker. "Against the Celtics, we've got to do more than show up."[5] Indeed, billed as the prohibitive favorites to win the NBA title entering the season, the Lakers had performed somewhat below expectations during the regular schedule. Although they won the Western Division by a comfortable seven-game margin, they did so with an unspectacular 55–27 mark. Moreover, the pairing of expensive off-season acquisition Wilt Chamberlain with perennial All-Stars Elgin Baylor and Jerry West had hardly produced team harmony. Chamberlain and Baylor developed an intense personal dislike for one another, and Chamberlain thought Lakers coach Bill "Butch" van Breda Kolff played favorites with Baylor and West.

The big center also bristled at being asked to play in a high post offense, feeling this diminished his overall scoring effectiveness inside. "It has been a hard year," conceded Chamberlain, who in addition to his on-court troubles had to deal with the death of his father at the beginning of the season. "That's why with all the problems, winning the championship would mean more than it ever has. It has been difficult to adjust to my father's death, but nobody seems to take that into consideration. Instead, everybody says 'Wilt's not doing this,' or 'he's not doing that.' Anytime I am involved, whatever the thing is, it is blown up all out of proportion. It has happened all through my career, so I guess I should be getting used to it."[6]

Despite all the internal discord, the Lakers had a relatively easy time advancing through the first two rounds of the playoffs, beating San Francisco in six games and wiping out Atlanta in five. Now facing their old nemesis, an aging and battered Celtics squad that had defeated them in seven previous championship series encounters, the Lakers held the not unreasonable hope that this would be their year to finally knock off Boston. In fact, they were almost gleeful that the Celtics were their opponent in the finals. "If we can win the championship," admitted Lakers general manager Fred Schaus, "I'd rather it be over Boston. It'd be much, much more satisfying."[7] Yet for the Lakers to prevail in the best-of-seven championship series, they needed standout performances from their "Big Three": Baylor, West, and Chamberlain. And if any Laker was capable of rising to such an occasion, it was Elgin Baylor. A career 27.4 points per game scorer, Baylor was arguably the finest cornerman ever to suit up in the NBA as he combined power, grace, and ability in a way that led people to call him "the Willie Mays of Basketball." As teammate Jerry West once observed, "Often times you like to pattern yourself after a great player, but with Elgin it's hard to do. He does things the average guy can't do. Often, you'd like to do some of the things Elg does, but if you don't have his tremendous strength and body control, the best you can do is just think about it."[8]

Like many individuals marked for athletic greatness, Baylor came from very humble roots. The son of a railroad brakeman, he had grown up in an impoverished black section of Washington, D.C., in the 1950s. Since blacks were not welcome on the city playgrounds, Baylor did not begin playing basketball until he was 14. He more than made up for the lost time, however, when he reached Springarn High, an all-black high school where he set a District of Columbia single-game scoring record with 68 points and became the first African-American to be named to the All-Metropolitan team. "He never shot much unless we needed the points," recalled Dave Brown, Baylor's high school coach. "And even back then he was never excitable. In one big game, they got four quick fouls on him. I moved him outside and he made 44 points."[9] But due to his poor performance in the classroom, Baylor was not swamped with many college scholarship offers upon graduation. Disappointed but hardly defeated, Baylor decided to attend the College of Idaho in Cardwell, Idaho, which boasted a grand total of 450 students in its enrollment. An all-around athlete, Baylor went there on a football scholarship until his coach, Sam Vokes, who also doubled as the school's varsity basketball coach, determined his unique talents would be better put to use on a basketball court.

The soundness of Vokes's judgment became apparent when Baylor tossed in 31 points a contest as a freshman hoop starter and was named to the small college All-American squad. Still, playing in Caldwell was hardly a true test of his athletic abilities, and when the opportunity arose to play big-time college basketball at the University of Seattle, Baylor did not pass it up. Although he had to sit out a year due to his status as a transfer student, Baylor bore no ill signs from the inactivity. He finished third in the nation in scoring in 1957 and soared to number one the following season with a 32.5 points per game average. But with his college eligibility running out, Baylor decided to make himself available for the 1958 NBA draft, a prospect that filled him with considerable anxiety. "Seattle was a small school and I knew the NBA would be a big step," he later explained to author Terry Pluto. "I figured I'd make the league, but I had my doubts. Was I good enough to start? How would my moves work?"[10] These doubts were soon abandoned, however, when he dropped 25 points in his first contest with the Lakers, the team that had the good fortune of selecting him as their number one draft pick. He went on to average 24.9 points per game that first season to firmly establish himself among the league's scoring elite. "This kid is the best rookie I've ever seen," gushed Syracuse Nationals coach Paul Seymour.[11]

To prove his rookie year was no fluke, Baylor continued to improve upon his scoring average in the seasons ahead, peaking at a career-high 38.2 points in 1962. He would also record individual game point totals of 64 and 71 points, the latter holding up as the league's scoring standard until Wilt Chamberlain came along to break it in 1962. Not coincidentally, Baylor acquired a reputation for being an unstoppable force on offense as he showcased a series of spectacular high-flying, acrobatic moves that heretofore had never been seen in the sport. Indeed, he was Michael Jordan before there was a Michael Jordan. As one wag put it, "He never has really broken the law of gravity, but he is awfully slow about obeying it."[12] "Baylor had an uncanny ability to control his body while in the air," confirmed former NBA referee Earl Strom in his 1990 autobiography, *Calling the Shots*. "He would go up and hang and twist and lean and get his shot off and in the basket in ways that you thought surely impossible on this planet. He was an excellent passer and made some mediocre teammates successful as a result. He was often double- and triple-teamed and still managed to get the job done."[13] Also working to Baylor's advantage were the attitudes of opposing defenders who were flat out intimidated by the bruising physicality his sturdy 6-foot-5-inch, 225-pound body was capable of inflicting upon them. "You try to lean on him and he'd fend you off with his left arm, using it like a hammer," marveled former NBA guard Rod Thorn.[14]

While opponents may have panicked at the mere sight of him stepping out onto a basketball floor, Baylor himself took a calmer, more detached view of things. Indeed, when a DC-3 plane carrying the Lakers home from a 1960 game in St. Louis lost power in the middle of a winter snowstorm, Baylor forever endeared himself to his teammates by serenely laying down in the aisle of the aircraft with a blanket. "If I'm gonna go," he explained, "I'm gonna go in style."[15] The plane survived, and so did Baylor's overall sense of purpose. For the future Hall of Famer never lost sight of the formidable odds it took for him to become a star in the NBA. African-Americans "all work hard to get into this league," he once said, "because it is one chance we have. And besides, we have to be that much better to beat out a white player. And then everyone asks where the white players are. I've seen many of them come into this league, and they've had great talent. But they didn't last—they married some money or got a good outside job, things that don't happen to us. . . . You give us a chance in other things, and you'll get your white players back right away." Nor was Baylor pliant when confronted head-on with the soul-deadening constrictions of Jim Crow. Once, in Charleston, West Virginia, he and two other black teammates were denied hotel accommodations because of their skin color. Instead of playing in a scheduled game against Cincinnati the following day, Baylor quietly yet firmly protested his unfair treatment by not suiting up. When fellow Laker and Charleston native Rod Hundley implored him to rethink his action, Baylor maintained a dignified mien. "Rod," he said, "I'm a human being. I'm not an animal put in a cage and let out for a show. They won't treat me like an animal." Thus made aware of his teammate's heartfelt feelings, a sympathetic Hundley replied, "Baby, don't play."[16]

Tragically, Baylor's greatness on the court was diminished by a succession of debilitating knee injuries, the most serious of which occurred late in the 1964–65 season. After coming down from a jump shot, Baylor felt something "pull" in his left knee. "I didn't know what it was," he later said. "I forgot about the ball as soon as I felt it. But I could run. I went up and down the court a few times, but it hurt so much and I didn't know what it was, so I decided I better get out." He was quickly ushered to a nearby hospital where the prognosis was worse than he could have possibly imagined. His left patella, a thick, triangular bone that holds the kneecap in place, had been shorn entirely away from the joint. "If he can move around again, that would accomplish a great deal," said Dr. Robert Kerlan, the renowned orthopedic specialist who performed the surgery to sew the knee back together. "Perhaps he might be able to play again well enough to prolong his career a few years. Will he ever be outstanding again? I'm not optimistic."[17]

Barely able to walk and sporting a hip-to-ankle cast, Baylor bravely embarked on a strenuous rehabilitation program to strengthen the knee and to see if he could still compete effectively on a basketball floor. The initial results were not encouraging. Although he made the Lakers' opening day lineup the next season, he was a pale shadow of his former self. He had trouble making cuts to the basket, and players he used to dominate defensively were running right past him. "I'm just sick about it," said Jerry West. "This is a hard thing to watch. Elg is one of the finest men in the world and the best player I ever saw. To see him crippled and scoring less points than some of the subs on the other team just makes you want to cry."[18] Things soon went from bad to worse when he strained ligaments in his right knee, thus requiring another hip-to-ankle cast. When he returned from this mishap and continued to perform listlessly, Dr. Kerlan called him into his office for a bucking-up session. "It was about a month before the season ended," Kerlan remembered, "I sat him down and told him it was now—he had to find out right now. I told him that he either had to go out and test it and find out, or otherwise he might as well come over and rest with me."[19]

Baylor took the advice to heart and embarked on an offensive tear for the remaining 20 games of the regular schedule, averaging 25 points and 14 rebounds a contest without experiencing any major physical setbacks. "Wasn't I a beast, baby?" he joked with teammates.[20] In the playoffs, he was even better, scoring 26.8 points per game and grabbing 197 rebounds. While not as explosive going to the hole as he had been prior to his knee injuries, he nonetheless remained an offensive force to be reckoned with, posting scoring averages of 26.6, 26, and 24.8 over the next three seasons. "It was an amazing recovery, certainly," Kerlan said, "but only if you consider it as simply overcoming an injury. The man is often the most important thing, and in view of the sort of man that Elgin is, then maybe we should have even expected it."[21]

If any doubts still remained about Baylor's ability to perform at a high level, they should have been erased after Game 1 of the 1969 NBA finals. All Baylor did was score 24 points to help the Lakers overtake the Celtics, 120–118, before a record crowd of 17,554 at the Los Angeles Forum. But alas, his sterling effort was overshadowed by an even greater performance from Jerry West, who scored a career playoff high of 53 points to go with 10 assists. "The big story for us the entire game was West," conceded Baylor in a personal diary account of the series that was later published in *Sport* magazine. "He was leading us in driving and scoring inside against Russell more than I can ever remember us doing it before. This was our big plan for the night. We knew that Wilt [Chamberlain] freezes Russell and that Bill can't afford to switch off without leaving Wilt open for an easy one. And if Russell tries to come after us, we could try to force him into foul trouble."[22]

It also didn't upset Laker plans that Emmette Bryant, the Celtic charged with the unenviable task of guarding West, had run into some unexpected foul trouble himself. Indeed, he had picked up three quick personal fouls before five minutes had even elapsed in the contest. "They were some bad calls," Bryant complained afterward. "And they put me in the hole. One more foul and I don't get to play much the rest of the game. I had to give West some room. I had to give him some shots. Some shots I wouldn't normally give him, because I couldn't get that fourth foul."[23] By halftime, West had scorched Boston for 26 points, but the Lakers found themselves trailing by a hoop at 58–56. This was by no accident because the Celtics, behind the dazzling play of John Havlicek (37 points, 12 rebounds) and Bill Russell (16 points, 27 rebounds), were more than holding their own against a tough Lakers defense. "Boston played extremely well—and we were not bad, either, I guess," said Lakers coach Butch van Breda Kolff. "Boston ran pattern stuff more than I expected. They shot mostly outside. I believe that was partly design, partly our defense."[24]

Yet like the Lakers, the Celtics could not pull away as there were 27 lead changes and 14 ties overall. It wasn't until the tense final seconds, in fact, that the game was decided. With 23 seconds remaining and the Lakers ahead 115–114, West uncorked an 18-foot jumper from the top of the key that fell just shy of the basket. "The ball bounced off the rim and the backboard," Wilt Chamberlain said. "Then, it bounced off someone else and it came to me."[25] Standing a mere three feet away from the basket, the 7-foot-2-inch Chamberlain had little difficulty stuffing the ball through the hoop to give the Lakers a 3-point advantage. Down but certainly not out, the Celtics came roaring back with a Russell layup after a goaltending violation had been assessed against Chamberlain with 7 seconds left. "I'll always try to block a shot like that when I get a chance," Chamberlain said.[26] With the regulation game clock counting down, the Celtics were forced to foul West, who nailed both his charity attempts to give the Lakers a comfortable 119–116 lead. The comfort soon turned to alarm, however, when Sam Jones (21 points, 6 assists) nailed one of his patented bank shots with a second to go. But the Celtics could not capitalize as they were unable to get off another shot before time expired. A conversion by Baylor after the buzzer rounded out the scoring for Los Angeles.

"We were fortunate to win a game like that," West exclaimed afterward. "As a sports fan, I wish I just could have been a spectator for this one." Chamberlain adopted a more subdued tone in his comments. "The way I look at it is that we got the breaks at the end," he said. "Was this a psychological win? Let's say we're one up with three to go."[27] As for

Russell gets ready to face Jerry West
Courtesy of the *Boston Herald*

the Celtics, although they lost, to a man they could not disguise the un-
abashed admiration they felt toward West. "Not only did he get 53
points, but he also got 10 assists," said John Havlicek. "If we could have
held him to his playoff average [about 30 points a game], I guess we
could have won by 20. We actually played really well."[28] Russell had no
argument with the former Ohio State All-American on this last point.
"Everybody is talking about West making 53 points and all the changes
that can be made to play against him," he wrote in the special *Boston*

Globe column chronicling his impressions during the playoffs. "But I have to look at it as a coach. Overall we played a good game but we still lost by only 2 points. It wouldn't make any difference if he got 100 points and we won by 1 or 2 points. The win is the important thing. You can't let one man's scoring throw you into a panic. A 2-point ballgame can go either way and it just didn't go ours."[29]

The breaks continued to go against the Celtics in Game 2 as a late Los Angeles rally sparked by Elgin Baylor gave the Lakers a 118–112 decision over their visiting arch rivals. The 11-year veteran scored the Lakers' last 12 points, while notching 32 points overall on 11 of 15 shooting. "He won it for us . . . he was the man," said Jerry West, who didn't do too badly himself with 41 points and 8 assists.[30] Baylor attributed his success to good fortune and having fresh legs. "I'd spent enough time on the bench during the game [15 minutes]," he revealed, "that I was ready for that all-out assault at the end, but when you end up with a scoring spree like that, and hit on 11 of 15 for the game, you know there's a little luck involved."[31]

Baylor, who also hauled down 10 rebounds, "went to work" on the Celtics in the final minutes with his team trailing by 4 points. He drained a jumper from the left corner and sank two free throws to put the Lakers up, 110–108, with 2:30 to go. The Celtics countered with a successful baseline move by Russell over Chamberlain and a running jumper by Havlicek, but Baylor answered each score with baskets of his own, including a 17-footer and a pair of free throws. The latter conversions were particularly significant because they put the Lakers ahead "for good" with less than a minute remaining. Baylor would add two more free throws in the closing seconds, but as *Los Angeles Times* reporter Mal Florence noted, "they were just window-dressing points."[32]

"We just keep coming back and that's the mark of a good team," said Chamberlain whose final stat sheet read 19 boards and 4 points. The 7-foot-2-inch center made the postgame remark while nursing a sore jaw with an ice pack. He had incurred the injury while contesting a loose ball with Don Nelson. Chamberlain's chin had made contact with Nelson's head "with a resounding whack," leaving the former Laker turned Celtic with "a king-sized headache." "It's too bad my head didn't cut Wilt's chin," a still groggy Nelson cracked. "Then he would have had to shave that beard off."[33]

One Celtic definitely not in a joking mood was Bill Russell. Staring at a 0–2 series deficit and the possibility of a Lakers sweep, Russell tried to make sense of the defeat as his team enplaned home for the next two games. "We had some strange things happen to us in the game," he confessed in his *Globe* column. "For example, Los Angeles got 79 shots and we got 112. That's a difference of 33 shots—33 shots that we had. And the rebounds were even. The trouble is that they got 20 more free throws. In fact, they made more free throws than we attempted. What happened was that L.A. outscored us by 18 points at the line. So the difference, you might say, was at the foul line because we outscored them from the floor. But, overall, I don't think we played too well. We were good in spots and scored, but the defense broke down."[34]

If there was any silver lining for Russell and the Celtics, it had to be the continued fine play of John Havlicek. Coming off two consecutive playoff series in which he averaged 27.2 and 21.5 points respectively, "Hondo" was showing no signs of letting up against the Lakers. He had already poured in a combined 79 points in the first two games, and he relished the prospect of doing even more damage back in the friendlier confines of Boston Garden. "I'm not discouraged because both [L.A.] games could have gone either way," he said. "We're going home now, and maybe all we need is the home crowd."[35]

Game 3 demonstrated the essential logic behind Havlicek's thinking. In front of an unusually supportive audience of 14,033 at the Garden, the Celtics overcame a poor third quarter to down the Lakers, 111–105, and register their first win of the series. Havlicek carried the bulk of the scoring load with 34 points, but got a big assist from ex–Ohio State teammate Larry Siegfried, who came off the bench to contribute 28. Together they accounted for over half the Celtics' offense and provided a number of crucial baskets down the stretch. "They're a money pair," praised Lakers guard Johnny Egan.[36] Ironically, Siegfried almost didn't suit up for the game as the combined effects of a lingering hamstring injury and a hip pointer made his playing status questionable. "When I saw him get off the plane yesterday," Celtics team physician Thomas A. Silva said, "I didn't think he would be able to play. But thanks to a lot of therapy and Larry's great motivation, he was able to make it."[37]

Typically, Siegfried didn't try to sugarcoat his condition after the game. "Yeah, I hurt out there," he told reporters. "The hip point didn't bother me but I knew if I got hit on it, I'd lie down on the floor and cry, and that's painful. It bothers me when I roll over on it in bed, which is why I've been getting only three hours sleep a night, if you can call it sleep.

Sam Jones works for a shot
Courtesy of the *Boston Herald*

The hamstring pull is what hurts during the game. It tightens up real bad. I even sat on heated pads when I was on the bench, but I don't know which hurt more, the heat or the pain. But excluding the circumstances, I played as well as I think I can play. I penetrated, I dribbled, I shot pretty well and I played pretty good defense." Among those who agreed with Siegfried's performance evaluation was Jerry West. "If you could point to one man as the difference in this game, it was probably Siegfried," the Lakers guard said. "He did so many things. And let me tell you, he wasn't scoring cheap baskets. He was shooting from downtown. And when he does that, it's tough to stop."[38]

Toughness was also exhibited by the Celtics after they blew a 57–40 lead at halftime. Outscored 38–21 in the third quarter, the Celtics entered the final frame tied with Los Angeles, 78–78. But a 24–10 streak in the middle of the period, fueled by an opportunistic running game and the bull's-eye marksmanship of Havlicek (9 points) and Siegfried (6), put the Celtics back in command. The Lakers still had an important ace left up their sleeve, however. Little-known and undervalued Johnny Egan, the "other guard" of the Lakers offense who averaged 8.5 points per game in 1968–69, heated up to score seven straight baskets down the stretch. A subsequent 3-point play by Chamberlain with 23 seconds left pulled the Lakers to within four at 109–105. Fortunately for the Celtics, the visitors could get no closer as Havlicek dropped in two foul shots with 13 seconds remaining to clinch the victory.

When probed afterward by reporters about being nervous during the Lakers' third quarter rally, Bill Russell was candid in his remarks. "Of course I was," he said. "I look over to the Los Angeles bench and there's Elgin Baylor and Jerry West having a breather. And we still have the fourth quarter to play. . . . But we regained our poise and started to play basketball again. We played defense and ran. That's how we got the lead in the first place." On the Lakers' side, Jerry West blamed general fatigue for his team's loss. "We really tired after our comeback drive," he said. "We just died— becoming sloppy and passive. I think the pace of the game had a lot to do with it. And a comeback from so far behind takes a toll on a team. I know I was really tired. How many buckets did I make in the last quarter—one of nine? I didn't have much left so I asked out." But then, West and his teammates knew going into the contest they were in for a ferocious fight, despite their 2–0 advantage in the finals. "We knew the Celtics wouldn't quit," the Lakers sharpshooter said. "They never have and never will."[39]

The Celtics proved that again in Game 4 as Sam Jones hit a dramatic off-balance, game-winning shot with a second to play to lift his team to a wild 89–88 victory over the Lakers. "I thought Sam's shot was going to miss when he put it up," Russell confessed. "I said to myself—'Oh, damn!' But the ball looked like it had fingers and just crawled in."[40] To Lakers coach Bill van Breda Kolff, the basket represented a nightmare come true. "I've lost tough ones before," he sighed, "but never any tougher."[41] Elgin Baylor concurred: "It was a lucky shot. But [Jones] made it. And that's what counts. He slipped, went up off balance and still put the ball in the hoop."[42]

An improbable series of events set the stage for the victory shot, starting with a nondescript out-of-bounds play initiated by Baylor under the Los Angeles basket with 14 seconds remaining. Protecting an 88–87 Lakers lead, Baylor passed the ball to Johnny Egan, who promptly had it stolen away from him by Boston's Emmette Bryant. "He slapped me right on the arm and knocked the ball loose," Egan said. "It was the key play in the game and [the officials] didn't call it."[43] Bryant immediately flicked a pass to Jones, who launched a 15-foot jumper from the right of the key. The ball bounced off the front of the rim, but the Celtics retained possession and called time-out with 7 seconds to play. While contemplating his options in the huddle, player-coach Russell was successfully lobbied by Havlicek and Siegfried to use a play straight out of their old Ohio State playbook. "There's just enough time for it," said Havlicek, who had introduced the play to his teammates at an earlier practice session during the Philadelphia series.[44] The play called for the use of a triple screen to give the intended shooter, in this case Jones, a clean look at the basket. "We walked through it one time in the huddle, just so everyone would be sure of what he had to do," said Jones, who had 16 points and 4 rebounds.[45] When play resumed, Bryant inbounded the ball to Havlicek, who then "broke" to form a defensive barrier alongside Bailey Howell and Don Nelson near the free throw line. While this was taking place, Jones wheeled around the screen on the right to receive the anticipated pass from Havlicek. After momentarily stumbling on the parquet floor, Jones tossed up a prayer that hit both the front and back rims of the basket before finally dropping.

"I didn't think the ball was going in," said Jones. "In fact, I didn't think it was going in the right general direction and I didn't think it was even going to make the front rim. I slipped as I tried to plant my

Fans flood the floor after Sam Jones's game-winning shot in Game 4 of the NBA finals

right foot to take the shot, and if there had been more time remaining I
doubt if I would have taken the shot—probably passing it instead. But
I knew there wasn't much time left, so I just put the ball up and as best I
could—purposely putting more spin on it than usual so Russ might have
a shot at a rebound." When informed that Russell had taken himself out

of the ballgame to insert a superior foul shooter in his place, Jones responded, "He wasn't? Oh my gosh!"[46]

A similar feeling of amazement struck Jerry West (40 points, 4 assists), who watched in anguish as Jones's ball crashed through the net. "I guess if the Good Lord wants you to win you win," he said. "That shot wasn't even a good one. But we played dumb basketball. Maybe we deserved to lose."[47] In truth, it seemed that neither team wanted to win. Poor ball handling, atrocious shooting, and sloppy overall play made the contest at times seem like a bad school yard pickup game. Fifty turnovers were committed along with a surfeit of errant passes too numerous to tabulate. "If it wasn't a playoff game, it would have stunk the place out," said Russell, who had 6 points and 29 rebounds. "It was an illustration of how not to play basketball, and we were just fortunate both clubs were playing that way."[48]

Indeed, the Celtics found themselves trailing by only 3 points entering the final period. They continued to stay close as Siegfried netted four of the team's first five baskets in the quarter. The Lakers grimly held on to the lead, however, until Bailey Howell notched two free throws and a jumper from the left baseline to put the Celtics ahead, 86–83, with just under 5 minutes left. Undaunted, the Lakers retook the lead, 88–86, when the Celtics offense inexplicably went catatonic for the next 4 minutes and the "unstoppable" West came up big with a jumper and three conversions. An intentional foul on Bryant with 15 seconds remaining resulted in a Boston free throw that cut the advantage to 88–87. But the Lakers could not hold on to the ball on the subsequent inbounds pass by Baylor, thus permitting the last-second heroics of Jones. "We had it and we let it get away," van Breda Kolff said bluntly. Bryant, however, had a different take on the situation as he rubbed his green-trimmed Celtics home jersey afterward. "Four-leaf clovers," he said, "were flying all over the place."[49]

The Lakers were in no need of such talismans in Game 5 as they trounced the visiting Celtics, 117–104, to seize a three games to two series advantage. "There is no real explanation for what happened," said Sam Jones, who led all Boston scorers with 25 points. "They just played good ball and hit well, that's all." While West again led the Lakers with 39 points and 9 assists, he received considerable help from Keith Erickson, the 6-foot-5-inch UCLA product who was a surprise starter at the forward spot. Aside from banging his way to 16 points and 10 rebounds on offense, Erickson also did a superior job on defense, helping limit John Havlicek to only 18 points on 6 of 21 shooting. "I just tried to play him tight," said Erickson, who proved to be a persistent thorn in Boston's side all during the contest.[50]

Equally vexing from the Celtics' perspective was arch foe Wilt Chamberlain, easily submitting one of his best performances in the playoffs. Though he scored only 13 points, he dominated the inside paint with 31 rebounds and 7 blocks. Moreover, his aggressive offensive rebounding "afforded" his team a number of second- and third-chance scoring opportunities, which allowed the Lakers to decisively outshoot the Celtics, 106–89. Chamberlain's mastery became particularly evident in the third quarter as the Lakers expanded what had been a precarious 49–45 halftime lead to 10 points. "Wilt was tremendous," Baylor later recounted. "He was going to the boards and completely outplaying Russell. Then, when Russell got his fourth foul, we started going to Wilt even more and Wilt was working him over pretty good. I think the Celtics knew they were beaten then, and Russell looked more tired than anyone."[51] Indeed, Russell, who managed a meager 7 points and 13 rebounds for the game, did wear a fatigued look about him, an understandable occurrence given the 35-year-old pivotman was playing over 40 minutes for the fifth straight time in the series. Nor was he in much of a mood afterward to discuss the situation with reporters. "Gentlemen," the usually quotable Russell said, "I have absolutely no comment."[52]

Irrespective of these factors, the Celtics still managed to stay within shouting distance at 107–100 late in the contest. But a breakaway drive and two free throws by Johnny Egan and another basket by Erickson off a Chamberlain steal safely put the game away for the Lakers. The victory came at a steep price, however. With 3 minutes left, West pulled the hamstring muscle in his left leg after colliding with Emmette Bryant for a loose ball. "I tried to run back on defense, but it hurt," West vividly recalled in his autobiography. "I asked out and went down to the dressing room where the doctor looked it over. At first I didn't think it was serious, but when I realized it was it was depressing. We had won a big game and now led, three games to two, but we did not have a happy dressing room."[53] To be sure, West's teammates grew distraught at the thought of being without their leading scorer heading into Game 6. As Chamberlain told Doug Krikorian of the *Los Angeles Herald-Examiner,* "I can't explain now how much West's loss would mean to us." Ever the fierce competitor, West did his best to allay these fears, insisting he would be ready to perform in the next contest. "The biggest thing in my life right now is to be an NBA champion," he said. "You just don't know how much it means to me. If I can crawl, I'll be out there playing."[54]

Such doggedness had always been a trademark quality of Jerry West. Since debuting as a pro in 1960, West had endured his share of injuries, including an assortment of serious leg maladies and several painful face contusions. As *Los Angeles Times* columnist Jim Murray once wrote, "His nose got broken more often than the pole vault record. He not only led the league in jump shots, he led it in nosebleeds. Also gauze. Bauer & Black made so much money off him he should have been listed on the cotton exchange. One night in West Virginia, a stranger asked, 'Which one's West?' 'Wait a minute,' a spectator told him. 'He'll be the one bleeding.' His nose looks like a freeway cloverleaf."[55]

Yet West continued to sacrifice his body night in, night out on the hardwood because this fit his all-out approach to the game. As former Lakers general manager Lou Mohs observed, "West gets hurt not because he's frail, but because he goes all out and take chances others won't. . . . And he'll get hurt again, because that's the only way he knows how to play."[56] Indeed, to West there was no substitute for victory on the court. "There are many reasons for playing this game," he once told Bill Libby of *Sport* magazine, "but winning is the best one. Individual performances don't mean much if they don't contribute to team victories. Individual performances usually are misjudged anyway. The guys that score big get the headlines, but it's the guy that makes the key steal or the key block or the key rebound or the key basket to stem a rally or start one who wins games, and he's usually overlooked in the writeups. I try to do a lot of things to contribute to victory, and some are recognized and some aren't."[57]

His most "recognized" contribution was his uncanny ability to score in crunch time, for which he earned the appellation "Mr. Clutch." "I'm embarrassed by the nickname, 'Mr. Clutch,'" he said. "I'm also proud of it. I know I've never been just another player on the Lakers. I want the responsibility. I want the ball in the clutch. I want the shot. I know I can make it. Because I've made it many times. I've also missed it many times. I've blown baskets and kicked the ball away and thrown it away and had it stolen from me in tight spots. I could cut my throat at such times. But I'm not afraid of such times. They stir me up. They bring out the best in me."[58] Lou Mohs believed such fearlessness was what made West unique as an athlete. "Under emotional stress, the average person's bodily functions go out of kilter," Mohs maintained. "Jerry and a few others have themselves under such control that they are not subject to normal human frailties and can operate with complete mechanical perfection. If there is any response to pressure at all, there is a heightening of this mechanical operation, a refining of talent. Jerry is actually better under stress—cooler, more calculating. Everyone wants to be this way, but wanting it is not enough. It has to be inside of you, and Jerry has it."[59]

West's opponents did not disagree. "I don't know who said it first," said former New York Knicks guard Mike Riordan. "I think maybe it was K.C. Jones, about the only one who could stop Jerry is West himself. All you can do is play him as tight as you can without fouling him. He amazes me every time I see him. Once I picked him up full court and he still comes down and scores. Once he used up his dribble, I got on him tighter and it didn't even matter. Two points. You feel it's all for nothing. Nobody's going to stop him, but the harder he works, the more tired he gets faster."[60] Even referees couldn't resist tipping their caps. "Jerry was so methodical," former NBA official John Vanak told author Terry Pluto. "He wore you out with his jump shot, his relentless defense, and unlike a lot of guards, he had enough guts to go under the basket for rebounds. He seldom complained about an official's call, and when he did you had to ask yourself, 'Did I kick that one?' He commanded that much respect in the league."[61]

At 6 foot 2 and 175 pounds, West was hardly an imposing specimen by NBA standards, but he did possess one physical attribute that set him apart from most of his basketball contemporaries: quickness. "Straightaway speed doesn't mean much," he said. "It's how fast you can move your hands and feet in a limited area of court. I know the defensive players now and, depending on who I'm facing, I vary my moves and shots, the arc and everything, just the way a pitcher changes speeds. I have more percentage shots, the shots I can hit, than most players." Along with this speed came an impassioned desire to be consistent in his efforts at all times. "That's the important thing in sports—consistency," West said. "You're better off with the guy who scores 20 points two games in a row than the one who scores 5 one night and 45 the next night. It's harder for me to get up for every game than it was some years ago. I'm more selective. But if I play bad in a game, I don't want to play bad two games in a row. I think I've achieved a reasonable level of consistency."[62]

Regrettably, West could not achieve a similar level of congruity with his own emotions off the basketball floor. After a bad individual outing or a tough loss, he often fell into a deep personal funk. "It used to be a big problem for Jerry. . . . He'd get down on himself—never on anybody else, or even the officials—but his depressions would last as long as a week or 10 days," revealed Fred Schaus, West's longtime coach in college and in the pros.[63] For his part, West never denied having these black moods. "I just can't wind down after a losing game," he once confessed. "I can't sleep. It's hard enough at home, but at least I have my family, and I'm at home. On the road, it's terrible. I replay the game, try to get rid of it that way, but it doesn't always work. I've taken to reading when I get back to the hotel."[64] Notwithstanding, the playing brilliance he so frequently displayed on the basketball court made his coaches and teammates overlook such emotional digressions. As Jim Murray wrote, "The game of basketball was invented precisely for people like West. Too frail for football, too nervous for baseball. Too young for chess, and too restless for crew. And too coordinated to sit still."[65]

The story of Jerry West begins along the rural back roads of Cheylan, West Virginia, in the 1950s. It was here that this solitary electrician's son first took up the game that would ultimately lead him to NBA superstardom. "I think I became a basketball player because it is a game a boy can play by himself," he later said. "I've always been the sort of person who likes to be by himself some. I've always been a guy who lives inside of himself a lot. I'm my own worst critic. I'm not easily satisfied. I think in the beginning I turned to basketball because I could practice it alone."[66] After receiving instruction on the basics of the game from his older brother David, who tragically lost his life during the Korean War, West went on to become a local high school standout, averaging 25.8 points in 60 games for Consolidated East Bank High School.

As he looked toward college, West had the luxury of sorting through 60 scholarship offers, many coming from the most prestigious basketball programs in the country. Some of the offers, however, went far beyond what was considered proper under then-existing NCAA recruitment guidelines, including one school's tender of a free car and a $300 a month allowance. "I'd be lying if I said I wasn't tempted," West later wrote. "I hadn't had a whole lot, so I was tempted all right. But I was warned that if I got caught taking more than I should, my career might be ruined, so I was scared, too. And I wasn't brought up to do the wrong thing and I knew it wouldn't sit right with me, so I was sort of turned against it, too."[67]

Eventually West decided to attend West Virginia University in nearby Morgantown because he liked Mountaineer coach Fred Schaus's "soft-sell" approach and he didn't want to stray too far away from home. It was a fateful decision that helped cement West Virginia's reputation as a perennial hoop powerhouse in the late 1950s, as West became one of the brightest stars in all of college basketball. Indeed, during West's three varsity seasons at the school, in which he averaged a sparkling 24.6 points a contest, the Mountaineers never lost a home game and compiled an overall record of 81–12. In 1959, West led the team all the way to the NCAA championship game, where they were nosed out by the University of California, 71–70. Individually, West earned tournament MVP honors after scoring 28 points in the finale. This accolade along with being named NCAA Player of the Year the following season made West a national celebrity. His newfound notoriety was confirmed when he arrived at the governor of West Virginia's office for a scheduled appointment. West innocently gave the receptionist his name. "You don't have to tell me who you are," he was told. "You're better known than the governor."[68] West's fame soared still higher when he was selected to represent the United States on the 1960 Olympic basketball team along with such other collegiate notables as Jerry Lucas, Walt Bellamy, and Oscar Robertson. The team went on to take the gold medal in Rome, leaving West with the greatest thrill of his life. "It was something you read about as a kid and always hoped you could do," he later recalled.[69]

Unfortunately, West did not experience a similar rush of excitement when he joined the Lakers as the second overall pick in the 1960 NBA draft. Confined to the bench for most of his rookie year, West found the opportunities few and far between to exhibit his superior playing skills. Interestingly enough, this was in accordance with the wishes of Fred Schaus, who had left his West Virginia coaching post for the Lakers job. Schaus, however, elected to bring West along slowly with limited playing time off the bench. He feared the pro game would be a difficult transition for his young star. Naturally, West saw things differently. "I should have been a starter," he complained bitterly in his autobiography years later. "I was better than any of our other guards. I knew it and Fred should have known it. . . . You learn more playing than sitting. And the team wasn't so good that it couldn't afford to let me play and learn. Actually they needed what I could give them."[70] Despite the lack of playing time, West managed to score 17 points a game, the only instance in his 14-year professional career that he averaged less than 20.

West's fortunes took a dramatic upturn the following season as he made his first NBA All-Star team and finished fifth in the league in scoring with a 30.8 point average. Of even greater import, his 2,310 total points were the most recorded by any guard in the NBA. "I have a lot more confidence now," West told *Sports Illustrated* at the time. "Last season I was afraid of making a mistake, because I might hurt the team and make myself look bad. I can do a lot more with the ball, too. I was strictly a right-handed shot and I didn't drive much, so the defense was playing me a whole step to the right and tight. Now I can go to my left and shoot with my left hand, and I'm driving a lot. The driving has helped a great deal. I don't have hands in my face every time I go up for a jump shot, and I'm getting five or six more foul shots a game."[71] West maintained this level of playing excellence in the seasons ahead as he teamed up with All-Star forward Elgin Baylor to form one of the most explosive scoring duos in NBA history. Together, they led the Lakers to six NBA final appearances in the 1960s. Yet with each successive loss to Boston in the championship round, West grew increasingly frustrated. As he revealed in a 1965 interview, "I guess—I feel I've accomplished about all there is to accomplish in basketball as an individual. I was an All-America, an All-Pro and I've made the All-Star team. . . . But there is one thing I'd really like to do before I quit—I'd like to help the Lakers win an NBA championship."[72]

With the Celtics only one game away from elimination in the 1969 NBA finals, the moment seemed especially ripe for West and the Lakers to turn that illusive dream into a reality. They couldn't pull it off in Game 6, however. Paced by Don Nelson's 25 points and 9 rebounds, the Celtics upended the visiting Lakers, 99–90, to even the series at three victories apiece and force a deciding game the following evening in Los Angeles. "We just played a very bad game," said Lakers coach Bill van Breda Kolff. "We didn't do very much right."[73] The numbers backed him up. Connecting on only 30 of 74 shots, the Lakers could not keep their vaunted offense from unraveling. Figuring prominently in this collapse was the uneven play of West, who netted 26 points in 39 minutes.

While impressive on the surface, these final numbers actually represented a 13-point drop-off from his series average.

"When the game started I didn't know what I could do," West said. "I had to find out how much movement and drive I had. As it was, I couldn't drive because when I pushed off it felt like I didn't have any strength. And this hurt me, I had real good luck driving before I got hurt and today my right leg took that away from me."[74] He concluded that if he had been "100 percent" healthy, the Lakers would have easily taken the game and the series. Chamberlain reached a similar conclusion. "We just didn't adjust," he said. "This is the first time I've played together with Jerry when he's been hurting like this and we couldn't do the thing we usually do."[75] One skeptical Celtic not buying any of these explanations was Bill Russell. "I don't think West's leg inhibited him," he said. "I still drew my two fouls on him as usual."[76]

Regardless of the state of West's health, the Celtics were relentless in applying their pressure defense, especially in the third quarter when they prevented Los Angeles from scoring more than two baskets in a row. "I think," declared an upbeat Russell, "that's the first time we outscored someone in the third period [in the series]. It was only one. But we'll take it."[77] The Lakers attempted to climb back into the game by scoring six straight points at the start of the fourth period, but the Celtics responded with five "quickies" from Don Nelson to stamp out the comeback.

Nelson had initially entered the contest with 4:13 to go in the first quarter when the normally reliable John Havlicek and Bailey Howell went stone cold from the field. "If we need scoring, my job is to score," said Nelson. "If Sam and Havlicek are going good that's not my job. You've got to evaluate the situation and see what the team needs."[78] The team needed instant offense and he provided it with 10 clutch points to close out the period. But the biggest lift of the day was provided by a home Garden crowd of 15,128, who gave Sam Jones a rousing farewell standing ovation during the pregame introductions. Jones, who was playing in his last home game as a Celtic, had difficulty composing himself during the spontaneous tribute. "I was just looking at the flags," said Jones, "and I was thinking, 'Please. Can't we have just one more.'"[79]

In spite of the tough loss, the Lakers expressed confidence that they would be the ones sipping victory champagne at the conclusion of Game 7. "If we play our game," said West, "we'll win. Everyone on the team wants this one so badly that I just can't imagine us losing. I think the victor will be the club that controls the rebounds, and with Wilt we should do this." Chamberlain did not find fault with this prediction. "I definitely think we are going to beat them," he said. "We definitely deserve to. We've proved across 82 games that we are a better team, and now we have to do so again in one game. It doesn't seem fair, but that's the NBA."[80] For their part, the Celtics were somewhat more subdued in their comments. "It's anybody's game—whoever wants it most," said Don Nelson. Added Sam Jones, "We can win if we get our defense going and get the ball. But it's tough against the Lakers. They've got two 7-footers under those boards, Wilt and [reserve center] Mel Counts, and it's tough for us to get the ball." As for Russell, he resisted the temptation to issue any brash predictions and opted instead to lament the impending retirement of Jones. "We'll miss him," Russell said. "We'll miss him because he was one of the great basketball players of all time. But, we'll miss him as a person more. You see, when we're in this room together, we're not basketball players. We're men. When we lose a player we can make an adjustment in our style and keep going. But when we lose a man like Sam, well, we're going to miss him."[81]

A different kind of sentiment seized Lakers owner Jack Kent Cooke. Certain of a triumph, Cooke had thousands of victory balloons raised to the Forum's rafters with the understanding they would be released when the Lakers made their inevitable appointment with destiny. In addition, arrangements were made for the University of Southern California Marching Band to come out from beneath the stands and play "Happy Days Are Here Again." Word of the victory celebration soon spread to the Celtics, who understandably took a dim view of the planned festivities. "We thought this was pretty funny," John Havlicek later wrote. "We were used to being champions, and we never even had champagne in the locker room. We certainly didn't hold their players responsible for this idea. We knew it was Cooke, who was intent on outdoing anything the NBA had ever seen. But this gave us additional incentive at a crucial time."[82]

The extra motivation was evident from the opening tip-off as the Celtics connected on 8 of their first 10 shots to post an early 24–12 lead. Havlicek provided the main offensive punch here as he scored 10 of his team-high 26 points in the first period. When he cooled down in the second quarter, teammate Emmette Bryant picked up the slack with a shooting exhibition of his own, collecting 15 points. "We were running," Bryant later recounted. "Plus Wilt [Chamberlain] had a personal vendetta against [Russell]. He didn't want Russ to score, get many rebounds or anything. So we used Russ to set a lot of screens because Wilt wouldn't switch see, because if he switched then Russ got a mismatch with [a smaller] guy. He got a dunk or something. And so we just ran screens off on Russ and got wide open shots for the whole game."[83]

Despite the offensive outburst, Los Angeles managed to draw within 59–56 at the half as the fast-breaking Celtics attack got bogged down in the slackening pace of the Lakers half-court game. At this critical juncture, however, Havlicek impressed upon his teammates the need to reestablish the running game. "I told them to get me the ball," Havlicek recalled. "If they gave it to me, I would run, and therefore make everyone else run. I was right in my prime then. I could practically go for days without stopping. I was so pumped up I could have played solely on adrenaline, anyway."[84]

The team enthusiastically responded to his floor leadership. Indeed, as the third quarter unfolded, the Celtics built a 15-point lead behind the sizzling offense of Don Nelson, who tallied 13 points in the session. True to form, the Lakers refused to wave the white flag. They began to whittle away at the Celtics advantage, until it got down to single digits midway through the fourth quarter. Then seeming disaster struck the home team. With the Celtics still in front, 103–94, Chamberlain committed the most controversial act of his Hall of Fame career. He took himself out of the ballgame after injuring his right knee at the 5:45 mark. An amazed Russell couldn't believe what he was witnessing. "I didn't think he'd been hurt that badly," Russell later wrote, "and even if he was, I wanted him in there. We were close—oh, so close—to finishing with a great game. I was almost moaning. 'Oh, man, don't do that. Don't leave,' I thought to myself."[85] Chamberlain, who had uncharacteristically picked up five fouls in the third quarter, offered a different version of events, claiming he had seriously damaged his knee. "It hurt bad," he told writer David Shaw in his 1973 biography *Wilt*, "like when you bang your crazy-bone against a wall as hard as you can. I had to be helped from the floor."[86]

In Chamberlain's absence, the Lakers mounted a furious rally, cutting the Celtics lead down to 1 point at 103–102 with 3 minutes to play. Ironically, one of the main catalysts in the comeback drive was Mel Counts, Chamberlain's replacement in the pivot. The ex-Celtic, who

Wilt goes down with 23 seconds showing on the clock
Courtesy of the *Boston Herald*

had 9 points and 7 rebounds on the day, held Russell scoreless and drained a 10-foot jumper that brought his team to within a free throw of the lead. Curiously, it was also around this time that Chamberlain approached Lakers coach Bill van Breda Kolff about reentering the contest. Laker veteran Tom Hawkins had a bird's-eye view of what transpired next. "I sat between them and Wilt asked Butch if he could come back," he recalled. "Butch said, 'We're doing well enough without you.' Wilt then just threw up his hands and walked to the other end of the bench."[87] Chamberlain later claimed the pain in his injured knee had receded enough to warrant his return to action and that only the recalcitrant attitude of van Breda Kolff prevented this from happening. "He was determined to prove he was the boss, even if it cost the Lakers the world championship," Chamberlain charged.[88] In his own defense, van Breda Kolff said his decision was based solely on the exigencies of the situation. "I would have put him back in if I felt he [Wilt] would have made the difference," he told reporters afterward.[89]

Even without Chamberlain's services, the Lakers found themselves on the verge of taking control of the game and winning the franchise's first NBA title since the 1953–54 season. It all came to naught, however. With 1:17 remaining, Don Nelson scooped up a loose ball near the foul line and hoisted a shot that one writer claimed "would have struck oil if the iron on the hoop hadn't gotten in the way."[90] The ball hit the back rim and squirted high in the air before finally falling straight through the hoop. "I wasn't even supposed to get the ball," Nelson later recalled, "but it was tipped out of John [Havlicek]'s hands and I picked it up. I was 12 feet out. I shot too quickly and didn't think it would go in, but it did."[91] The basket gave the Celtics a 3-point lead at 105–102 and essentially ended the Lakers' title hopes as Russell blocked a subsequent Counts drive from the baseline and Larry Siegfried and John Havlicek came through with clutch conversions. The Lakers could only counter with a pair of Baylor free throws and a meaningless layup by Johnny Egan at the final buzzer. "It is as if we aren't supposed to win," a dejected Jerry West said afterward. "I'll give them credit. They've got players who know how to win."[92]

As the Celtics ran triumphantly from the court, a mischievous thought entered the mind of team general manager Red Auerbach. "What I want to know," he mused, "is what they are going to do with those blankety-blank balloons. Anybody want to buy some balloons cheap?"[93] A few minutes later, within the confines of the joyous Boston dressing room, a jubilant Don Nelson pondered a different question. "What can I say?" he said of his championship-clinching basket. "It was a lucky shot—the luckiest of my life."[94] If there was anyone happier than Nelson at that particular moment, it might have been Sam Jones, who finished with 24 points. After 12 glorious seasons with the Celtics, in which he scored 15,411 points and earned 10 championship rings, he fittingly was departing from the game as a winner. "We've got the greatest team in the world," he exclaimed. "We read in the paper where it would be a crime if we won again. Well, I guess it's just a crime then."[95] As he began to take off his Boston uniform for the last time, Jones drew attention to the fact that the trunks he was wearing belonged to Bailey Howell. "We switched pants early in the season," he explained. "Maybe it's superstition, but they do fit me better than my own."[96] Where the championship fit in the context of Bill Russell's long and celebrated career became a hot topic among reporters. "How can I say this is the most satisfying?" retorted Russell, who amassed 6 points and 21 rebounds in the deciding game. "I've been on 11 world champions. I will say this though. I consider myself fortunate to be associated with a great bunch of guys. Everyone contributed—and I mean everyone. It's a study of comradeship and friendship. Among my top accomplishments? I've passed the point of accomplishments. I've done all there is to do."[97] That included seizing the opportunity to take a verbal swipe at Chamberlain. "I've been reading that the big center of the Los Angeles team said that we've been lucky," he remarked. "Now you can see that it just isn't so. . . . Winning this wasn't unexpected. I never thought of losing. And this wasn't the toughest playoff series I've ever been in. I've been in a lot of these type of games and they've all been exciting."[98]

Unlike his coach, John Havlicek did not hesitate to rank the championship as the greatest in all his years with the Celtics. "This is my most satisfying championship because it's the one we've had to work the hardest for," he said. "Yes, I think it was the biggest of all my thrills. This has got to be one of the greatest comebacks of all time. Time and again all season we had to bounce back—and did. We've had more talent in other seasons but none with more guts."[99] He credited Russell for making it all possible. "He plays a great game," the Celtics team captain said, "he coaches a great game and he's still able to substitute individuals well. That's impossible, but he does it. That has made us a winner."[100]

Sew It Up!

Russell and Celtics sew it up
Courtesy of the *Boston Herald*

Unsurprisingly, the atmosphere in the Lakers locker room next door was like a scene from a wake. "I just hate to sit here and listen to all that noise over in the other locker room," confessed an emotional Jerry West, who had a game-high 42 points. "It's very difficult to sit here and try to appear happy . . . because I'm not. We lost. They're a fine team, but I think we were the best team. I had no idea we'd lose—even in the last quarter when we were 15 points behind. I guess it's just not meant for me to play on a world championship team."[101] Not even the knowledge he would receive a new automobile for having been named the series most valuable player cheered him up. "What significance is the car?" he scoffed. "I'd give it away right now if we could have won the title."[102] One thing West did win was the admiration of his opponents. After the final buzzer had sounded, a number of Celtics rushed up to embrace West for his outstanding play. "You were great, baby," Sam Jones said.[103] The accolades continued to flow in the Boston locker room. "He is the master," Siegfried declared. "They can talk all they want about the others, build them up, but he is the one. He is the only guard."[104] Added John Havlicek, "I just told him that it was a tough break, and that we all love him and have the greatest respect for him as a player."[105]

Love was hardly the word to describe the extreme ill will that now existed between Chamberlain and van Breda Kolff. Still fuming about his benching at the end of the contest, Chamberlain (18 points, 27 rebounds) could barely keep his emotions in check for reporters. "I can just read it now," he said, "how everyone is going to blame me for this loss. It's inevitable. I could say a lot of things now but I'm not because then everyone would accuse me of sour grapes."[106] Nevertheless, he could not resist taking a shot at his erstwhile coach. "We lacked the proper direction," he said of the underlying reason for the Lakers' loss. "When [the Celtics] started on their third quarter spree, we weren't doing anything correctly. This was when someone should have called a timeout, and make the proper moves."[107] When asked specifically to comment on van Breda Kolff's decision not to use him down the stretch, Chamberlain expressed bewilderment. "Yes, I asked to come back in," he said evenly. "I felt I could have come back. For me it was the most frustrating championship I've lost because I wasn't able to do anything about it because of my knee. I don't know when I'll be in this position again."[108] To his credit, van Breda Kolff did not back down from the controversy and vigorously defended his actions. "All I know," he said, "is that after Wilt came out we scored some points. . . . Mel Counts was playing extremely well. He gives us another outside threat and if he gets fouled he makes the foul shots. . . . If we made some shots, it would have been a great move. We didn't . . . but we came close, didn't we?" As for

Russell arrives at Logan
Courtesy of the *Boston Herald*

the Celtics performance, the Lakers coach had nothing but high praise. "That's the Celtics' strength—balance," he said. "Don't get me wrong, it's nice to have Jerry West to go to, but it would be nice to have four guys with him. You can't beat balance. The Celtics' balance was only getting old, that's why we stayed close. Four years ago? Sam Jones and those guys would have run away from us."[109]

After most of the writers and players had departed from the Celtics dressing room, a young *Boston Globe* reporter named Leigh Montville decided to approach Russell and ask him about a rumor that claimed he was planning to retire from basketball. It was hardly a task he relished carrying out, however. All season long, Montville, who would go on to

The banners are hoisted

write for *Sports Illustrated,* had covered the Celtics, and while he came to greatly enjoy many of the players on the team, particularly personalities like Satch Sanders and Larry Siegfried, Russell represented something of an enigma to him. He never quite knew what to expect from the mercurial Celtics player-coach. "He was the hardest of any guy there to get close to," Montville later remembered. "I mean, at least for me—a 25-year old guy. He liked [middle-aged *Globe* columnist] Bud Collins because maybe he saw a peer . . . but to me he saw an insignificant little shit. You could catch him [on a particular day] . . . and he might be very good. He would talk to you and be very nice. You'd say, 'Wow, we're okay, Bill and me.' And the next day he'd come to practice and you'd go, 'Hi Bill!' and he'd walk by you like he never fucking saw you, never met you in his life. I don't know what that was, whether it was the star thing. Because I've seen it a million times since [with celebrities]. . . . But he was the only guy like that on that team."[110]

As Montville prepared to pose his question to Russell, he could not help but notice that Russell was chatting with Jim Brown, the former star running back of the Cleveland Browns. "They were probably the two most political black athletes of our time, two angry men," Montville said. "Here's this 5-9, red-headed, freckle-faced honky writer. I went over to [Russell], 'Hello, I heard the rumor that you are going to retire after this.' Jim Brown just looked at me and said, 'The man has just won the fucking world title. Why do you ever think he's going to fucking retire?'" Startled by the vehemence of Brown's response, Montville obligingly crept away after Russell responded to his inquiry with a firm "Nah."[111]

The weary Celtics leader, however, still had to deal with one final demand of his time. As he was exiting up a flight of stairs, an usherette suddenly stepped in front of him and held out a pencil and paper. "You've refused all these years," she said brightly. "How about signing this now, just for once."[112] Unimpressed by her line of reasoning, Russell resumed his walk.

Afterword

Not long after Russell announced his retirement and the 1969 NBA championship had officially entered the record books, the Celtics began a swift descent into mediocrity. Without their Hall of Fame center, the team finished the 1969–70 season with a disappointing 34–48 record and did not qualify for the playoffs for the first time since 1949.

Despite high hopes, Russell's replacement in the pivot, former San Diego Rockets center Henry Finkel, turned out to be a certifiable bust with a less than awe-inspiring 9.7 scoring average. "After Russ left," Havlicek later said, "we still had a lot of capable people, but we had no dominating figure at center. I don't say that condemning Henry. We expected him to do a job like Russell did, and that wasn't fair."[1]

Adding to the Celtics' difficulties was the inexperienced coaching of Tom Heinsohn, who had left his regular broadcasting job to direct the team. Loud, profane, and demonstrative, Heinsohn initially had difficulty getting through to his players, as they had grown accustomed to the subtler leadership qualities of Russell. "It wasn't the easiest year to be coach of the Boston Celtics," he later remarked.[2] Indeed, Heinsohn faced constant challenges to his authority throughout the season, even from members of the Boston media who condescendingly dismissed him as a "coaching puppet" for Red Auerbach.[3]

Still, Heinsohn was shrewd enough to realize the team's future lay in the hands of younger players like Don Chaney and first-round draft pick

Jo Jo White of Kansas. He quickly incorporated them into the starting lineup, thus providing the Celtics with a foundation that would lead them to the 1974 championship, the franchise's first without Russell. The team would win another title in 1976 before handing the baton off to Larry Bird, Kevin McHale, and Robert Parish for three more championships in the 1980s.

By this time, however, the principal cast of the 1969 champions had long since gone their separate ways. Emmette Bryant, the journeyman guard whose outstanding play helped lift his teammates in that postseason, played only one more year with the Celtics, as he had a major falling out with Tom Heinsohn over playing time. He was put on the expansion list at the conclusion of the 1969–70 season and lasted two more years with the expansion Buffalo Braves. He became an assistant coach at Columbia University for a year before joining Bill Russell's coaching staff in Seattle for the 1973–74 season. "I enjoyed it [at Seattle]," he said. "But it was tough from the standpoint of having played with all these guys and now I had to be a disciplinarian. That didn't work too good."[4] A fling at scouting also didn't work out, but he eventually found his niche as a recreation specialist with the juvenile department of the state of Washington, a job he has held since 1975. Notwithstanding, he always has fond memories of the 1969 championship. "We were lucky to make the playoffs," he said. "The goal was always to get into the playoffs. . . . I enjoyed it immensely, just the camaraderie as a team."[5]

Larry Siegfried's playing days were also numbered following the 1968–69 season. Plagued by back problems, the moody guard saw his scoring average plummet to single digits as he was unable to reclaim his shot. He struggled on for three more years before finally calling it quits with the Atlanta Hawks in 1972. His affiliation with professional basketball did not end there, however. After serving as an assistant coach with Ohio State University, he spent three years as an assistant under Johnny Egan with the Rockets. He went on to become a motivational speaker for schools and universities around the country and currently can be found teaching incarcerated individuals in the Ohio state prison system. He never forgot how special it was to be a Celtic in the 1960s. "If I could do one thing," he told a reporter in 1984, "it would be to have everyone understand what it was like to be part of the Boston Celtics during the great years. All of those championships were a by-product of good people doing the right things. As time progresses, those teams become even greater because there aren't any teams anymore—just individuals, and it's wrong."[6]

After earning his second championship ring in 1969, Bailey Howell played only two more seasons in the NBA. He finished his career with the Philadelphia 76ers in 1971 with a career 18.7 scoring average. It was not an easy final year, however. With his playing skills noticeably diminished due to injury, Howell struggled to regain some semblance of his old form. He averaged only 10.7 points, but he still cut a highly respected figure in the Philadelphia locker room. "He's got a wry sense of humor that seems to put everyone around him in good spirits," said 76ers coach Jack Ramsey. "When he's out on the court, he's the hardest-driving competitor you'll ever see. He's always driving. He hates to lose."[7] While he had always thought about coaching as a possible career option when he called it quits as a player, he came to the realization that this course was impractical. "I thought at my age I didn't have the time to take an assistant coaching job," he later said. "I thought it was critical for my family that I didn't move three or four times in the next 10 years after I retired. I didn't think I could pay my dues as an assistant. I think my not going into coaching has been a blessing."[8]

Indeed, he became a successful sales and promotional representative with Converse sneakers as he returned to his old stomping grounds in Mississippi. In 1997 he received one of the highest honors in basketball when he was inducted into the Basketball Hall of Fame in Springfield, Massachusetts. Yet the memory of the 1968–69 season and his teammates still holds a special place in his heart. "All of those fellows had been there before," he said. "They all knew what type of effort and sacrifice it took to win. And they knew how much reward there was in winning personally and as a group. I think it was a big advantage. We had a lot of competitors on that team. We had all the ingredients other than youth. We had all the ingredients to be a championship team . . . but we had to go out on the court and do it."[9]

Upon his departure from the Celtics, Sam Jones served the dual role of basketball coach and athletic director at Federal City College in Washington, D.C. "The people at the school want to play big time basketball," Jones told reporters in 1969. "They heard I was retiring and they agreed to hold it open for a year if I took the job."[10] Alas, his tenure at the inner city school was largely unsuccessful. Under his watch, the basketball team could not pull off a winning season. In addition, the school's football program had to be dropped after 47 players failed to meet the requisite academic standards. Eventually, he left Federal City to take over the head coaching job at North Carolina Central University. But following a woeful 5–16 record during the 1973–74 season, he abruptly resigned his post and served a year as an assistant coach with the NBA's New Orleans Jazz. He later performed some scouting duties for the Celtics and worked for the Nike Corporation. His vast contributions to the game were recognized in 1983 when he was inducted into the Basketball Hall of Fame.

Don Nelson wasn't sure what he would do when he finally hung up his Celtics jersey for good in 1976. For a time he thought joining the officiating ranks might be his best option. "Yes," he later said, "I was serious about officiating. I wanted to stay in the game in some way. Sure, I wanted to coach, but how did I know I'd get a job? There are very few around. I talked to Red [Auerbach] and he suggested I go into college coaching. I didn't want to do that, so I began to think about officiating."[11] As fate would have it, however, a professional coaching opportunity did fall into Nelson's lap for the upcoming 1976–77 season. Milwaukee Bucks head man Larry Costello was looking for an assistant and placed a call to Nelson. The 14-year NBA veteran enthusiastically accepted the offer and spent most of training camp teaching the Bucks how to run the fast break properly.

But when Costello unceremoniously submitted his resignation in November, Nelson was tapped to replace him. "The first night," Nelson recounted, "I called the team together and told them that I had no idea what kind of reception they could expect before the home crowd that night. All I asked of them was to pass and fast break and keep hustling. I told them to be ready for anything, including people throwing things. They went out and played hard and never gave anybody a chance to boo. It's really been that way ever since."[12]

To be sure, under Nelson's leadership, the Bucks became a perennial playoff team, even going so far as to memorably sweep the Larry Bird–led Celtics in the 1983 Eastern Conference semifinals. All told, his teams won seven consecutive division titles to go along with seven consecutive 50-win seasons. For his efforts, he was twice named NBA Coach of the Year. From Milwaukee Nelson went on to have successful coaching runs with the Golden State Warriors and the Dallas Mavericks. Still, the memory of the 1969 championship burns bright. "We weren't the most dominant team," he said. "We just weren't expected to go very far."[13]

Tom Sanders also had trouble staying away from the game. Following his retirement as a player in 1973, he agreed to take over as head coach of the Harvard University men's squad. In four seasons with the Crimson, his teams compiled an unspectacular 40–60 record and made no post-season tournament appearances. Still, he never regretted his decision to go to the Ivy League school. "Coaching at Harvard was really fun . . . ," he later said. "Level has nothing to do with it. Their philosophy is something I really like. [Harvard grants no athletic scholarships.] There are 22 professional teams, 200-odd pro ball players. But I don't think that the only worthwhile goal of college players should be to play pro ball."[14]

Indeed, he believed such thinking was indicative of a misplaced set of priorities—or worse. "It's the responsibility of adults to prepare kids for that or for alternative goals," he said. "Too many institutions allow individuals—coaches or athletic directors, maybe—to take advantage of the self-indulgent goal that many kids have to play pro ball. A coach should help players realize their ability to make it in the pros or other things. Any institution should help the kids there fulfill all their potential. That's what I felt I had Harvard's cooperation in doing."[15]

Sanders went on to serve as an assistant coach under Tom Heinsohn for the Celtics in the late 1970s. Following Heinsohn's dismissal in the middle of the 1977–78 season, Sanders took over the head coaching reins and led the team to a disappointing 23–39 mark over parts of two seasons. He eventually ended up as vice president of NBA Player Programs for the league office in New York. In this job he would provide young players with financial and personal advice. "When you talk about players, you're talking sometimes about a macho bunch who don't feel that they may want to ask for any help," he said. "You've got to really keep on putting it out there for the times players want to take advantage of it. They're going through the kinds of stresses and strains that happen when you have a relationship where the gentleman is always on the road. Dealing with kids, dealing with how to say no to people who are asking for favors from tickets to money."[16]

Unlike most of his teammates, John Havlicek still had several outstanding years of basketball left in him after the 1969 championship. He consistently averaged over 20 points a game and played a key veteran leadership role in helping the Celtics rebuild after Russell's retirement.

Russell laughs it up with Havlicek and Heinsohn
Courtesy of the *Boston Herald*

"It marked quite a transition for me," he later told Mark Goodman of *Sport* magazine. "I had been the kid, the sixth man, and I liked it that way. Auerbach had always told me, 'It's not who starts the game, but who finishes it.' I believed it. Suddenly, I was the veteran. I remember in 1970, when we played an early exhibition game at Florida State, we walked onto the court and a referee asked, 'Are these the Celtics?' It was unnerving. I was at the peak of my physical abilities, but we had lost so many veterans that we had to struggle. I blew up a couple of times in the lockerroom . . . because we just weren't learning to execute."[17]

But the team did turn around and Havlicek was able to take home two more championships before retiring in 1978. By then, his reputation as being one of the all-time greats in his sport was secure. "There was no one in the game I respected more," said Hall of Famer Jerry West. "He and Russell were the best. They were incredible competitors."[18] In retirement, Havlicek continued to do well as a successful commercial spokesman and an enterprising businessman. He ended up owning several Wendy's Old Fashioned Hamburger restaurants and even earned a diploma from the chain's management institute. "Remember," he informed the *Boston Globe*, "I'm a guy that used to fold his socks over coathangers. I like that stuff, the details. How many hamburgers there are in a bag of meat. What the temperature of the grease should be in the french-fry cookers. The levels of condiments. The calibrator you put under the soda dispenser. If it isn't equalized, you can be making a lot of money or losing a lot. I know all those things now."[19]

Russell's post-Celtics career was far more turbulent. Just months after winning the 1969 title, Russell abruptly ended his marriage of 13 years and moved to California to pursue a career in movies. "It was a time of excitement mixed with fear," he later wrote in his autobiography. "Every breath I took felt a little frosty. I was excited because I was venturing into the outside world after 13 years in a compression chamber. Fans were about to become people, and I was about to become a person instead of a star. I wanted to read everything I could get my hands on, to poke around in every layer of life. I felt liberated and tingly, the way college seniors are supposed to on graduation day."[20]

He also took the opportunity to publicly get a few things off his chest, most notably his anger at Wilt Chamberlain for peremptorily removing himself from Game 7 of the 1969 finals. "Any injury short of a broken leg or a broken back isn't good enough," Russell told a college audience in Madison, Wisconsin. "When he took himself out of that final game, when he hurt his knee; well, I wouldn't have put him back in the game either, even though I think he's great."[21] Not surprisingly, Chamberlain took strong exception to these statements. "He is a man and I suppose, subject to his own opinion," the big center said. "Why he has chosen to enlighten the world with it, only he knows."[22] While the two would reconcile, it took over two decades before they were on speaking terms again.

By then, however, they were able to joke about their legendary rivalry. "I asked him as recently as four or five years ago," Chamberlain said during a 1999 public tribute to Russell, "'Bill why don't you let me have one of those [championship] rings that you can't wear?' He gave me that big cackle of his. When you hear him laugh like that, you wonder whether he's laughing with you or laughing at you. I knew right then and there he was laughing at me. So I said, maybe I could show you the finger that I'd use [for the ring]. Then I gave him the old finger."[23]

In California, Russell's movie career fizzled from the outset. "How many parts are there for a black man 6 feet 10?" he asked sardonically.[24] To stay active, he became a call-in talk show host for a Los Angeles radio station and toured the college lecture circuit as a celebrity speaker. In the latter capacity, he was unflinchingly honest about his former life as an NBA superstar. Before a student group at Houston Baptist College in 1973, for example, Russell revealed that he had played two games under the influence of the drug Dexedrine. Needless to say, the entire episode proved very disconcerting. "Because of the Dexedrine, I felt like I was blocking shots with my shoes," he said. "After the game, I went to the dressing room, showered, dressed and went back to our hotel for a sandwich. I went to my room and turned on the TV. I watched until 2 A.M. The station had signed off about 1. But I kept watching. I turned off the TV and still couldn't fall asleep. I couldn't even close my eyes. I was awake all night."[25]

Such candor became useful when Russell agreed to work as a color commentator for the ABC-TV telecasts of NBA games in the early 1970s. Unlike most sportscasters of his day, Russell was not afraid to state the unvarnished truth as he saw it. When broadcast partner Keith Jackson once observed that a particular player was having a "rough game," Russell was quick to jump in and correct him. "No Keith," he said, "he's having a bad game."[26] Still, Russell went out of his way not to be overly critical in his analysis. "When you hear me talking about basketball," he said, "I happen to be fond of the game and 99 percent of the players. So what I do is tell the truth without hurting anybody. I try not to hurt anybody."[27] And one way to avoid the latter was through humor. When Jackson once asked him how he would play against Milwaukee Bucks center Kareem Abdul-Jabbar, Russell deadpanned, "First, I'd speak to him."[28]

As for describing the overall Xs and Os of a contest, Russell was a firm believer in keeping things simple for the home viewing audience. "I have a tremendous advantage in covering basketball," he said. "I remember. I rarely get technical about a game. I played with what was the smartest team in pro sports. When Red Auerbach put in a new play, it used to take hours, literally hours, to learn the play. Then, when the game begins we'd forget it. How can you explain it to fans in two minutes? It would just confuse them."[29]

As much as he found network broadcasting both personally and financially rewarding, Russell decided to return to coaching in 1973 as the leader of a young but talented Seattle Supersonics squad. "What I'm trying to do is turn around a whole group of guys who have been doing things another way," he said. "What I want them to do is execute in a game what we've spent so much time on in practice. We're still losing our poise too much in clutch situations. And if the opposition keeps theirs—well, it's a case where we've gone and beaten ourselves again. Earlier in the season, with just a few seconds left on the clock, we called time to set up a play against the Knicks which might have won for us. But somebody blew the pass in and we didn't even get the shot off. Maybe we wouldn't have gotten the basket anyway. But the point is we should at least have gotten the ball in the air."[30]

Following an extended period of adjustment, his inexperienced charges began to rapidly buy into his program of intelligent play and tight defense. "Man, he's a fabulous cat," said Seattle starting forward Spencer Haywood. "For a while we didn't understand what he wanted from us. I guess we just had too many bad habits to break. But now that we're starting to get it all together, I can see that what Russell says is going to work."[31] Although the Sonics would post only a 36–46 mark in their first year under Russell, they would go on to have winning records in two of their next three seasons and make the playoffs. All the while, Russell found the people of Seattle a refreshing contrast to those he had come into contact with in Boston during his playing days. "They don't invade my privacy, but they're friendly to me and nice to me," he said. "It's one of those places where you don't mind taking a walk because the people just say hello."[32]

Still, after only four seasons with the Sonics, Russell abruptly resigned as coach, citing his difficulty relating to a new generation of ballplayers as the main reason for his surprise move. Indeed, he thought the NBA had become a haven for too many overpriced and selfish athletes. As he later wrote, "Since it is my habit simply not to talk to people I don't like, I found it harder and harder to have discussions with many of the players. It was obvious to them that I didn't like them, and naturally they didn't like me either."[33]

He returned to network broadcasting, this time with CBS-TV, and quickly ran into controversy. While doing a game with former San Francisco Warriors star Rick Barry in 1981, Barry observed that Russell had a "watermelon" smile when a picture of Russell flashed across the screen. Outraged by this racially insensitive remark, Russell barely acknowledged Barry for the rest of the broadcast. "Of course, I was offended by that," Russell told an interviewer in 1984. "But that was three years ago, and I know Rick is not what he sounded like. I'll have no problems working with Rick."[34]

Russell was less forgiving when it came to his induction ceremony at the Basketball Hall of Fame in Springfield, Massachusetts. Unwilling to be associated with an institution he felt was founded by racists, Russell caused a major public uproar by refusing to have anything to do with the ceremony. "It's unthinkable," exclaimed former University of Kentucky coach Adolph Rupp, who ironically had his own well-deserved reputation as a racist to contend with. "Why it's the dream of every basketball player to be inducted into the Hall. If he insists on declining he should not even be talked about in the future. I say if he doesn't want it, forget about it."[35]

Russell was undeterred in his decision, however. "Well, first of all, I know the guys, and knew most of them that started [the Hall]," he told television talk show host Phil Donahue. "I didn't have respect for them. All of them are in it. And to me, it has no more value than if you and I decided we're going to pick the ten best-dressed men list . . . and then after we did that, we decided that the whole world has to [accept it]. . . . I just don't want to be in it."[36]

Following another ill-advised stab at coaching with the Sacramento Kings in the late 1980s, Russell dropped out of the public eye for several years. It was only with the dawn of the new millennium that Russell began to resurface. "I was comfortable with going home and closing the door, but [my agent] Alan [Hilburg] and my daughter and a few friends said that wasn't right," he told Richard Sandomir of the *New York Times* in 2000. "They said I shouldn't take my accomplishments in silence. While I'm not completely comfortable with this, I can put myself in a frame of mind where I'm not uncomfortable."[37] To this end, Russell agreed to make a number of public appearances around the country, in addition to writing a best-selling book on personal business management and endorsing several commercial products. "My message is team effort," he claimed. "Almost all successful organizations are team efforts. What you have to find out in a team is what are your strengths and how to use them effectively, and how not to overuse them and underuse them."[38]

At the same time, Russell became active again in the Boston community, working as a consultant with the Celtics. "It may sound like a return, but I never actually left," he contended. "I have always been visible in Boston. Don't you realize that? My person and my image never disappeared. It's just that there were things I wanted to do. But I never lost contact with the Celtics' organization."[39] Russell also took the time to state that he was not the "perpetually angry man" that so many people made him out to be during his 13 years wearing the green. "If you become embittered by anything, you've just thrown away any chance you have of being happy," he said. "And I've always felt that I owe it to myself, to my family, to be as happy as possible. Look, when I was playing for the Celtics, I was having the time of my life. Most of the time, I went to bed looking forward to tomorrow. The experiences I had here, the positive experiences, far outweighed the negative experiences. I really had a good time. . . . I mean, I had a good time!"[40]

His greatest moment of all would occur on May 26, 1999, when fans, family members, old teammates, and an all-star cast of basketball and show business celebrities feted him during a moving public tribute at the Fleet Center in Boston. Ostensibly arranged to re-retire Russell's number (the Celtic great had reluctantly agreed to the honor some two decades earlier during a quirky ceremony without fans), the gala was more a celebration of his life and many accomplishments both on and off the court. Typically, Russell appeared uncomfortable amid all the hoopla, which included taped tributes from President Bill Clinton, Michael Jordan, and former U.S. senator Bill Bradley. "I really think of myself as Charlie Russell's kid," he told the gathering. "This kind of stuff is foreign to me. I really don't understand it."[41] What he did seem to grasp, however, was how special his time with the Celtics had been. "But thank God I came here, because I found a family," he said. "Coming to the Celtics was finding a family. Everyone was so generous and kind to me. With Red, I realized I had found a friend. [Being a Celtic] became a way of life more than just an existence."[42]

And arguably the man most responsible for creating this way of life was at long last receiving his public due. It was thus only fitting that when a voice from the crowd shouted, "We love you, Bill," an emotional Russell could think of only one appropriate response.

"I love you, too," he said.[43]

Notes

Preface

1 Bill Russell, "I'm Not Involved Anymore," *Sports Illustrated,* August 4, 1969.
2 Bill Russell and Taylor Branch, *Second Wind: The Memoirs of an Opinionated Man* (New York, 1979), 168.
3 Ibid.
4 *Boston Globe,* May 27, 1999.
5 *Boston Globe,* June 20, 1993.
6 *Boston Globe,* May 12, 1992.
7 Ibid.

CHAPTER 1
A Divided City with a Winning Tradition

1 John Powers, *The Short Season: A Boston Celtics Diary, 1977–78* (New York, 1979), 3.
2 Jeff Greenfield, *The World's Greatest Team: A Portrait of the Boston Celtics, 1957–69* (New York, 1976), 9.
3 Bob Ryan, *The Boston Celtics: The History, Legends, and Images of America's Most Celebrated Team* (Reading, Mass., 1990), 13.
4 Ibid.
5 Bob Cousy as told to Al Hirshberg, *Basketball Is My Life* (Englewood Cliffs, N.J., 1958), 68.
6 Harvey Araton and Filip Bondy, *The Selling of the Green: The Financial Rise and Moral Decline of the Boston Celtics* (New York, 1992), 75.
7 Ibid., 81.
8 *Springfield Union,* June 6, 1973.

9 J. Anthony Lukas, *Common Ground: A Turbulent Decade in the Lives of Three American Families* (New York, 1986), 56.
10 Stephan Thernstrom, *The Other Bostonians: Poverty and Progress in an American Metropolis, 1880–1970* (Cambridge, Mass., 1973), 194.
11 Thomas H. O'Connor, *The Hub: Boston Past and Present* (Boston, 2001), 236.
12 Ibid., 237.
13 Mel King, *Chain of Change: Struggle for Black Community Development* (Boston, 1981), xxvi.
14 *Boston Globe,* June 3, 1967.
15 *Boston Globe,* June 4, 1967.
16 *Boston Globe,* June 6, 1967.
17 Thomas H. O'Connor, *Bibles, Brahmins, and Bosses: A Short History of Boston* (Boston, 1984), 169.
18 *Boston Globe,* November 6, 1967.
19 *Boston Herald-Traveler,* April 7, 1968.
20 Lukas, *Common Ground,* 34.
21 Emmett H. Buell Jr. with Richard A. Brisbin Jr., *School Desegregation and Defended Neighborhoods: The Boston Controversy* (Lexington, Mass., 1982), 29.
22 Jackie Robinson, *I Never Had It Made: An Autobiography* (Hopewell, N.J., 1995), 29.
23 Glen Stout and Richard A. Johnson, *Red Sox Century* (Boston, 2000), 242.
24 *Boston Globe,* November 26, 2000.
25 Peter Golenbock, *Fenway: An Unexpurgated History of the Boston Red Sox* (New York, 1992), 225.
26 Dan Shaughnessy, *The Curse of the Bambino* (New York, 1990), 57.

27 *Boston Globe,* November 26, 2000.

28 Major League Steering Committee, "The Race Question," August 27, 1946, in *The Jackie Robinson Reader: Perspectives on an American Hero,* ed. Jules Tygiel (New York, 1997), 130–31.

29 Roger Kahn, *The Era, 1947–1957—When the Yankees, the Giants, and the Dodgers Ruled the World* (New York, 1993), 66.

30 *Boston Globe,* November 26, 2000.

31 Shaughnessy, *The Curse of the Bambino,* 57.

32 *Boston Globe,* April 3, 1977.

33 George Sullivan, *The Picture History of the Boston Celtics* (New York, 1982), 68.

34 *Boston Globe,* April 3, 1977.

35 *Boston Globe,* February 26, 1999.

36 *Boston Globe,* April 3, 1977.

37 Richard A. Johnson, *A Century of Boston Sports* (Boston, 2000), 121.

38 *Boston Herald,* September 9, 1964.

39 *Boston Herald,* February 9, 1986.

40 *Boston Herald American,* September 6, 1979.

41 Ibid.

42 *Boston Record,* September 9, 1964.

43 News clipping, "The Walter Browns," by Harold K. Banks, Boston Herald Library.

44 News clipping, "Walter Brown Puts Business, Pleasure Together in Garden," by Frederick McCarthy, Walter Brown File, Boston Herald Library, Boston, Mass.

45 *Boston Record,* November 21, 1958.

46 Ibid.

47 Sullivan, *The Picture History of the Boston Celtics,* 8.

48 Neil D. Isaacs, *Vintage NBA: The Pioneer Era (1946–56)* (Indianapolis, Ind., 1996), 7.

49 Sullivan, *The Picture History of the Boston Celtics,* 152.

50 *Boston Globe,* January 14, 1964.

51 News clipping, "Red Auerbach Resigns Tri-Cities Post to Pilot Hub Quintet" by George C. Carens, Red Auerbach File, Boston Herald Library.

52 News clipping, "The Amazing Auerbach" by Joe Fitzgerald, Boston Herald Library.

53 Curt Gowdy with John Powers, *Seasons to Remember: The Way It Was in American Sports, 1945–1960* (New York, 1993), 124.

54 *Boston Globe,* April 3, 1977.

55 Ibid.

56 Ibid.

57 Tom Whalen, "Bob Cousy Talks About Life with the Boston Celtics," *The Bates College Student,* February 6, 1985.

58 Jack Ramsey, "The Red Behind the Green," *The Final Game, Official Commemorative Game Program and Magazine,* April 21, 1995.

59 *Boston Globe,* October 24, 1968.

60 Irv Goodman, "The Winning Ways of Red Auerbach," *Sport,* March 1965.

61 Irv Goodman, "Hothead on the Boston Bench," *Sport,* February 1956.

62 Dan Shaughnessy, *Ever Green: The Boston Celtics—A History in the Words of Their Players, Coaches, Fans, and Foes, from 1946 to the Present* (New York, 1990), 12.

63 Irv Goodman, "Cousy, Sharman, Russell & Co.," *Sport,* March 1958.

64 Arnold Auerbach and Paul Sann, *Red Auerbach: Winning the Hard Way* (Boston, 1966), 153.

65 Goodman, "The Winning Ways of Red Auerbach."

66 Auerbach and Sann, *Winning the Hard Way,* 183.

67 News clipping, "The Amazing Auerbach," by Joe Fitzgerald, Red Auerbach File, Boston Herald Library.

68 Ibid.

69 Bill Bradley, *Life on the Run* (New York, 1995), 107.

70 News clipping, "The Amazing Auerbach," by Joe Fitzgerald, Red Auerbach File, Boston Herald Library.

71 Gilbert Rogin, "They All Boo When Red Sits Down," *Sports Illustrated,* April 5, 1965.

72 Ibid.

73 *Boston Globe,* January 5, 1985.

74 Frank Deford, "No. 2 in the Rafters, No. 1 in Their Hearts," *Sports Illustrated,* January 14, 1985.

75 Goodman, "The Winning Ways of Red Auerbach."

76 Auerbach and Sann, *Winning the Hard Way,* 14.

77 Goodman, "The Winning Ways of Red Auerbach."

78 Isaacs, *Vintage NBA,* 71.

79 Auerbach and Sann, *Winning the Hard Way,* 40.

80 Ibid., 41.

81 *Boston Globe,* January 5, 1985.

82 Sullivan, *The Picture History of the Boston Celtics,* 200.

83 *Christian Science Monitor,* November 21, 1962.

84 Sullivan, *The Picture History of the Boston Celtics,* 18.

85 Ramsey, "The Red Behind the Green."

86 Greenfield, The World's Greatest Team, 33.

87 Terry Pluto, *Tall Tales: The Glory Years of the NBA, in the Words of the Men Who Played, Coached, and Built Pro Basketball* (New York, 1994), 267.

88 Rogin, "They All Boo When Red Sits Down."

89 *Boston Globe,* January 5, 1985.

90 *Boston Herald,* January 4, 1985.
91 Phil Berger, "The Sport Interview: Red Auerbach," *Sport,* June 1979.
92 *Boston Globe,* April 29, 1966.
93 *Boston Globe,* April 19, 1966.
94 *Christian Science Monitor,* April 20, 1966.
95 Ibid.
96 *Boston Globe,* April 19, 1966.
97 Quotes from "Changing the Game: Contributions of the African-American Athlete," February 28, 2001, www.NBA.com.
98 Ibid.
99 *Boston Globe,* April 19, 1966.
100 *Boston Herald-Traveler,* April 24, 1966.
101 *Boston Globe,* April 19, 1966.
102 Ibid.
103 Magazine clipping, "Player Bill Russell Takes a Look at Coach Russell." by Bob Hoobing, Russell Scrapbook, Sports Museum of New England, Boston, Mass.
104 Phil Berger, "What a Coach Means to a Pro Basketball Team," *Sport,* December 1968.
105 *Boston Herald American,* June 17, 1973.
106 Hoobing, "Player Russell Takes a Look at Coach Russell."
107 *Boston Herald,* April 13, 1967.
108 Joe Fitzgerald, *That Championship Feeling: The Story of the Boston Celtics* (New York, 1975), 177.
109 Ray Fitzgerald, *Champions Remembered: Choices from a Boston Sports Desk* (Lexington, Mass., 1982), 73.
110 *Boston Globe,* April 3, 1967.
111 Sullivan, *The Picture History of the Boston Celtics,* 85.
112 Frank Deford, "This One Was Worth Shouting About," *Sports Illustrated,* May 13, 1968.
113 John Havlicek as told to Bob Sales, "Behind the Celtics Startling Comeback," *Sport,* August 1968.
114 *Boston Globe,* May 12, 1992.

CHAPTER 2
The Eagle with a Beard

1 Frank Deford, "The Ring Leader," *Sports Illustrated,* May 10, 1999.
2 Ibid.
3 Ed Linn, "Bill Russell's Private World," *Sport,* February 1963.
4 Darren Duarte interview of Bill Russell on *Basic Black,* WGBH-TV, November 2002.
5 Bill Russell as told to William McSweeney, *Go Up for Glory* (New York, 1980), 15–16.
6 Ibid., 21.
7 Bruce Lee, "Bill Russell, K.C. Jones, Unstoppable San Francisco," *Sport,* April 1964.
8 Linn, "Bill Russell's Private World."
9 Russell and Branch, *Second Wind,* 68.
10 William Johnson, "Triumph in Obscurity," *Sports Illustrated,* April 22, 1968.
11 Ibid.
12 Russell and Branch, *Second Wind,* 119.
13 Ibid., 120.
14 Lee, "Bill Russell, K.C. Jones, Unstoppable San Francisco."
15 Russell and Branch, *Second Wind,* 122.
16 Deford, "The Ring Leader."
17 Lee, "Bill Russell, K.C. Jones, Unstoppable San Francisco."
18 K.C. Jones with Jack Warner, *Rebound: The Autobiography of K.C. Jones and an Inside Look at the Champion Boston Celtics* (Boston, 1986), 55.
19 *Boston Globe,* May 26, 1999.
20 Auerbach and Sann, *Winning the Hard Way,* 88.
21 Ibid.
22 *Boston Globe,* May 26, 1999.
23 Auerbach and Sann, *Winning the Hard Way,* 90.
24 *Boston Globe,* May 26, 1989.
25 Brad Herzog, *The Sports 100: The One Hundred Most Important People in American Sports History* (New York, 1995), 285–86.
26 Linn, "Bill Russell's Private World."
27 *Springfield Daily News,* October 31, 1980.
28 Russell as told to McSweeney, *Go Up for Glory,* 46.
29 Russell and Branch, *Second Wind,* 216.
30 *Boston Globe,* December 23, 1956.
31 *Boston Globe,* May 27, 1999.
32 Ibid.
33 Ibid.
34 Sullivan, *The Picture History of the Boston Celtics,* 39.
35 Ibid.
36 *The Sporting News,* May 14, 1970.
37 News clipping, Jim Murray Column, January 14, 1965, Bill Russell File, Naismith Memorial Basketball Hall of Fame.
38 Bill Russell with Tex Maule, "I Am Not Worried About Ali," *Sports Illustrated,* June 19, 1967.
39 Richard Hofstadter and Beatrice K. Hofstadter, *Great Issues in American History: From Reconstruction to Present, 1864–1981* (New York, 1982), 451.
40 Russell as told to McSweeney, *Go Up for Glory,* 137.
41 Linn, "Bill Russell's Private World."
42 *Boston Globe,* June 15, 1988.
43 *Boston Globe,* May 26, 1999.
44 *Boston Globe,* June 15, 1988.
45 Ibid.
46 *The Sporting News,* March 14, 1970.

47 Russell as told to McSweeney, *Go Up for Glory*, 165.
48 William M. Kunstler, "Bill Russell," *Sport*, December 1986.
49 Tony Kornheiser, "Nothing but a Man" in *ESPN SportsCentury*, ed. by Michael Mac-Cambridge (New York, 1999), 184.
50 Linn, "Bill Russell's Private World."
51 *Boston Globe*, November 12, 2000.
52 Fitzgerald, *Champions Remembered*, 71.
53 Russell as told to McSweeney, *Go Up for Glory*, 130.
54 Ibid.
55 *Boston Globe*, May 26, 1999.
56 Sullivan, *The Picture History of the Boston Celtics*, 200.
57 Bill Russell with David Falkner, *Russell Rules: Eleven Lessons on Leadership from the Twentieth Century's Greatest Winner* (New York, 2001), 10–11.
58 George Plimpton, "Sportsman of the Year, Bill Russell," *Sports Illustrated*, December 23, 1968.
59 Jones with Warner, *Rebound*, 56.
60 *Boston Globe*, May 27, 1999.
61 Ibid.
62 Pluto, *Tall Tales*, 127.
63 *Boston Herald*, November 22, 1981.
64 *Boston Globe*, May 26, 1999.
65 Ibid.
66 Ibid.
67 Bill Russell with Bob Ottum, "The Psych . . . And My Other Tricks," *Sports Illustrated*, October 25, 1965.
68 Ibid.
69 Deford, "The Ring Leader."
70 Russell with Ottum, "The Psych . . . And My Other Tricks."
71 Deford, "The Ring Leader."
72 *Boston Globe*, May 26, 1999.
73 Russell with Ottum, "The Psych . . . And My Other Tricks."
74 Jones with Warner, *Rebound*, 85.
75 Bob Cousy and Bob Ryan, *Cousy on the Celtic Mystique* (New York, 1988), 34.
76 Jeremiah Tax, "The Man Who Must Be Different," *Sports Illustrated*, February 3, 1958.
77 *The Sporting News*, March 14, 1970.
78 Tommy Heinsohn and Joe Fitzgerald, *Give 'em the Hook* (New York, 1988), 64.
79 *Boston Herald*, May 27, 1999.
80 *Boston Globe*, May 26, 1999.
81 Ken Shouler, *The Experts Pick Basketball's Best Fifty Players in the Last Fifty Years* (Lenexa, Kans., 1998), 154.
82 Plimpton, "Sportsman of the Year, Bill Russell."
83 Russell as told to McSweeney, *Go Up for Glory*, 145.
84 Russell and Branch, *Second Wind*, 230.
85 Ibid., 140.
86 Ibid., 132.
87 Bob Sales, interview with author.
88 Tom Heinsohn, interview with author.
89 *Boston Globe*, October 15, 1988.
90 Russell as told to McSweeney, *Go Up for Glory*, 153.
91 *Springfield Union*, June 6, 1973.
92 Edward Linn, "I Owe the Public Nothing," *Saturday Evening Post*, January 18, 1964.
93 Fitzgerald, *Champions Remembered*, 72.
94 Fred Katz, "The Unknown Side of Bill Russell," *Sport*, March 1966.
95 Russell as told to McSweeney, *Go Up for Glory*, 55.
96 *Boston Globe*, October 17, 1979.
97 Ibid.
98 Russell and Branch, *Second Wind*, 183.

CHAPTER 3
Getting Under Way

1 *Time*, September 13, 1968.
2 Tariq Ali and Susan Watkins, *1968: Marching in the Streets* (New York, 1998), 162.
3 *Life*, September 6, 1968.
4 Craig Hamrick, "About Dark Shadows," www.laraparker.com.
5 *Salem Evening News*, September 24, 1968.
6 *Christian Science Monitor*, May 3, 1968.
7 Sullivan, *The Picture History of the Boston Celtics*, 197.
8 *Boston Globe*, November 5, 1968.
9 Tommy Heinsohn with Leonard Lewin, *Heinsohn, Don't You Ever Smile? The Life and Times of Tommy Heinsohn and the Boston Celtics* (New York, 1976), 164.
10 Heinsohn with Lewin, *Heinsohn, Don't You Ever Smile?* 163.
11 *Boston Herald-Traveler*, October 25, 1968.
12 Ibid.
13 *Boston Globe*, March 21, 1967.
14 Sullivan, *The Picture History of the Boston Celtics*, 198.
15 Larry Siegfried, interview with author.
16 Ibid.
17 *Boston Record-American*, March 23, 1967.
18 Larry Siegfried, interview with author.
19 Pluto, *Tall Tales*, 358.
20 *Boston Record*, March 23, 1967.
21 *Boston Herald-Traveler*, February 1, 1970.
22 *Boston Record-American*, December 16, 1965.
23 *Christian Science Monitor*, May 3, 1968.
24 *Boston Herald*, May 13, 1984.
25 Sullivan, *The Picture History of the Boston Celtics*, 197.

26 *Boston Herald-Traveler,* September 24, 1968.
27 Sullivan, *The Picture History of the Boston Celtics,* 197.
28 Araton and Bondy, *The Selling of the Green,* 64.
29 Greenfield, *The World's Greatest Team,* 145.
30 Arnold Auerbach and Joe Fitzgerald, *Red Auerbach: An Autobiography* (New York, 1977), 166.
31 *Boston Globe,* September 29, 1968.
32 *Boston Globe,* September 27, 1968.
33 Ibid.
34 Cousy as told to Hirshberg, *Basketball Is My Life,* 156.
35 *Seattle Times,* March 29, 1983.
36 Ibid.
37 *Boston Globe,* December 17, 2000.
38 *Seattle Times,* March 29, 1983.
39 *Boston Globe,* December 17, 2000.
40 *Seattle Times,* March 29, 1983.
41 Leonard Koppett, *Twenty-four Seconds to Shoot: The Birth and Improbable Rise of the NBA* (Kingston, N.Y., 1999), 197–98.
42 *Boston Globe,* May 12, 1992.
43 *Salem Evening News,* October 15, 1968.
44 *Boston Herald-Traveler,* October 19, 1968.
45 *Boston Herald-Traveler,* October 22, 1968.
46 Powers, *The Short Season,* 3.
47 Ibid., 4.
48 *Boston Globe,* April 30, 1995.
49 Ibid.
50 Kareem Abdul-Jabbar with Mignon McCarthy, *Kareem* (New York, 1990), 127.
51 Ramsey, "The Red Behind the Green."
52 Ibid.
53 *Boston Globe,* October 24, 1968.
54 Ibid.
55 *Salem Evening News,* September 24, 1968.
56 Joe Fitzgerald, *The Boston Celtics: Fifty Years* (Del Mar, Calif., 1996), 35.
57 *Christian Science Monitor,* February 27, 1961.
58 News clipping, "Excitement the Very Least of Celtics' Announcer Johnny Most," by Dave Langworthy, Johnny Most File, Boston Globe Library, Boston, Mass.
59 *Boston Herald American,* November 10, 1974.
60 *Boston Phoenix,* January 8, 1993.
61 *Boston Globe,* December 15, 1964.
62 *Boston Globe,* January 5, 1992.
63 *Boston Globe,* January 9, 1972.
64 *Boston Globe,* February 7, 1973.
65 *Boston Globe,* January 7, 1993.
66 *Boston Phoenix,* January 8, 1993.
67 *Boston Globe,* January 5, 1993.
68 *Boston Globe,* January 4, 1993.
69 *Boston Herald,* February 8, 1979.
70 *Boston Globe,* April 14, 1985.
71 *Boston Globe,* January 4, 1993.

72 *Boston Globe,* November 4, 1968.
73 Russell and Branch, *Second Wind,* 124.
74 John Devaney, "What Makes Havlicek Run . . . And Run . . . And Run," *Sport,* February 1969.
75 *Boston Globe,* February 28, 1971.
76 Don Kowett, "John Havlicek's Latest Exercise in Exorcism," *Sport,* May 1974.
77 Devaney, "What Makes Havlicek Run."
78 John Underwood, "The Green Running Machine," n.d., in Nomination Files, Naismith Memorial Basketball Hall of Fame (hereinafter NMBHF).
79 *Christian Science Monitor,* April 10, 1978.
80 Devaney, "What Makes Havlicek Run."
81 Ibid.
82 Underwood, "The Green Running Machine."
83 *Boston Globe,* May 12, 1976.
84 Kowett, "John Havlicek's Latest Exercise in Exorcism."
85 Mark Goodman, "A Fond Farewell to Hondo Havlicek," *Sport,* May 1978.
86 Sullivan, *The Picture History of the Boston Celtics,* 192.
87 *Boston Herald American,* September 20, 1980.
88 *Boston Globe,* February 5, 1963.
89 *Christian Science Monitor,* April 10, 1978.
90 *Boston Herald,* April 30, 1984.
91 *Boston Herald American,* October 13, 1978.
92 Kowett, "John Havlicek's Latest Exercise in Exorcism."
93 *Boston Herald American,* January 30, 1977.
94 Ibid.
95 *Boston Globe,* April 29, 1969.
96 Kowett, "John Havlicek's Latest Exercise in Exorcism."
97 *Christian Science Monitor,* April 10, 1978.
98 Phil Pepe, *Greatest Stars of the NBA* (Englewood Cliffs, N.J., 1970), 151–52.
99 *Boston Globe,* April 16, 1965.
100 *Boston Herald,* May 30, 1984.
101 *Boston Record-American,* January 17, 1967.
102 Pepe, *Greatest Stars of the NBA,* 152.
103 Sullivan, *The Picture History of the Boston Celtics,* 82.
104 *Los Angeles Times,* November 20, 1968.
105 Ibid.

CHAPTER 4
Nobody Roots for Goliath

1 Kornheiser, "Nothing but a Man" in *ESPN SportsCentury,* 179.
2 Jerry West, *Mr. Clutch: The Jerry West Story* (New York, 1971), 193.
3 Tom Heinsohn, interview with author.

4 *Springfield Daily News,* November 7, 1985.

5 *Boston Globe,* May 26, 1999.

6 Red Holzman with Leonard Lewin, *A View from Above* (New York, 1980), 219–20.

7 *Boston Globe,* May 26, 1999.

8 George Vescey, *Pro Basketball Champions* (New York, 1970), 98.

9 *Boston Globe,* May 26, 1999.

10 Auerbach and Fitzgerald, *Red Auerbach: An Autobiography,* 179.

11 *Boston Globe,* May 26, 1999.

12 *Boston Globe,* May 20, 2001.

13 Ibid.

14 Jeremiah Tax, "The Tall Ones in Boston," *Sports Illustrated,* November 16, 1959.

15 *Christian Science Monitor,* November 9, 1959.

16 Ibid.

17 Wilt Chamberlain and David Shaw, *Wilt: Just Like Any Other Seven-Foot Black Millionaire Who Lives Next Door* (New York, 1973), 9.

18 *Daily News Sports Writer,* "A Century of Superstars: Wilt Chamberlain—Chosen by Our Readers as the Greatest Local Athlete of the Century—Is a Man Still Defending His Legacy," n.d., www.philly.com.

19 Chamberlain and Shaw, *Wilt,* 22.

20 Daily News Sports Writer, "A Century of Superstars."

21 *Philadelphia Daily News,* October 13, 1999.

22 Ibid.

23 Wilt Chamberlain with Bob Ottum, "My Life in a Bush League, Part I," *Sports Illustrated,* April 12, 1965.

24 Ibid.

25 Ibid.

26 Pluto, *Tall Tales,* 214.

27 Dick Schaap, "The Real Wilt Chamberlain," *Sport,* March 1961.

28 Chamberlain and Shaw, *Wilt,* 68.

29 Bill Libby, *Goliath: The Wilt Chamberlain Story* (New York, 1977), 32.

30 Chamberlain and Shaw, *Wilt,* 51.

31 Ibid.

32 Frank Graham Jr., "Is There a Defense against Wilt?" *Sport,* March 1958.

33 Ibid.

34 Schaap, "The Real Wilt Chamberlain."

35 Libby, *Goliath,* 41.

36 Schaap, "The Real Wilt Chamberlain."

37 Ibid.

38 *USA Today,* October 13, 1999.

39 Chamberlain and Shaw, *Wilt,* 97–98.

40 Holzman with Lewin, *A View from the Bench,* 70–71.

41 *Philadelphia Inquirer,* October 13, 1999.

42 Sullivan, *The Picture History of the Boston Celtics,* 34.

43 *Boston Globe,* March 26, 1960.

44 Ibid.

45 Ibid.

46 Wilt Chamberlain as told to Tim Cohane, "Basketball Has Ganged Up on Me," *Look,* March 1, 1960.

47 Ibid.

48 Ibid.

49 *New York Times,* March 26, 1960.

50 Ibid.

51 *New York Times,* March 27, 1960.

52 *Boston Globe,* March 26, 1960.

53 Chamberlain and Shaw, *Wilt,* 118.

54 Fitzgerald, *Champions Remembered,* 5.

55 Sullivan, *The Picture History of the Boston Celtics,* 191.

56 John Havlicek and Bob Ryan, *Hondo: Celtic Man in Motion* (Englewood Cliffs, N.J., 1977), 132.

57 *Philadelphia Inquirer,* October 13, 1999.

58 *USA Today,* October 12, 1999.

59 Ibid.

60 Pluto, *Tall Tales,* 224.

61 *Philadelphia Inquirer,* October 13, 1999.

62 Daily News Sports Writer, "A Century of Superstars."

63 Holzman with Lewin, *A View from the Bench,* 77.

64 Alexander Wolff, *Basketball: A History of the Game* (New York, 1997), 122.

65 Libby, *Goliath,* 126.

66 Holzman with Lewin, *A View from the Bench,* 79.

67 Leonard Shecter, "The Startling Change in Wilt Chamberlain," *Sport,* March 1967.

68 Ibid.

69 Chamberlain and Shaw, *Wilt,* 183.

70 Shecter, "The Startling Change in Wilt Chamberlain."

71 Chamberlain and Shaw, *Wilt,* 183.

72 Rick Barry with Bill Libby, *Confessions of a Basketball Gypsy: The Rick Barry Story* (Englewood Cliffs, N.J., 1972), 65.

73 Libby, *Goliath,* 151.

74 Ibid., 154.

75 Chamberlain and Shaw, *Wilt,* 191.

76 Tami Sheheri and Janon Fisher, "FBI Probed Wilt Chamberlain for Gambling," www.apbnews.com, February 14, 2000.

77 *New York Post,* February 14, 2000.

78 Chet Walker with Chris Messenger, *Long Time Coming: A Black Athlete's Coming-of-Age in America* (New York, 1995), 206.

79 Libby, *Goliath,* 176.

80 Roland Lazenby, *The Lakers: A Basketball Journey* (New York, 1993), 170.

81 William Nack, "I've Made My Own Bed, I've Got to Lie in It," *Sports Illustrated,* February 20, 1984.

82 Ibid.
83 *The Sporting News,* December 21, 1968.
84 Ibid.
85 Ibid.
86 Libby, *Goliath,* 179.
87 Frank Deford, "On Top—But in Trouble," *Sports Illustrated,* January 27, 1969.
88 Arnold Hano, "Wilt, West and Baylor: Do Three Superstars Make a Super Team?" *Sport,* March 1969.
89 Leonard Lewin, "The Wilt Chamberlain Controversy," *Sport,* August, 1969.
90 Wilt Chamberlain, *A View from Above* (New York, 1991), 251.
91 Arthur Ashe and Arnold Rampersad, *Days of Grace: A Memoir* (New York, 1993), 238.
92 *USA Today,* October 13, 1999.

CHAPTER 5
Sinking in the East

1 Stephen E. Ambrose, *Nixon: The Triumph of a Politician, 1962–72* (New York, 1987), 221.
2 *Boston Globe,* December 18, 1968.
3 *Boston Herald-Traveler,* December 1, 1968.
4 *Time,* October 25, 1968.
5 *Boston Herald-Traveler,* December 3, 1968.
6 Red Holzman with Leonard Lewin, *The Knicks* (New York, 1971), 70.
7 *Boston Globe,* January 17, 1969.
8 Tom Heinsohn, interview with author.
9 Heinsohn with Lewin, *Heinsohn, Don't You Ever Smile?* 157–58.
10 News clipping, "Red Puts More Than Color in TV," by Tim Horgan, Boston Celtics Scrapbook, Sports Museum of New England (hereafter SMNE).
11 Heinsohn with Lewin, *Heinsohn, Don't You Ever Smile?* 156.
12 News clipping, "Red Puts More Than Color in TV."
13 Ibid.
14 Heinsohn with Lewin, *Heinsohn, Don't You Ever Smile?* 155–56.
15 Ibid.
16 Ibid.
17 Heinsohn, interview with author.
18 Ibid.
19 Ibid.
20 *NBA Newsletter,* April 28, 1986, NMBHF.
21 Ibid.
22 Sullivan, *The Picture History of the Boston Celtics,* 39.
23 *Boston Herald,* May 5, 1986.
24 Ibid.
25 Russell and Branch, *Second Wind,* 141.

26 *Boston Herald,* May 5, 1986.
27 *Boston Herald,* February 13, 2000.
28 *Boston Herald,* May 5, 1986.
29 Heinsohn and Fitzgerald, *Give 'em the Hook,* 25.
30 Ibid.
31 Al Hirshberg, *Basketball's Greatest Stars* (New York, 1963), 72.
32 *Boston Herald,* May 5, 1986.
33 Ibid.
34 Heinsohn and Fitzgerald, *Give 'em the Hook,* 167.
35 *Boston Herald-Traveler,* December 22, 1968.
36 *Boston Globe,* December 19, 1968.
37 *Boston Globe,* January 11, 1969.
38 *Boston Globe,* January 14, 1969.
39 Ibid.
40 *Boston Globe,* January 17, 1969.
41 *Boston Herald,* March 9, 1975.
42 *Boston Globe,* March 27, 1974.
43 Ibid.
44 Greenfield, *The World's Greatest Team,* 139.
45 *Des Moines Register,* September 3, 1983.
46 Ibid.
47 *Boston Globe,* March 27, 1974.
48 Ibid.
49 *Boston Herald,* January 29, 1980.
50 Ibid.
51 *Boston Herald American,* March 9, 1975.
52 Greenfield, *The World's Greatest Team,* 139.
53 *Christian Science Monitor,* April 24, 1968.
54 *Boston Herald,* May 13, 1986.
55 *Des Moines Register,* September 3, 1983.
56 *Christian Science Monitor,* April 24, 1968.
57 *Boston Herald-Traveler,* February 25, 1966.
58 News clipping, "Don Nelson, Ex-Pessimist," by Harvey Robbins, Don Nelson File, Boston Globe Library.
59 Joe Fitzgerald, *That Championship Feeling: The Story of the Boston Celtics* (New York, 1975), 166.
60 *Christian Science Monitor,* April 28, 1969.
61 *Boston Herald-Traveler,* February 25, 1966.
62 *Christian Science Monitor,* April 28, 1969.
63 *Boston Herald,* May 13, 1986.
64 *Boston Globe,* January 24, 1969.
65 *Boston Herald-Traveler,* January 25, 1969.
66 Ibid.
67 Sullivan, *The Picture History of the Boston Celtics,* 191.
68 *New York Times,* January 4, 1978.
69 Coles Pjhinizy, "Sanders of Harvard," *Sports Illustrated,* March 4, 1974.
70 Joe McGinniss, "One Celtic's Formula," *Sport,* February 1967.
71 Ibid.
72 *Boston Herald American,* March 30, 1980.
73 McGinniss, "One Celtic's Formula."
74 Ibid.

75 Fitzgerald, *That Championship Feeling,* 111.
76 *New York Times,* January 4, 1978.
77 News clipping, "Satch a Synonym for Celtics Pride," by Harvey Robbins, Tom Sanders File, Boston Globe Library.
78 McGinniss, "One Celtic's Formula."
79 *Boston Globe,* January 19, 1973.
80 *Boston Globe,* November 24, 1963.
81 News clipping, "He Was the Prototype Celtic, This Man They Call 'Geezer,'" by Bob Ryan, Tom Sanders File, Boston Globe Library.
82 McGinniss, "One Celtic's Formula."
83 *Boston Globe,* December 26, 1965.
84 Ibid.
85 Greenfield, *The World's Greatest Team,* 137.
86 *Boston Globe,* January 26, 1969.
87 *Boston Herald-Traveler,* January 26, 1969.
88 *Boston Herald-Traveler,* January 27, 1969.
89 *Boston Globe,* January 27, 1969.
90 Ibid.
91 Ibid.

CHAPTER 6
Limping into the Playoffs

1 *Beverly Times,* January 31, 1969.
2 *Beverly Times,* January 30, 1969.
3 *New York Times,* February 1, 1969.
4 *Boston Globe,* February 3, 1969.
5 *Boston Herald-Traveler,* February 3, 1969.
6 *Boston Globe,* February 3, 1969.
7 Ibid.
8 *Boston Globe,* February 4, 1969.
9 *Boston Herald-Traveler,* February 4, 1969.
10 Ibid.
11 Ibid.
12 *Boston Herald-Traveler,* February 5, 1969.
13 *Boston Herald-Traveler,* February 7, 1969.
14 *Boston Globe,* February 10, 1969.
15 Ibid.
16 Ibid.
17 *Boston Herald-Traveler,* February 12, 1969.
18 News clipping, Joe Looney Feature, Bailey Howell File, NMBHF.
19 Jack Zanger, "Bailey Howell Made It in a Hurry," *Sport,* February 1962.
20 Pluto, *Tall Tales,* 360.
21 *Boston Herald-Traveler,* January 12, 1969.
22 Havlicek and Ryan, *Hondo,* 107.
23 Bailey Howell, interview with author.
24 *Christian Science Monitor,* May 1, 1968.
25 Havlicek and Ryan, *Hondo,* 107.
26 Ibid.
27 D. Leo Monahan, "The Case of the Happy Cornerman," Sunrise, December 1966, NMBHF.
28 Jack Zanger, "The Better-Late-Than-Never Celtic," *Sport,* March 1969.
29 News clipping, "Bailey Howell: The Rookie of Any Other Year," Anonymous, Bailey Howell File, NMBHF.
30 News clipping, "Howell Excels in NBA Wars," by AL Thomy, Bailey Howell File, NMBHF.
31 Zanger, "Bailey Howell Made It in a Hurry."
32 *The Sporting News,* March 18, 1967.
33 Ibid.
34 *Boston Globe,* September 2, 1966.
35 Zanger, "The Better-Late-Than-Never Celtic."
36 News clipping, "Bailey Howell Finds Life with Celtics Enjoyable," Anonymous, Bailey Howell File, NMBHF.
37 *Boston Herald-Traveler,* January 12, 1969.
38 *The Sporting News,* January 11, 1969.
39 *Boston Globe,* May 4, 1968.
40 Ibid.
41 Zanger, "The Better-Late-Than-Never Celtic."
42 *Boston Herald-Traveler,* March 3, 1969.
43 *Boston Herald-Traveler,* March 30, 1969.
44 *New York Post,* April 7, 1969.
45 Emmette Bryant, interview with author.
46 Boston Celtics Basketball Club, *World Champion Boston Celtics 1968–1969 Yearbook* (Boston, 1968), 24.
47 Emmette Bryant, interview with author.
48 *The Sporting News,* April 26, 1969.
49 Emmette Bryant, interview with author.
50 Ibid.
51 Holzman with Lewin, *The Knicks,* 25.
52 Emmette Bryant, interview with author.
53 *The Sporting News,* April 26, 1969.
54 Emmette Bryant, interview with author.
55 *Boston Herald-Traveler,* March 30, 1969.
56 Emmette Bryant, interview with author.
57 *New York Post,* April 7, 1969.
58 *The Sporting News,* April 26, 1969.
59 Ibid.
60 Roland Lazenby, *The NBA Finals: A Fifty Year Celebration* (Indianapolis, Ind., 1996), 167.
61 Bob Ryan, *Celtics Pride: The Rebuilding of Boston's World Championship Basketball Team* (Boston, 1975), 36.
62 Lazenby, *The NBA Finals,* 167.
63 *Christian Science Monitor,* March 4, 1971.
64 *Boston Globe,* March 21, 1969.
65 Havlicek and Ryan, *Hondo,* 155.
66 *Christian Science Monitor,* March 4, 1971.
67 Dennis D'Agostino, "Don Chaney: Synonymous with Success," www.NBA.com, June 13, 2002.
68 *Boston Record-American,* May 4, 1967.
69 *Boston Globe,* March 26, 1969.

70 *Boston Globe,* November 5, 1982.
71 Ibid.
72 Ibid.
73 *Boston Herald-Traveler,* March 10, 1969.
74 *Boston Globe,* March 10, 1969.
75 Ibid.
76 *Boston Herald-Traveler,* February 9, 1969.
77 Al Hirshberg, "The Celtics' Cinderella Star," *Sport,* January 1962.
78 George Walsh, "Jones and Jones at Court," *Sports Illustrated,* March 20, 1961.
79 *Boston Record-American,* May 1, 1968.
80 *Boston Herald-Traveler,* February 9, 1969.
81 Ibid.
82 *Boston Globe,* March 1, 1963.
83 Ibid.
84 Hirshberg, "The Celtics' Cinderella Star."
85 Walsh, "Jones and Jones at Court."
86 *The Sporting News,* February 15, 1969.
87 Pluto, *Tall Tales,* 256.
88 Ibid.
89 Russell and Branch, *Second Wind,* 151.
90 Pluto, *Tall Tales,* 255.
91 Hirshberg, "The Celtics' Cinderella Star."
92 *Boston Globe,* April 2, 1962.
93 *Boston Globe,* April 2, 1962.
94 Ibid.
95 *Boston Record-American,* May 1, 1968.
96 Russell and Branch, *Second Wind,* 152.
97 *Boston Globe,* May 1, 1968.
98 *Boston Herald-Traveler,* February 9, 1969.
99 *The Sporting News,* February 15, 1969.
100 Bailey Howell, interview with author.
101 *Beverly Times,* March 17, 1969.
102 *Boston Herald-Traveler,* March 17, 1969.
103 *Beverly Times,* March 17, 1969.
104 *Beverly Times,* March 18, 1969.
105 *Boston Herald-Traveler,* March 20, 1969.
106 Ibid.
107 *Boston Globe,* March 20, 1969.
108 *Boston Herald-Traveler,* March 24, 1969.
109 *Boston Globe,* March 24, 1969.
110 News clipping, "End of Era Staring C's in the Face," by Tim Horgan, Boston Celtics Scrapbook, SMNE.
111 *Sporting News,* March 22, 1969.

CHAPTER 7
A Philly Rout and a Big Apple Upset

1 *New York Times,* March 31, 1969.
2 James C. Humes, *Eisenhower and Churchill: The Partnership That Saved the World* (New York, 2001), 195.
3 *Time,* March 28, 1969.
4 *Beverly Times,* March 29, 1969.
5 *Philadelphia Inquirer,* April 9, 1969.
6 Joe Jares, "Four for the Bundle." *Sports Illustrated,* February 24, 1969.
7 Ibid.
8 Walker with Messenger, *Long Time Coming,* 159.
9 Jack Kiser, "Yesterday's Heroes, Hal Greer Is No. 8 on the NBA All-Time Scoring List. So Why Isn't He in the Hall of Fame?" *Basketball Digest,* December 1980.
10 Raymond Hill, *Unsung Heroes of Pro Basketball* (New York, 1973), 67.
11 Wayne Lynch, *Season of the 76ers: The Story of Wilt Chamberlain and the 1967 NBA Champion Philadelphia 76ers* (New York, 2002), 25–26.
12 *Basketball Weekly,* January 29, 1981.
13 *The Sunday Republican,* February 22, 1981, NMBHF.
14 *Philadelphia Inquirer,* February 20, 1982.
15 Hill, *Unsung Heroes of Pro Basketball,* 62.
16 Kiser, "Yesterday's Heroes."
17 Hill, *Unsung Heroes of Pro Basketball,* 59.
18 *The Parthenon Special Issue,* November 1981, NMBHF.
19 Hill, *Unsung Heroes of Pro Basketball,* 64.
20 Lynch, *Season of the 76ers,* 25.
21 *Boston Herald-Traveler,* March 27, 1969.
22 *Boston Globe,* March 27, 1969.
23 Ibid.
24 *Boston Globe,* March 28, 1969.
25 *Boston Herald-Traveler,* March 29, 1969.
26 *Boston Globe,* March 29, 1969.
27 *Boston Herald-Traveler,* March 29, 1969.
28 *Boston Globe,* March 31, 1969.
29 *Beverly Times,* March 31, 1969.
30 *Boston Globe,* April 2, 1969.
31 Ibid.
32 Ibid.
33 *Boston Globe,* April 5, 1969.
34 Ibid.
35 *Christian Science Monitor,* April 9, 1969.
36 Jares, "Four for the Bundle."
37 Willis Reed with Phil Pepe, *A View from the Rim: Willis Reed on Basketball* (New York, 1971), 84.
38 Jares, "Four for the Bundle."
39 *Christian Science Monitor,* April 9, 1969.
40 Walt Frazier with Neil Offen, *One Magic Season and a Basketball Life* (New York, 1988), 47.
41 *New York Daily News,* April 3, 1963.
42 *Christian Science Monitor,* April 9, 1969.
43 Russell and Branch, *Second Wind,* 166.
44 Phil Pepe, *The Incredible Knicks* (New York, 1970), 52.
45 Reed with Pepe, *A View from the Rim,* 22.
46 Arnold Hano, "Willis Reed and the Icing on the Cake," *Sport,* April 1970.
47 Ibid.

48 Pepe, *The Incredible Knicks.*
49 Reed with Pepe, *A View from the Rim,* 40.
50 Ibid., 49.
51 Pepe, *The Incredible Knicks,* 56.
52 Russell and Branch, *Second Wind,* 166.
53 *Christian Science Monitor,* December 27, 1968.
54 Jares, "Four for the Bundle."
55 Frazier with Offen, *One Magic Season and a Basketball Life,* 47.
56 Pete Axthelm, *The City Game: Basketball from the Garden to the Playgrounds* (Lincoln, Nebr., 1999), 65.
57 Bill Russell with David Falkner, *Russell Rules: Eleven Lessons on Leadership from the Twentieth Century's Greatest Winner* (New York, 2001), 123.
58 *New York Times,* April 7, 1969.
59 Ibid.
60 *New York Post,* April 7, 1969.
61 *Boston Herald-Traveler,* April 7, 1969.
62 Bob Spitz, *Shoot Out the Lights: The Amazing, Improbable, Exhilarating Saga of the 1969–70 New York Knicks* (New York, 1995), 31.
63 *Boston Herald-Traveler,* April 7, 1969.
64 *Boston Globe,* April 7, 1969.
65 Ibid.
66 *New York Daily News,* April 10, 1969.
67 *Boston Globe,* April 10, 1969.
68 Ibid.
69 *New York Post,* April 10, 1969.
70 *Boston Herald-Traveler,* April 10, 1969.
71 *Boston Herald-Traveler,* April 11, 1969.
72 Ibid.
73 *Boston Globe,* April 11, 1969.
74 *New York Times,* April 11, 1969.
75 *Boston Herald-Traveler,* April 11, 1969.
76 *Boston Globe,* April 11, 1969.
77 John McPhee, *A Sense of Where You Are: A Profile of Bill Bradley at Princeton* (New York, 1999), 74.
78 Frank Deford, "An Ivy Leaguer Is the Best," *Sports Illustrated,* December 7, 1964.
79 Axthelm, *The City Game,* 98.
80 *New York Times,* June 5, 1966.
81 Ibid.
82 *New York Times,* April 28, 1967.
83 *New York Times,* December 11, 1967.
84 *New York Times,* December 12, 1967.
85 Pepe, *The Incredible Knicks,* 88.
86 Curry Kirkpatrick, "An Answer to the Bradley Riddle," *Sports Illustrated,* March 18, 1968.
87 *Christian Science Monitor,* November 27, 1968.
88 Ibid.
89 Red Holzman with Harvey Frommer, *Red on Red* (New York, 1987), 76.
90 Milton Gross, "The Pros Tell Their Favorite Bill Russell Stories," *Sport,* November 1969.

91 *Boston Herald-Traveler,* April 14, 1969.
92 Ibid.
93 *Boston Globe,* April 14, 1969.
94 *New York Times,* April 14, 1969.
95 *Boston Globe,* April 14, 1969.
96 *New York Daily News,* April 14, 1969.
97 *New York Daily News,* April 15, 1969.
98 *New York Times,* April 15, 1969.
99 *New York Post,* April 15, 1969.
100 *Boston Globe,* April 15, 1969.
101 Ibid.
102 *New York Daily News,* April 15, 1969.
103 *Boston Globe,* April 17, 1969.
104 Spitz, *Shoot Out the Lights,* 37.
105 *New York Times,* April 20, 1969.
106 *Boston Herald-Traveler,* April 19, 1969.
107 *Boston Globe,* April 19, 1969.
108 *Boston Globe,* April 19, 1969.
109 Ibid.
110 *New York Post,* April 19, 1969.
111 *Boston Herald-Traveler,* April 19, 1969.
112 *Boston Globe,* April 19, 1969.
113 *Boston Herald-Traveler,* April 19, 1969.
114 *New York Post,* April 19, 1969.
115 *Boston Globe,* April 19, 1969.

CHAPTER 8
The Greatest Team in the World

1 *Time,* April 18, 1969.
2 *Life,* April 25, 1969.
3 *Time,* April 18, 1969.
4 *Boston Herald-Traveler,* April 23, 1969.
5 *Boston Herald-Traveler,* April 22, 1969.
6 *The Sporting News,* March 15, 1969.
7 *Boston Herald-Traveler,* April 22, 1969.
8 Jerry West, "My Career with Elgin," n.d., NMBHF.
9 Frank Deford, "A Tiger Who Can Beat Anything," *Sports Illustrated,* October 24, 1966.
10 Pluto, *Tall Tales,* 172.
11 Hirshberg, *Basketball's Greatest Stars,* 155.
12 Phil Berger, *Heroes of Pro Basketball* (New York, 1968), 90.
13 Earl Strom with Blaine Johnson, *Calling the Shots: My Five Decades in the NBA* (New York, 1990), 75.
14 Pluto, *Tall Tales,* 176.
15 Berger, *Heroes of Pro Basketball,* 92.
16 Deford, "A Tiger Can Beat Anything."
17 Ibid.
18 Phil Pepe, *Winners Never Quit* (New York, 1969), 34.
19 Deford, "A Tiger Can Beat Anything."
20 Berger, *Heroes of Pro Basketball,* 98.
21 Deford, "A Tiger Can Beat Anything."
22 Elgin Baylor, "Elgin Baylor's Playoff Diary," *Sport,* July 1969.

23 *Boston Globe,* April 24, 1969.
24 *Boston Herald-Traveler,* April 24, 1969.
25 *Boston Globe,* April 24, 1969.
26 *Los Angeles Times,* April 24, 1969.
27 Ibid.
28 *Los Angeles Herald-Examiner,* April 24, 1969.
29 *Boston Globe,* April 24, 1969.
30 *Los Angeles Herald-Examiner,* April 26, 1969.
31 Baylor, "Elgin Baylor's Playoff Diary."
32 *Los Angeles Times,* April 26, 1969.
33 Ibid.
34 *Boston Globe,* April 27, 1969.
35 *Los Angeles Herald-Examiner,* April 26, 1969.
36 *Boston Herald-Traveler,* April 28, 1969.
37 *Boston Globe,* April 28, 1969.
38 *Boston Herald-Traveler,* April 28, 1969.
39 Ibid.
40 *Boston Herald-Traveler,* April 30, 1969.
41 *Los Angeles Herald-Examiner,* April 30, 1969.
42 *Boston Globe,* April 30, 1969.
43 Ibid.
44 Frank Deford, "The Last Drop in the Bucket," *Sports Illustrated,* May 12, 1969.
45 *Boston Globe,* April 30, 1969.
46 *Boston Herald-Traveler,* April 30, 1969.
47 *Los Angeles Times,* April 30, 1969.
48 *Boston Herald-Traveler,* April 30, 1969.
49 *Boston Globe,* April 30, 1969.
50 *Los Angeles Herald-Examiner,* May 2, 1969.
51 Baylor, "Elgin Baylor's Playoff Diary."
52 *Los Angeles Times,* May 2, 1969.
53 West with Libby, *Mr. Clutch,* 199.
54 *Los Angeles Herald-Examiner,* May 2–3, 1969.
55 News clipping, Jim Murray Column, Jerry West File, NMBHF.
56 Berger, *Heroes of Pro Basketball,* 124.
57 Bill Libby, "The Courage and Splendor of Jerry West," *Sport,* March 1970.
58 Bill Libby, *We Love You Lakers* (New York, 1972), 100.
59 Berger, *Heroes of Pro Basketball,* 126.
60 Holzman with Levin, *A View from the Bench,* 65.
61 Pluto, Tall Tales, 191.
62 Libby, "The Courage and Splendor of Jerry West."
63 John Underwood, "The Eye of an Eagle and a Big Wingspread," *Sports Illustrated,* February 8, 1965.
64 Berger, *Heroes of Pro Basketball,* 127.
65 *Los Angeles Times,* February 13, 1966.
66 Libby, *We Love You Lakers,* 95.
67 West with Libby, *Mr. Clutch,* 36.
68 Berger, *Heroes of Pro Basketball,* 118.
69 West with Libby, *Mr. Clutch,* 72.

70 Ibid., 79.
71 Roger Williams, "The Long Leap Forward of Jerry West," *Sports Illustrated,* November 20, 1961.
72 Underwood, "The Eye of an Eagle and a Big Wingspread."
73 *Boston Globe,* May 4, 1969.
74 Ibid.
75 Ibid.
76 *Los Angeles Times,* May 4, 1969.
77 *Boston Globe,* May 4, 1969.
78 Ibid.
79 Ibid.
80 *Los Angeles Herald-Examiner,* May 5, 1969.
81 News clipping, "West Says, 'We'll Win,' Celts More Guarded," by George Sullivan, *Boston Celtics Scrapbook,* SMNE.
82 Havlicek and Ryan, *Hondo,* 113.
83 Emmette Bryant, interview with author.
84 Havlicek and Ryan, *Hondo,* 114.
85 Russell and Branch, *Second Wind,* 169.
86 Chamberlain with Shaw, *Wilt,* 218.
87 *Los Angeles Times,* May 9, 1969.
88 Chamberlain with Shaw, *Wilt,* 218.
89 *Los Angeles Times,* May 6, 1969.
90 *Los Angeles Herald-Examiner,* May 6, 1969.
91 News clipping, "Don Nelson, Ex-Pessimist," by Harvey Robbins, Don Nelson File, Boston Globe Library.
92 *Los Angeles Herald-Examiner,* May 6, 1969.
93 *Boston Herald-Traveler,* May 6, 1969.
94 Ibid.
95 Ibid.
96 *Boston Globe,* May 6, 1969.
97 *Boston Herald-Traveler,* May 6, 1969.
98 Ibid.
99 Ibid.
100 *Los Angeles Times,* May 6, 1969.
101 Ibid.
102 *Los Angeles Herald-Examiner,* May 6, 1969.
103 Vecsey, *Pro Basketball Champions* (New York), 31.
104 Deford, "The Last Drop in the Bucket."
105 *Los Angeles Herald-Examiner,* May 6, 1969.
106 Ibid.
107 Ibid.
108 *Boston Herald-Traveler,* May 6, 1969.
109 *Boston Globe,* May 6, 1969.
110 Leigh Montville, interview with author.
111 Ibid.
112 *Los Angeles Times,* May 6, 1969.

Afterword

1 Sullivan, *The Picture History of the Boston Celtics,* 91.
2 Ibid., 92.
3 Ibid., 90.

4   Emmette Bryant, interview with author.
5   Ibid.
6   *Boston Herald,* May 13, 1984.
7   *Philadelphia Inquirer,* February 7, 1971.
8   News clipping, "Whatever Happened to . . . Bailey Howell: A Celtic Great?" Bailey Howell File, NMBHF.
9   Bailey Howell, interview with author.
10 *Boston Herald-Traveler,* February 9, 1969.
11 *Boston Globe,* January 23, 1977.
12 Ibid.
13 *Boston Globe,* May 12, 1992.
14 *Boston Herald American,* March 30, 1980
15 Ibid.
16 *Boston Globe,* November 5, 2002.
17 Mark Goodman, "A Fond Farewell to Hondo Havlicek," *Sport,* May 1978.
18 *Boston Herald,* October 13, 1978.
19 *Boston Globe,* March 14, 1982.
20 Russell, *Second Wind,* 215.
21 *Boston Globe,* May 21, 1969.
22 *Boston Globe,* May 23, 1969.
23 *Boston Herald,* May 27, 1999.
24 *Boston Herald American,* May 17, 1973.
25 *Boston Globe,* February 18, 1973.
26 Jeff Greenfield, *The World's Greatest Team,* 168.
27 *Washington Post,* April 26, 1972.
28 *Boston Globe,* May 5, 1972.
29 *Washington Post,* April 26, 1972.
30 *Christian Science Monitor,* November 21, 1973.
31 Ibid.
32 Greenfield, *The World's Greatest Team,* 170.
33 Russell, *Second Wind,* 259.
34 *USA Today,* September 20, 1984.
35 News clipping, "Basketball Hall of Fame Needs Him," by Ed Comerford, Bill Russell File, NMBHF.
36 Donahue transcript, WGN-TV, October 19, 1979, NMBHF.
37 *New York Times,* June 16, 2000.
38 Ibid.
39 *Boston Globe,* November 8, 2000.
40 *Boston Globe,* November 12, 2000.
41 *Boston Globe,* May 27, 1999.
42 *Boston Herald,* May 27, 1999.
43 Ibid.

Bibliography

BOOKS

Abdul-Jabbar, Kareem, with Mignon McCarthy. *Kareem*. New York, 1990.

Ali, Tariq, and Susan Watkins. *1968: Marching in the Streets*. New York, 1998.

Ambrose, Stephen E. *Nixon: The Triumph of a Politician, 1962–1972*. New York, 1987.

Araton, Harvey, and Filip Bondy. *The Selling of the Green: The Financial Rise and Moral Decline of the Boston Celtics*. New York, 1992.

Ashe, Arthur R., Jr. *A Hard Road to Glory: A History of the African-American Athlete Since 1946*. New York, 1993.

Ashe, Arthur, and Arnold Rampersad. *Days of Grace: A Memoir*. New York, 1993

Auerbach, Arnold, and Joe Fitzgerald. *Red Auerbach: An Autobiography*. New York, 1977.

Auerbach, Arnold, and Paul Sann. *Red Auerbach: Winning the Hard Way*. Boston, 1966.

Axthelm, Pete. *The City Game: Basketball from the Garden to the Playgrounds*. Lincoln, Nebr., 1999.

Barry, Rick, with Bill Libby. *Confessions of a Basketball Gypsy: The Rick Barry Story*. Englewood Cliffs, N.J., 1972.

Berger, Phil. *Heroes of Pro Basketball*. New York, 1968.

Bjarkman, Peter. *The Biographical History of Basketball*. Chicago, 2000.

Boston Celtics Basketball Club. *World Champion Boston Celtics 1968–1969 Yearbook*. Boston, 1968.

Bradley, Bill. *Life on the Run*. New York, 1995.

Buell, Emmett H., with Richard A. Brisbin Jr. *School Desegregation and Defended Neighborhoods: The Boston Controversy*. Lexington, Mass., 1982.

Chamberlain, Wilt. *A View from Above*. New York, 1991.

Chamberlain, Wilt, and David Shaw. *Wilt: Just Like Any Other Seven-Foot Black Millionaire Who Lives Next Door*. New York, 1973.

Cousy, Bob, as told to Al Hirshberg. *Basketball Is My Life*. Englewood Cliffs, N.J., 1958.

Cousy, Bob, with Ed Linn. *The Last Loud Roar*. Englewood Cliffs, N. J., 1964.

Cousy, Bob, and Bob Ryan. *Cousy on the Celtic Mystique*. New York, 1988.

Crothers, Tim, and John Garrity. *Sports Illustrated Greatest Athletes of the 20th Century*. New York, 1999.

Fitzgerald, Joe. *That Championship Feeling: The Story of the Boston Celtics*. New York, 1975.

———. *The Boston Celtics: Fifty Years*. Del Mar, Calif., 1996.

Fitzgerald, Ray. *Champions Remembered: Choices from a Boston Sports Desk*. Lexington, Mass., 1982.

Fox, Larry. *Illustrated History of Basketball*. New York, 1974.

Frazier, Walt, with Neil Offen. *One Magic Season and a Basketball Life*. New York, 1988.

George, Nelson. *Elevating the Game: Black Men and Basketball*. New York, 1992.

Golenbock, Peter. *Fenway: An Unexpurgated History of the Boston Red Sox*. New York, 1992.

Gowdy, Curt, with John Powers. *Seasons to Remember: The Way It Was in American Sports, 1945–1960.* New York, 1993.

Greenfield, Jeff. *The World's Greatest Team: A Portrait of the Boston Celtics, 1957–69.* New York, 1976.

Halberstam, David. *The Breaks of the Game.* New York, 1981.

———. *Summer of '49.* New York, 1989.

Harris, Merv, *The Fabulous Lakers.* New York, 1972.

Havlicek, John, and Bob Ryan. *Hondo: Celtic Man in Motion.* Englewood Cliffs, N.J., 1977.

Heinsohn, Tommy, and Joe Fitzgerald. *Give 'em the Hook.* New York, 1988.

Heinsohn, Tommy, with Leonard Lewin. *Heinsohn, Don't You Ever Smile? The Life and Times of Tommy Heinsohn and the Boston Celtics.* New York, 1976.

Herzog, Brad. *The Sports 100: The One Hundred Most Important People in American Sports History.* New York, 1995.

Higgins, George. *Style Versus Substance: Boston, Kevin White, and the Politics of Illusion.* New York, 1984.

Hill, Raymond. *Unsung Heroes of Pro Basketball.* New York, 1973.

Hirshberg, Al. *Basketball's Greatest Stars.* New York, 1963.

Hofstadter, Richard, and Beatrice K. Hofstadter. *Great Issues in American History: From Reconstruction to Present, 1864–1981.* New York, 1982.

Hollander, Zander, ed. *The Pro Basketball Encyclopedia.* Los Angeles, 1977.

Holzman, Red, with Harvey Frommer. *Red on Red.* New York, 1987.

Holzman, Red, with Leonard Lewin. *A View from Above.* New York, 1980.

Holzman, Red, with Leonard Lewin. *The Knicks.* New York, 1971.

Humes, James C. *Eisenhower and Churchill: The Partnership That Saved the World.* New York, 2001.

Isaacs, Neil D. *All the Moves: A History of College Basketball.* Philadelphia, 1975.

———. *Vintage NBA: The Pioneer Era (1946–56).* Indianapolis, Ind., 1996.

Johnson, Richard A. *A Century of Boston Sports.* Boston, 2000.

Jones, K.C., with Jack Warner. *Rebound: The Autobiography of K.C. Jones and an Inside Look at the Champion Boston Celtics.* Boston, 1986.

Kahn, Roger. *The Era, 1947–1957—When the Yankees, the Giants, and the Dodgers Ruled the World.* New York, 1993.

King, Mel. *Chain of Change: Struggle for Black Community Development.* Boston, 1981.

Koppett, Leonard. *Twenty-Four Seconds to Shoot: The Birth and Improbable Rise of the National Basketball Association.* New York, 1999.

Lazenby, Roland. *The Lakers: A Basketball Journey.* New York, 1993.

———. *The NBA Finals: A Fifty Year Celebration.* Indianapolis, Ind., 1996.

———. *Mindgames, Phil Jackson's Long Strange Journey.* New York, 2002.

Libby, Bill. *We Love You Lakers.* New York, 1972.

———. *Goliath: The Wilt Chamberlain Story.* New York, 1977.

Lukas, J. Anthony. *Common Ground: A Turbulent Decade in the Lives of Three American Families.* New York, 1986.

Lupo, Alan. *Liberty's Chosen Home.* Boston, 1977.

Lynch, Wayne. *Season of the 76ers: The Story of Wilt Chamberlain and the 1967 NBA Champion Philadelphia 76ers.* New York, 2002.

Lyons, Louis M. *Newspaper Story: One Hundred Years of the Boston Globe.* Cambridge, Massachusetts, 1971.

MacCambridge, Michael, ed. *ESPN SportsCentury.* New York, 1999.

McPhee, John. *A Sense of Where You Are: A Profile of Bill Bradley at Princeton.* New York, 1999.

O'Connor, Thomas H. *Bibles, Brahmins, and Bosses: A Short History of Boston.* Boston, 1984.

———. *Building a New Boston: Politics and Urban Renewal 1950 to 1970.* Boston, 1993.

———. *The Hub: Boston Past and Present.* Boston, 2001.

Patterson, James. *Grand Expectations: The United States, 1945–1974.* New York, 1996.

Pepe, Phil. *Winners Never Quit.* New York, 1969.

———. *Greatest Stars of the NBA.* Englewood Cliffs, N.J., 1970.

———. *The Incredible Knicks.* New York, 1970.

Peterson, Robert W. *Cages to Jumpshots: Pro Basketball's Early Years.* New York, 1990.

Pluto, Terry. *Loose Balls: The Short, Wild Life of the American Basketball Association—as Told by the Players, Coaches, and Movers and Shakers Who Made It Happen.* New York, 1990.

———. *Tall Tales: The Glory Years of the NBA, in the Words of the Men Who Played, Coached, and Built Pro Basketball.* New York, 1994.

Powers, John. *The Short Season: A Boston Celtics Diary 1977–78.* New York, 1979.

Reed, Willis, with Phil Pepe. *A View from the Rim: Willis Reed on Basketball.* New York, 1971.

Robinson, Jackie. *I Never Had It Made: An Autobiography.* Hopewell, N.J., 1995.

Russell, Bill, and Taylor Branch. *Second Wind: The Memoirs of an Opinionated Man.* New York, 1991.

Russell, Bill, with David Falkner. *Russell Rules: Eleven Lessons on Leadership from the Twentieth Century's Greatest Winner.* New York, 2001.

Russell, Bill, as told to William McSweeney. *Go Up for Glory.* New York, 1980 (reprint).

Ryan, Bob. *Celtics Pride: The Rebuilding of Boston's World Championship Basketball Team.* Boston, 1975.

————. *The Boston Celtics: The History, Legends, and Images of America's Most Celebrated Team.* Reading, Massachusetts, 1990.

Sachare, Alex, ed. *The Official NBA Basketball Encyclopedia.* New York, 1994.

Salzberg, Charles. *From Set Shot to Slam Dunk: The Glory Days of Basketball in the Words of Those Who Played It.* New York, 1987.

Shaughnessy, Dan. *The Curse of the Bambino.* New York, 1990.

————. *Ever Green: The Boston Celtics—A History in the Words of Their Players, Coaches, Fans, and Foes, from 1946 to the Present.* New York, 1990.

————. *Seeing Red: The Red Auerbach Story.* Holbrook, Mass., 1994.

Shouler, Ken. *The Experts Pick Basketball's Best Fifty Players in the Last Fifty Years.* Lenexa, Kans., 1998.

Spitz, Bob. *Shoot Out the Lights: The Amazing, Improbable, Exhilarating Saga of the 1969–70 New York Knicks.* New York, 1995.

Stout, Glen, and Richard A. Johnson. *Red Sox Century.* Boston, 2000.

Strom, Earl, with Blaine Johnson. *Calling the Shots: My Five Decades in the NBA.* New York, 1990.

Sullivan, George. *The Picture History of the Boston Celtics.* New York, 1982.

————. *The Boston Celtics: Fifty Years.* Del Mar, Calif., 1996.

Tager, Jack. *Boston Riots: Three Centuries of Social Violence.* Boston, 2001.

Thernstrom, Stephan. *The Other Bostonians: Poverty and Progress in an American Metropolis, 1880–1970.* Cambridge, Mass., 1973.

Tygiel, Jules, ed. *The Jackie Robinson Reader: Perspectives on an American Hero.* New York, 1997.

Vecsey, George. *Pro Basketball Champions.* New York, 1970.

Walker, Chet, with Chris Messenger. *Long Time Coming: A Black Athlete's Coming-of-Age in America.* New York, 1995.

West, Jerry, with Bill Libby. *Mr. Clutch: The Jerry West Story.* New York, 1971.

Wilkens, Lenny, and Terry Pluto. *Unguarded: My Forty Years Surviving in the NBA.* New York, 2000.

Wolff, Alexander. *Basketball: A History of the Game.* New York, 1997.

MAJOR ARTICLES AND DOCUMENTS

Baylor, Elgin. "Elgin Baylor's Playoff Diary," *Sport,* July 1969.

Berger, Phil. "What a Coach Means to a Pro Basketball Team," *Sport,* December 1968.

————. "The Sport Interview: Red Auerbach," *Sport,* June 1979.

Chamberlain, Wilt, as told to Tim Cohane. "Basketball Has Ganged Up on Me," *Look,* March 1, 1960.

Chamberlain, Wilt, with Bob Ottum. "My Life in a Bush League, Part I," *Sports Illustrated,* April 12, 1965.

————. "My Life in a Bush League, Part II," *Sports Illustrated,* April 19, 1965.

D'Agostino, Dennis. "Don Chaney: Synonymous with Success," www.NBA.com, June 13, 2002.

Deford, Frank. "Some Old Pros Refuse to Die," *Sports Illustrated,* May 9, 1960.

————. "An Ivy Leaguer Is the Best," *Sports Illustrated,* December 7, 1964.

————. "A Tiger Who Can Beat Anything," *Sports Illustrated,* October 24, 1966.

————. "This One Was Worth Shouting About," *Sports Illustrated,* May 13, 1968.

————. "On Top—But in Trouble," *Sports Illustrated,* January 27, 1969.

————. "At the End, It Was Up to the Two Big Men Underneath," *Sports Illustrated,* April 21, 1969.

————. " . . . And That Old Celtics Wheel Rolls Again," *Sports Illustrated,* April 28, 1969.

————. "The Last Drop in the Bucket," *Sports Illustrated,* May 12, 1969.

————. "A Man for All Seasons," *Sports Illustrated,* February 15, 1982.

————. "No. 2 in the Rafters, No. 1 in Their Hearts," *Sports Illustrated,* January 14, 1985.

————. "The Ring Leader," *Sports Illustrated,* May 10, 1999

Devaney, John. "What Makes Havlicek Run . . . And Run . . . And Run," *Sport,* February 1969.

Dodd, Donald. "Mr. Basketball Bailey Howell," *Dawg's Bite,* December 11, 1982.

Elderkin, Phil. "New Lease on Life for Bailey Howell," *The Sporting News,* March 18, 1967.

———. "Sam Slipping . . . Celtics Pay the Price," *The Sporting News,* February 15, 1969.

———. "Like Paint . . . Bryant Clings to NBA Foes," *The Sporting News,* April 26, 1969.

———. "All I Owe Public Is My Best Effort," *The Sporting News,* March 14, 1970.

Goodman, Irv. "Hothead on the Boston Bench," *Sport,* February 1956.

———. "Cousy, Sharman, Russell & Co.," *Sport,* March 1958.

———. "The Big Collision: Wilt vs. Russell," *Sport,* December 1959.

———. "The Winning Ways of Red Auerbach," *Sport,* March 1965.

Goodman, Mark. "A Fond Farewell to Hondo Havlicek," *Sport,* May 1978.

Graham, Frank, Jr. "Is There a Defense Against Wilt?" *Sport,* March 1958.

Gross, Milton. "The Pros Tell Their Favorite Bill Russell Stories," *Sport,* November 1969.

Hafner, Dan. "Wilt Growing Weary of Barrage of Harpoons," *The Sporting News,* March 15, 1969.

Hannum, Alex, with Frank Deford. "Old Days and Changed Ways," *Sports Illustrated,* November 25, 1968.

Hano, Arnold. "Wilt, West, and Baylor: Do Three Superstars Make a Super Team?" *Sport,* March 1969.

———. "Willis Reed and the Icing on the Cake," *Sport,* April 1970.

Havlicek, John, as told to Bob Sales. "Behind the Celtics Startling Comeback," *Sport,* August 1968.

Heinsohn, Tommy, with Bob Ottum. "Of Charley Horses and Little Old Ladies," *Sports Illustrated,* October 26, 1964.

"Heinsohn Paints Word Pictures for the NBA on CBS," *NBA Newsletter,* April 28, 1986.

Hirshberg, Al. "The Celtics' Cinderella Star," *Sport,* January 1962.

Hoobing, Bob. "Player Bill Russell Takes a Look at Coach Russell," n.d., Russell Scrapbook, Sports Museum of New England, Boston, Mass.

Hunt, George P. "Editor's Note, Education of a Wanderer," *Life,* April 25, 1969.

Husock, Howard. "Remembering Johnny Most at his Legendary Best," *Boston Phoenix,* January 8, 1993.

Janoff, Murray. "The New Bill Bradley: Knick Terror," *The Sporting News,* March 22, 1969.

Jares, Joe. "Four for the Bundle," *Sports Illustrated,* February 24, 1969.

Johnson, William, "Triumph in Obscurity," *Sports Illustrated,* April 22, 1968.

Katz, Fred. "The Unknown Side of Bill Russell." *Sport,* March 1966.

Kirkpatrick, Curry. "An Answer to the Bradley Riddle," *Sports Illustrated,* March 18, 1968.

———. "It's the End of a Long, Long Run," *Sports Illustrated,* April 10, 1978.

Kiser, Jack. "Yesterday's Heroes, Hal Greer Is No. 8 on the NBA All-Time Scoring List. So Why Isn't He in the Hall of Fame?" *Basketball Digest,* December, 1980.

Kowett, Don. "John Havlicek's Latest Exercise in Exorcism, *Sport,* May 1974.

Kunstler, William M. "Bill Russell," *Sport,* December 1986.

Lee, Bruce. "Bill Russell, K.C. Jones, Unstoppable San Francisco," *Sport,* April 1974.

Letter. Arnold "Red" Auerbach to Lee Williams, August 20, 1974, Player Files, Naismith Memorial Basketball Hall of Fame, Springfield, Mass.

Lewin, Leonard. "The Wilt Chamberlain Controversy," *Sport,* August 1969.

Libby, Bill. "The Courage and Splendor of Jerry West," *Sport,* March 1970.

Linn, Ed. "Bill Russell's Private World," *Sport,* February 1963.

———. "I Owe the Public Nothing," *Saturday Evening Post,* January 18, 1964.

McGinniss, Joe. "One Celtic's Formula," *Sport,* February 1967.

Montville, Leigh. "And They All Say 'This is It,'" *Sports Illustrated,* May 19, 1986.

———. "Blowin' Smoke," *Sports Illustrated,* November 16, 1992.

Nack, William. "I've Made My Own Bed, I've Got to Lie in It," *Sports Illustrated,* February 20, 1984.

O'Neil, Paul. "Jackie's Wedding: For the Beautiful Queen Jacqueline, Goodbye Camelot, Hello Skorpios," *Life,* November 1, 1968.

Pjhinizy, Coles. "Sanders of Harvard," *Sports Illustrated,* March 4, 1974.

Plimpton, George. "Sportsman of the Year, Bill Russell," *Sports Illustrated,* December 23, 1968.

Ramsey, Jack. "The Red Behind the Green," *The Final Game, Official Commemorative Game Program and Magazine,* April 21, 1995.

Rogin, Gilbert. "We Are Grown Men Playing a Child's Game," *Sports Illustrated,* November 18, 1963.

———. "They All Boo When Red Sits Down," *Sports Illustrated,* April 15, 1965.

Russell, William F. "I'm Not Involved Anymore," *Sports Illustrated,* August 4, 1969.

Russell, Bill, with Tex Maule. "I Am Not Worried about Ali," *Sports Illustrated*, June 19, 1967.

Russell, Bill, with Bob Ottum. "The Psych . . . And My Other Tricks," *Sports Illustrated*, October 25, 1965.

Schaap, Dick. "The Real Wilt Chamberlain," *Sport*, March 1961.

Shecter, Leonard. "The Startling Change in Wilt Chamberlain," *Sport*, March 1967.

Sheheri, Tami, and Janon Fisher. "FBI Probed Wilt Chamberlain for Gambling," www.APBNews.com, February 14, 2000.

Tax, Jeremiah. "The Man Who Must Be Different, *Sports Illustrated*, February 3, 1958.

———. "Here Comes the Big Fellow at Last," *Sports Illustrated*, October 26, 1959.

———. "The Tall Ones in Boston," *Sports Illustrated*, November 16, 1959.

Transcript. *Donahue Television Show*, October 19, 1979, WGN-TV, Chicago, Ill.

Underwood, John. "The Eye of an Eagle and a Big Wingspread," *Sports Illustrated*, February 8, 1965.

———. "The Green Running Machine," n.d., in Nomination Files, Naismith Memorial Basketball Hall of Fame, Springfield, Mass.

Vecsey, George. "Bill Russell's Most Trying Season, *Sport*, April 1967.

Walsh, George. "Jones and Jones at Court," *Sports Illustrated*, March 20, 1961.

Weiss, Dick. "A Case for Hal Greer," *Basketball Weekly*, January 29, 1981.

Whalen, Tom. "Bob Cousy Talks about Life with the Boston Celtics," *The Bates College Student*, February 6, 1985.

Williams, Roger. "The Long Leap Forward of Jerry West," *Sports Illustrated*, November 20, 1961.

Zanger, Jack. "Bailey Howell Made It in a Hurry," *Sport*, February 1962.

———. "The Better-Late-Than-Never Celtic," *Sport*, March 1969.

NEWSPAPERS AND PERIODICALS

Basketball Digest
Basketball Weekly
Beverly Times
Boston Advertiser
Boston Globe
Boston Herald
Boston Herald American
Boston Herald-Traveler
Boston Phoenix
Boston Record
Boston Record-American
Cedar Rapids Gazette
Christian Science Monitor
Des Moines Register
Life
Look
Los Angeles Herald-Examiner
Los Angeles Times
New York Daily News
New York Post
New York Times
Philadelphia Inquirer
Quincy Patriot Ledger
Salem Evening News
San Francisco Chronicle
Seattle Times
Sport
The Sporting News
Sports Illustrated
Springfield Daily News
Time
USA Today
Washington Post
Worcester Evening Gazette

INTERNET SITES

National Basketball Association, www.nba.com
APB Online, Inc., www.apbnews.com
The Lara Parker Site, www.laraparker.com
Philly.com, The Region's Home Page, www.philly.com

TELEVISION INTERVIEW

Darren Duarte interview of Bill Russell on *Basic Black*, WGBH-TV, November 2002

INTERVIEWS WITH THE AUTHOR

Emmette Bryant
Tom Heinsohn
Bailey Howell
Leigh Montville
Don Nelson
Bob Sales
Larry Siegfried

Index